PRAISE
RUNNING TOWARDS GUNFIRE

"If you want to read about combat in Iraq at the boots-on-the-ground level, this book is for you. Jason Angell has penned a plainspoken, tough but compassionate story about the Marines in his unit. Their courage, their fears, and their hopes. Operating daily in a difficult place against a brutal but worthy adversary, they never quit, never faltered, and most importantly, never stopped believing in each other. None of us came back the same from the fight, but the great majority served well, with courage, honor and virtue. This is their story."

—GENERAL ROBERT NELLAR, USMC (Ret.), thirty-seventh commandant of the Marine Corps

"At that period, 2005 and 2006, Ramadi gained notoriety as the most dangerous place on the face of the earth. Jason Angell served there, and he served with great honor and distinction as a member of a Marine ANGLICO team. This is his story."

—MAJOR GENERAL JOHN GRONSKI, USA (Ret.); former commanding officer of 2nd Brigade, 28th Infantry–Ramadi, Iraq

"The US war in Iraq has become a distant memory, and first-person accounts of the harsh, gritty combat US service members experienced are important to the historical record. Jason Angell's memoir, *Running Towards Gunfire*, is one of the rare books that takes readers on a retrospective journey from the perspective of a marine's experience of fighting in Ramadi circa 2005 during the Iraq war.

"He transforms from an eager and willing participant whose innocence is replaced by pragmatism after his first firefight and, after many more, finally succumbs to fatal acceptance he may be killed.

Angell's unvarnished, thoughtful writing allows readers to assess the actions of those on the ground versus being a vigorous defense of US policy in the wake of 9/11.

"As a fellow combat veteran and Marine, I cannot recommend this sobering story enough for those who seek to understand modern warfare and the people who fought it. Buy this book."

—IVAN F. INGRAHAM, USMC Raider (Ret.),
acclaimed author of *The Patrol*

"A superbly written story that shares the gut-wrenching emotion of combat and how US marines and soldiers, bent by war, fought and survived in the deadliest city on earth."

—MAJOR SCOTT A. HUESING, USMC (Ret.),
bestselling author of *Echo in Ramadi*

"*Running Towards Gunfire* reveals the heart of why American marines fight with ferocity and courage. Jason describes a warrior's battlefield report of the Marine fighting spirit in the most complicated urban warfare in Ar Ramadi, Iraq, and the courageous love between brothers in battle. The heart of combat is clearly described through the ultimate competition between two irreconcilable forces, both utilizing every means necessary in the arena with only one victor. *Running Towards Gunfire* is a heart-pounding account of marines using every type of attack aircraft, technology, and coordination in a complex urban battlefield to relentlessly kill a fanatical enemy."

—MAJOR FRED GALVIN, USMC (Ret.), author of *A Few Bad Men: The True Story of US Marines Ambushed in Afghanistan and Betrayed in America*

"Jason Angell expertly captures the intensity of navigating a small ANGLICO team through the battlespace to bring additional fire support to a roulette wheel of units. The complexity of those operations and the emotional toll that it had on Angell and his marines rings true throughout."

—ISAAC G. LEE, author of *Hangar 4: A Combat Aviator's Memoir*

"Angell writes with the clarity and authenticity of a man who has seen and done hard things in his nation's service and who has reflected on them deeply. With his detailed descriptions of his men and their missions, Angell paints a vivid picture of the day-to-day life and work of our nation's finest warriors in the most difficult conditions imaginable. This book is a must-read for anyone seeking to understand the reality of war and the lives of those who prosecute it."

—DONOVAN CAMPBELL, author of *Joker One: A Marine Platoon's Story of Courage, Leadership, and Brotherhood*

"*Running Towards Gunfire* dives deep into the experiences of marines fighting a brutal insurgency in Ramadi, Iraq. This gripping first-person account sheds light on the realities of modern urban combat, taking readers on a journey alongside these courageous fighters. Prepare to be transported to the heart of the action as marines forge bonds and fight for survival in some of the most intense battles of the Iraq War. This unflinching look at urban warfare is a must-read for anyone who wants to understand the courage, camaraderie, and sacrifice of the men on the front lines."

—HOLLIE MCKAY, author of *Only Cry for the Living: Memos from Inside the ISIS Battlefield*

Running Towards Gunfire:
Courage and Brotherhood in Ramadi

by Jason Angell

© Copyright 2024 Jason Angell

ISBN 979-8-88824-418-0

Published by

 **köehlerbooks** ™

3705 Shore Drive
Virginia Beach, VA 23455
800-435-4811
www.koehlerbooks.com

RUNNING TOWARDS GUNFIRE

COURAGE AND BROTHERHOOD IN RAMADI

JASON ANGELL

VIRGINIA BEACH
CAPE CHARLES

TABLE OF CONTENTS

This book is dedicated to the US Marines, soldiers, airmen, and sailors that served in Iraq, especially the city of Ramadi. We were once giants.

PROLOGUE

This book is not about politics. It isn't about leadership, history, or counterinsurgency strategies, although these topics are certainly discussed and significant. I didn't write this to fit a narrative or push any views about the global war on terror or the war in Iraq. This book is based solely on my memories, some after-action reports, and limited discussions with a few of the men I had the pleasure of serving with. If I got something wrong, which I inevitably did, that wasn't my intention.

I started writing this not long after my first child, Scarlett, was born in 2007. I believe my daughter and my two sons will eventually want to know what their father did during this war, just as I wanted to know what my father did in Vietnam or what my maternal grandfather did in World War II and during the Korean War. My children need to know this part of me. For a brief period of my life, I was a hunter of men. I battled insurgents and tried to kill them before they could kill me or my marines while standing shoulder to shoulder with some of the most courageous individuals I have ever met. We stood in the narrow zone of chaos between civilization and anarchy—places that are difficult to describe and put into context for those who have never experienced such a world.

Many of the topics covered in this book are not easy to discuss. Killing during war—the associated violence and raw emotions—can easily be mistaken for bloodlust. I think it is crucial for readers to understand the reality of Ramadi, Iraq, after Fallujah was cleared in the fall of 2004 through the surge in 2007. Ramadi was the most dangerous city on the planet at that time. The battlefield was in people's homes and neighborhoods, on rooftops and alleyways, as we tried to bring security to the citizens and return home in one piece.

When I first arrived in Ramadi in the summer of 2005, I wanted to be there. This was about being part of something bigger than myself. Like countless young men throughout history, I was drawn to the military by the promise of excitement and adventure. In the Marine Corps, and especially in Ramadi, we found it, and it almost killed us.

INTRODUCTION

In an instant, time stopped. I heard no sounds. I felt no movement. My mind focused squarely on the flash that had ripped a hole in the darkness. After almost seven months in Iraq, I instinctively knew what was happening in those milliseconds, but strangely, I questioned it.

What the fuck is that?

The explosion was so close that I had no time to blink before the gut-wrenching concussion slammed into our vehicle, instantly followed by the loud clap of the detonation echoing through the urban canyon. Shrapnel peppered our gun truck. I was thrown to the left as the blast picked up our vehicle and dropped it back down in the middle of the road.

As quickly as the blast had come, it was gone, leaving us in hazy silence and confusion. Dust filled the vehicle. Stunned, no one spoke a word as we rolled forward on momentum. An odd but familiar metallic taste permeated my mouth as the pungent smell of cordite filled my nose.

I thought of my marines.

"Anyone fuckin' hit?" I yelled, running my hands down the length of my legs. A piercing ring resonated in my ears. I felt nauseous. Thankfully, I was in one piece. The expletive-laced replies from my marines came back almost in unison. Although pissed off and angry, they were alive and physically in one piece. I thanked God, a compulsion that had become all too common in Ramadi.

Sergeant Anderson swung right in the turret behind the machine gun, leaning into the weapon mount waiting to release a barrage of automatic-weapons fire.

"You see anyone? You got PID [positive identification]?" I yelled, grabbing the radio handset and scanning through the front right window. My head spun from the explosion; I was dizzy but pushed through it.

"Negative. Not yet," Anderson shouted back. He searched for a target, his night vision goggles (NVG) exposing the darkness in shades of green. We all expected the night to erupt in gunfire and more explosions.

"Just fuckin' shoot, Anderson," echoed from the backseat. "Light 'em up."

I hurriedly replied, "Negative. Wait for a target, dude. You don't know who's out there."

I completely trusted Anderson's decisions. My comment was directed at the passenger, a marine from our unit who was hitching a ride with us. We didn't blindly shoot into the darkness. We didn't want to kill civilians, and we didn't want to shoot our fellow marines or soldiers. Anderson was a professional and knew the risk of a blue-on-blue incident.

I keyed the handset. "Wild Eagle Two-Two from Five-Seven."

I had to force myself to speak calmly. *Calm down, Angell. Relax, think, and then speak.* I kept trying—no response. Through my NVGs, I looked into the side mirror of the vehicle. Wild Eagle Two-Two's gun truck was silhouetted by the infrared headlights of the escort vehicle behind it. They weren't moving. They were stopped in the middle of Route Michigan, in the middle of Ramadi, Iraq, one of the most dangerous cities on the planet in 2006.

"Stop," I told Sergeant Dyer. He quickly hit the brakes. "Murray's gun truck isn't moving."

In front of us, though, the lead escort vehicle's outline grew smaller and smaller as they continued west. "Gunfighter Three, this is Wild Eagle Five-Seven. We're stopping. Our other vehicle is hit and immobile," I explained to the convoy commander as I watched his vehicle disappear into the darkness.

"Negative. Get out of the kill zone" was the cold response.

I cursed them below my breath but knew the tactic. You had to get out of the kill zone. They had no choice; neither did we. Frustrated, I replied with a verbal jab.

"Copy. We're stopping. I'm not leaving my fellow marines."

There was no way my team and I were going to leave Captain Shane Murray, Corporal Donnelly, or the rest. I kept trying to reach them on the radio but received nothing in return.

The city was silent and dark. We were only about a mile from Camp Corregidor, but it might as well have been a hundred. We felt alone and feared for the fate of Murray and his team, although no one uttered such a thought.

"All right. Fuckin' turn it around. Let's get it over with," I told Sergeant Dyer, shaking my head. Anxious and nervous, we had no idea what was happening in or around their gun truck, but we had to do something. I had to make a decision. The disturbing thought that Murray and his marines might be dead danced in my head.

Turning around was easier said than done. Attached to our gun truck was a small trailer with the gear, packs, and belongings we were moving from Camp Corregidor to Camp Ramadi as our time in Iraq wound down. Sergeant Dyer backed up, moved forward, and then backed up and moved forward again in an attempt to turn the gun truck. We all expected to get hit by another IED. We sat bracing for it, waiting. Some of us even plugged our ears. We had become accustomed to the feeling; we knew it would happen, and we wanted to get it over with. There was no other choice. *Deal with it.*

We had become experts at dealing with it: dealing with the confusion, with the monotony, the boredom; dealing with the excitement and adrenaline, the longing for family and home, the fear, the heat, the frustration; dealing with the nonsensical rules of engagement, the film of dirt and sand coating everything we touched, and the horrible smell of this country; dealing with this godforsaken city and its apathetic citizens. We dealt with the piercing screams of

Iraqi women who had seen their husbands and sons gunned down. We dealt with watching young children running through raw sewage to escape a firefight. The only thing we really wanted to deal with was the enemy, the insurgents. But this was Ramadi. We were forced to deal with all of it. This was our war.

The enemy was an ambush attacker, typical of guerrilla fighters throughout history. He attacked at the time and place of his choosing and only when he held the tactical advantage, when we least expected it.

Over time, you come to accept that death can grab you by the hand and take you into the unknown abyss in an instant. It's the only way to survive and still be able to operate and accomplish your mission day in and day out for seven to thirteen months at a time. Before long, this acceptance becomes mundane. You grow accustomed to seeing death around every corner. You and your fellow marines and soldiers, your brothers, laugh when an insurgent's bullet misses your head by millimeters. You are amused at how surreal and crazy the whole situation is. You run towards gunfire. You are addicted to the violence that old men and women in Washington, DC, say is just and righteous. You feel a thousand feet tall. You're an alpha male, a fucking warrior, a Spartan. You are a combat marine who will give your life to protect your brothers.

Everything changes when you see home on the horizon. As it approaches, you start thinking about reuniting with your wife, your children, your friends and family. The possibility that you might leave Iraq alive becomes real. You no longer laugh at death. It becomes clear that death means business, so you had better respect that because you are both in the same line of work. He's just more efficient.

At this point in our deployment, we had become quite accustomed to extreme violence and its ever-present companion. We were a key element of a small ad hoc task force that brought together the unique capabilities of US Army snipers, scouts, and US Marine Corps ANGLICO (Air Naval Gunfire Liaison Company) teams. We cast aside interservice rivalries, stepped out of the road-bound gun trucks, abandoned conventional operations, and jumped into the world of hunting insurgents in their backyard and from their own homes. We became the ones hiding in the shadows, bringing death unto our enemy when he least expected it—when we held the advantage.

We were ANGLICO. We brought death from above. We were United States Marines.

CHAPTER ONE:
THE BEGINNING

The Marine Corps was in my blood, although I didn't always know it. My father, Jim Angell, enlisted in the Marines in the mid-1960s and volunteered for Vietnam. He served his four years and got out as a sergeant. He never really talked about his time in the Marine Corps or about Vietnam until I became a marine myself. But I knew he was proud of his service, and he had every right to be. He is part of the less than 1 percent of Americans who have served their country during wartime.

After the Marine Corps, my father became a cement mason and ended up in Houston, Texas, in the '70s because of its booming economy. Until I was in the sixth grade, we lived in a blue-collar 1950s-style house not far from a bayou in the suburbs. I have fond memories of that neighborhood where I played baseball, caught frogs and turtles, and pretended to fight battles in exotic places.

I once made an ignorant remark typical of a child as me and some buddies ran by my father with toy guns, screaming our war cries.

"War is fun," I yelled.

My dad stopped me in my tracks, bent down, and grabbed my skinny little eight-year-old arm to say, "Son, there is nothing fun about war."

That day, that moment, stuck with me. I would remember it the first time I saw gunfire shot in anger two decades later, during my war.

International conflict and combat captured my attention from a very young age. At six years old, I watched on TV as the Soviets rolled armored columns into Afghanistan. Although I wasn't sure what it meant, I knew it was important. A few years later, I was mesmerized by footage of British Royal Marines, with their thick mustaches, fighting over a speck of no-man's-land called the Falkland Islands in the South Atlantic. I sat awestruck as the nightly news showed the HMS *Sheffield* sink after being hit by an Exocet missile, the Argentinian A4 Skyhawks banking and yanking mere feet above the water and dodging fire from the British armada.

Over a year later, I woke up one Sunday morning to find my father drinking his coffee and glued to the news, our loyal Dalmatian at his feet. This time the situation didn't concern the Brits. It was more personal. Flak-jacket and helmet-clad US Marines were searching for their wounded and dead brothers under smoldering hulks of debris and concrete, caught in a civil war in a faraway place called Beirut. Those images were imprinted on my young mind.

The summer before my sixth-grade year, we moved to San Leon, a small, rural fishing community along the brown coastal waters of Galveston County, Texas. My dad had been a part-time shrimper, making extra money on the side, but now made it a full-time job as the Houston economy declined. He built a shrimp boat with his own hands while we were still in Houston. Our Pentecostal neighbors called him Noah.

Living along Dickinson Bay in San Leon cemented my love of the outdoors. My buddies and I fished, hunted, combed for stone crabs at the water's edge, and camped and swam in the bays and canals along the coast. We were hardly ever inside, even during the sweltering, humid summers. When I needed money, I'd mow yards or work on my dad's boat.

I was never particularly good at school or sports, although I managed to get by. While I'm sure I could have excelled if I had tried, I only wanted to hang out with my friends, get into trouble, and chase girls. But when I became a junior at Dickinson High School, I felt a growing restlessness that would haunt me for years. I wanted to see new things. So, I moved to my mother's house in Fort Collins, Colorado, chasing a young lady I had met the previous summer.

After high school, I had no serious plans for college. I moved back to Texas, found a job washing cars, and spent most of my time hanging out with my buddies. When my parents asked me to pay rent since I wasn't attending college, I slept on a friend's couch. We did nothing but get into trouble—getting into fights, drinking, and chasing girls. This was a period rife with unquestionably bad decisions that could have altered the course of my life. And I knew it.

One morning, a Marine recruiter approached a friend and me at the carwash. He talked a little about the Corps, handed us his card, and went on his way. The young sergeant was confident and professional. My buddy joked about giving the recruiter the names of our other friends as a gag. Military recruiters can be relentless when they believe you might be interested in joining. But this Marine recruiter commanded respect, which caught my attention.

About a week later, another friend was considering joining the Army. They had a buddy program, so he asked if I wanted to enlist. I told him I might be interested if he wanted to enlist in the Marine Corps.

"There's no fucking way I'm going into the Marines. Those guys are crazy," he said.

I laughed, but in the back of my mind, I liked the idea of joining an organization others thought was nuts.

My fun times in Texas were short lived. In June 1992, I was driving to a friend's house after a party at around one in the morning. A GT Mustang pulled up next to me in my lowered Chevy S-10 Blazer. He wanted to race, so I obliged. He blew past me. A police officer saw us and pulled me over. It reminds me of the adage that you don't have to outrun a bear; you just have to be faster than your companion.

I was arrested on suspicion of DWI. Thankfully, when I submitted to a breathalyzer test at the police station in Dickinson, I came up legal; I'd only had one beer since I was too busy talking to a young lady. But my Blazer had already been towed, so the police held me overnight for public intoxication. I was bailed out the next day by a friend. A few weeks after this reality check, I left Texas to live with my mother again.

Seven months after that, I enlisted in the Marine Corps.

■ ■ ■

My drive to join the Marine Corps didn't rest solely on trying to stay out of trouble. The Marine Corps is the answer for many young men ready to take on the world. I was no exception. I wanted to be a warrior and wasn't content staying in one place, doing the same thing. My father had served his country in the Marine Corps, and I was a patriotic young man, so it seemed only natural. I enlisted and volunteered for the infantry; if I was going to join, I might as well go all the way.

In February 1993, I found myself trembling on painted yellow footprints as a large Marine drill instructor screamed at me for being an idiot mere moments after getting off the bus in San Diego. My right leg shook uncontrollably.

The next three months were demanding and tough, but I made it through, earned an expert rifle badge, and graduated on May 14, 1993. I was as green as they came, but everyone starts somewhere.

After ten days of leave, I reported to the School of Infantry (SOI) aboard Camp Pendleton, California. For the next three months, I learned the skills needed to be a rifleman in the infantry. It was a great time, although it was filled with petty games instigated by my Marine instructors. Day in and day out, we hiked through the scrub brush of the Southern California hills, learned how to use the various weapon systems found in an infantry platoon, and were taught the basic skills of a junior marine on a fire team. We spent our weeks training in the field, and we'd return on Friday afternoons to clean weapons before getting a couple of days off.

The first time I ever heard of ANGLICO, or anything like it, was as a student at SOI. We were coming back to the barracks after a day of training. The hike was about eight miles long, so the instructors stopped us halfway through. Sitting on my pack, drinking water, I spotted movement out of the corner of my eye. From a thickly wooded area in a draw leading to a dry riverbed popped out four marines camouflaged from head to toe.

They wore Vietnam-era boonie hats, what marines call covers, with grass woven in to help them blend into the environment. In the early '90s, the boonie cover was forbidden, especially for students at SOI. Their hands, necks, and faces were covered with various blends of camouflage paint. They were loaded down with gear. Most notably, they all wore huge rucksacks about three times the size of ours and didn't seem fatigued. Each one had an antenna sticking out of their pack, the handset connected to the H-harness at the shoulder. These guys were pros.

As I watched them, I noticed all the other marines watching too. As soon as these men pushed through the thick vegetation, they gathered in a circle, each member facing in a different direction with their M16s pointed out and ready. One of the marines grabbed his radio handset and spoke into it. A low rumble in the distance grew abruptly louder. As the ear-busting noise peaked, we all jumped in shock at the unexpected flash from a pair of jets streaking just above the treetops in the canyon.

The jets were gone as fast as they had appeared. I glanced back over at the four marines, but they were gone, having melted back into the thick bushes and trees after directing their mock bombing run on make-believe targets.

Later that evening, after a few hours of cleaning our weapons, gear, and barracks, we were dismissed for two days of much-needed liberty. I changed into regular street clothes and walked down to the SOI convenience store, called the PX (post exchange), to get a Dr. Pepper and make a phone call home. There I noticed those marines I'd seen earlier. They were still covered in camouflage paint and had their packs on the ground with their rifles leaning against their rucksacks.

As I strolled through the PX entrance, one of the marines headed in as well. He was right in front of me at the checkout counter, getting a can of Copenhagen tobacco. He glanced at me and said, "What's up, man" as if we knew each other. I quickly inspected his collar.

"Good evening, Corporal," I said nervously. At this point, I'd only been in the Marine Corps for about five months. As a private first class (PFC), I was outranked by almost everyone—and they made sure I knew it. It came with the territory.

Astonishingly, the corporal replied without yelling.

"Doing good now that the captain gave us a chance to get some chew," he said with a smile. "Been in the field for about six days straight, humping these hills with all this shit on my back."

"What unit are you with, Corporal?" I asked, setting my drink on the counter, feeling like an idiot—but I wanted to know more.

"I'm with 1st ANGLICO," he replied, handing the clerk a five-dollar bill.

I was stumped. "What's that, Corporal?"

He laughed. "I get that question all the time, 1st Air Naval Gunfire Liaison Company, ANGLICO. We work in small teams with US allies, Army, SOF, or by ourselves, blow shit up with air, arty, and naval guns, jump out of planes; it's not your average grunt shit, devil dog."

"Wow" was about all I could push out. "Sounds pretty cool."

His response was immediate. "It is, and I love it—great training, always going somewhere new, and no stupid games. Well, I've gotta go. We've got a ten-click patrol to some LZ. See you later, marine." And with that, he was gone.

Outside, as I opened my Dr. Pepper, the captain, two sergeants, and corporal threw on their huge packs, laughing as they headed off into the towering hills of Camp Pendleton. They were the real deal. I wanted to be in a unit like that.

■ ■ ■

At the end of August 1993, I graduated from SOI as an 0311, an infantry rifleman. I was lucky enough to get posted to Camp Pendleton, so the powers that be bused most of us over to 62 Area on base. I was now a rifleman for the 3rd Battalion, 5th Marines, Lima Company, 3rd Platoon. Life in the Fleet Marine Force (FMF) was pretty good. When we weren't in the field training, which was all the time, we had nights and weekends off.

Going to the field in the fleet was vastly different from SOI and boot camp, but I caught on quick. Everything revolved around physical fitness, our ability to hump and run, and our tolerance for constant harassment. If we fell out during a hike or run, the corporals and senior lance corporals made us pay when the officers weren't looking—a punch here, a gut check there, coupled with a session of digging a large hole behind the barracks. I was lucky; I could hack almost anything the grunts threw at me, and I excelled after the initial shock common to most new marines. I also learned that some of the meanest, most psychotic marines in the Marine Corps were "senior" lance corporals.

Like most marines, we played hard and trained hard. I grew tight with the platoon, and before long we were really going crazy. We went down to Tijuana, where we could drink beer at eighteen and seek the elusive "donkey show" that was more fiction than fact. What made it even better was the number of college girls frequenting the various clubs along Revolution Avenue. When that got old, we obtained a few fake IDs and hit the bars and clubs of Orange County, California. Life was good.

As 1993 ended, my platoon spent weeks in the field doing patrols, live-fire exercises, company training, twenty-five-mile hikes, and amphibious landings. I loved it and had outgrown my homesickness for the most part.

But a car accident brought my time in the Marine Corps to a screeching halt.

■ ■ ■

Upon being medically discharged for a severe leg injury, I decided to stay in Southern California and go to college with the thought of possibly returning to the Marine Corps one day as a commissioned officer.

College was awesome. Unlike high school, I excelled at my studies and wanted to learn. The Marine Corps had instilled in me a sense of pride, personal responsibility, and a drive to succeed; I was disciplined and motivated. When the dean's list came out after my first semester, I was on it. But I didn't give up my work-hard, play-hard mentality. During my senior year at California State University, Fullerton, I partied a lot with some excellent friends. This was when I met my wife.

Joni and I first laid eyes on each other in the early fall of 1999. A buddy and I were at a bar called Off Campus Pub across the street from the university. It wasn't exactly glamorous, but she was there with her sister and friends. I noticed her big smile, beautiful eyes, tight black outfit, and dark, silky hair. We hit it off, and by the end of the night, she had given me her phone number. After the "mandatory" two-day waiting period, I attempted to call. She had given me the wrong number. I was disheartened but laughed it off. It happens to the best of us.

Two months later, we ran into each other again. She looked just as I remembered her. Of course, I teased her about giving me the wrong number. Joni claimed it was a mistake. We dated for the next two months, but I wouldn't be staying in Southern California after graduating, so I knew it wouldn't last. We were simply enjoying each other's company.

In February 2000, four months before I graduated, I got the call that the Marine Corps had accepted me into their Officer Candidate School (OCS) program for the ten-week summer Platoon Leaders Class (PLC).

The selection officer and I had been forced to jump through a few hoops over the past year. All the Navy doctors said I was in tip-top condition, but the "disabled vet" status caused problems for the bureaucrats. Finally, I was told to go to the Veterans' Administration (VA) hospital in Long Beach to get a physical. I needed one of the doctors to certify that I no longer had a disability.

This was probably the least painful experience I have ever had with the monstrous VA. I drove down to Long Beach one morning and got an X-ray and a quick physical from an orthopedic doctor. The funny part was trying to explain why I was there.

"You mean you're trying to get *off* disability?" he asked skeptically.

"Yes sir. I'm about to graduate from college, and I'm trying to go back into the Marine Corps as an officer. Headquarters Marine Corps won't let me go to OCS if I'm still designated as a disabled vet."

He grabbed the paperwork out of my hand, signed it right there, and said, "I've never had anyone here that wanted to get off disability."

With the pencil-pushing bureaucrats appeased, four days after graduating college, I arrived in humid Virginia for OCS.

■ ■ ■

For the next ten weeks, as a member of Alpha Company, I ran around the forest and swamps of Quantico while staff sergeants, gunnery sergeants, and Marine Corps officers evaluated our moral, intellectual, and physical qualities. Our days were filled with physical training (PT), classes, close-order drill, and more PT. The PT, much to my enjoyment, was significantly more challenging than at boot camp. Marine Corps officers are expected to be in peak physical condition and set the example. You can't lead marines while falling back during a long hike or run.

Attrition was the name of the game. The instructors sought reasons to kick candidates out, another difference from boot camp. The instructors weren't bullies; they were simply experts at identifying the weak, dishonest, and those who didn't stack up to the Corps' high standards. They didn't care what school you went to. What mattered was whether you possessed the qualities to lead three dozen marines into combat.

Our platoon watched a Harvard graduate break down and cry about six weeks into the course. This individual had consistently fallen out on runs, was unable to negotiate various obstacles, nodded off during classes, and was last at everything and a known complainer. He despised cleaning the bathroom—or as the Navy and Marine Corps call it, "the head." At one point during this chore, as I listened to him whine about being a Harvard graduate cleaning a toilet, I stopped my own scrubbing, looked over at him, and was brutally honest.

"You'll never lead marines."

I was right. And six weeks in, with no expression on our faces, no emotion, we all stood silently as he sobbed. That night, the MPs escorted him out of our barracks. He went home with nothing but a bad haircut and some stories he probably wasn't entirely honest about.

Our platoon, one of five in the company, started off with around eighty candidates and graduated with just over thirty. Almost fifty dropped on request, were booted out for injuries, or were kicked out for integrity issues. I enjoyed OCS and felt my prior enlisted experience gave me an edge. In the end, I graduated third in my platoon and in the top 5 percent in the company—facts that matter little in combat or anywhere else.

About six months after graduating from OCS, I was commissioned a second lieutenant and checked into the Basic School (TBS) on Quantico. TBS is a mandatory twenty-six-week course all newly commissioned Marine second lieutenants must attend. Future Marine aviators, lawyers, and ground combat officers come together after their commission to learn about weapon systems, infantry tactics, leadership, and Marine Corps doctrine. For ground officers such as myself, this is also where we receive our official military occupational specialty (MOS).

TBS, sometimes jokingly referred to as "the big suck" or "time between Saturdays," was a great course. The Marine Corps wants officers of exemplary character who are devoted to leading marines and able to make decisions, communicate, and act amid the fog of war. They want a warfighter who embraces the Marine Corps ethos and is physically tough and mentally strong, with a "bias for action." A bias for action comprises a willingness to take initiative, act boldly, and accept risk. Everything we did revolved around these tenets. We were always being evaluated, and we evaluated each other.

We lived in four-man rooms in a dormitory building complex with a large cafeteria called a chow hall, which was also used for various other events and had red carpet from wall to wall. This was a place of legends. Simply walking in could deflate the most self-involved egos.

Outside the chow hall was a small bar called the Hawkins Room—or "the Hawk." Yes, right there in O'Bannon Hall was a bar. We frequented that place as often as we could, drinking Shiner Bock beer and smoking cigars. Discussions usually revolved around getting into the "fleet" or which instructor was harder than the next. We thought we were tough, but we had no idea what tough was; most of that class would eventually find out when the nation went to war a couple of years later.

In April 2001, with about two and a half months left of TBS, I found out I was going to be an artillery officer. I had wanted to be an infantry officer, so I wasn't too happy about this.

Each year, TBS graduates about 1,700 second lieutenants. These officers must fill the ranks of various MOSs that fit the needs of the Marine Corp throughout the entire fleet. Each training class receives a certain number of slots per MOS. Some specialties, such as infantry and artillery, have more slots, while others have fewer, such as human intelligence or tanks. These slots, in turn, are divided into thirds—as are the students, depending on their class ranking. This method of assigning MOSs is called the "quality spread." I was in the bottom of the top third.

A large portion of the officers want the combat MOSs, such as tanks, infantry, artillery, and ground intelligence. Those slots go fast. My staff platoon commander, Captain Keith Perry, told me he had to argue with the other class instructors to get me one of those coveted slots. It was settled; I was an artillery officer.

In July 2001, I graduated from TBS and arrived at Fort Sill, Oklahoma, for Field Artillery School. This course, my last before finally entering the operating forces, was difficult. Ninety percent of it was academic. For five months, along with about ten other marines and 180 soldiers, I learned about gunnery, manual computations of trajectory, how the earth's rotation, drift, weather, elevation, and temperature affect artillery, and how to take all this into account when attempting to deliver timely, accurate, and effective artillery support. We learned the correct method for spotting and adjusting artillery as a forward observer and how to emplace a six-gun 155mm artillery battery.

The exams covering manual gunnery computations were not easy. The Marine Corps standard was to get an 85 percent or higher on these exams. The Army could receive 70 percent. Anything less, and you had to go see a Marine major to discuss your "failure." On two of these exams, I received an 83 percent and an 81 percent. The major chewed my ass. I graduated with an 84 percent, and considering the amount of studying required to get that grade, I was happy. But everything was inconsequential after September 11, 2001.

On that infamous day, our class was conducting an artillery shoot in the hills, requesting, spotting, and calling in artillery fire on old, rusty targets. It was a "move and shoot," meaning we'd identify a target, call artillery on it, move to a different location, and do it all again. After a couple of hours, some Army lieutenant came by our position to ask if we'd heard about what was happening. Some planes had hit the WTC towers and the Pentagon.

For the Marine instructors and students, things changed. Maybe it was a facade or the attitude beaten into all young marines and officers, but everything became more real for us. For some in my class, though, I wasn't too sure. A few soldiers weren't paying attention during one lecture. The course instructor, a short, stocky, shaven-headed Marine captain, spared no punches, making it clear that they would be fighting America's next war, and they had better grow up, or they would get people killed. Of course, his tone and language weren't quite as nice. Those second lieutenants, most of them West Point graduates, stared with their mouths open as the gruff marine read them the riot act.

Three months later, I graduated. As I left Oklahoma, I never looked back in my rear-view mirror. I was to be assigned to the 2nd Battalion, 11th Marine Regiment, an artillery battalion based out of Camp Pendleton. It was only a short forty-five-minute commute from my new apartment in Orange County. With thirty days of leave and a new apartment, I planned to enjoy my time off.

Plans are one thing; reality is entirely different. After about a week of getting my apartment in order and drinking beer with friends, I became restless. I was running daily, heading to Newport Beach to surf, watching the latest news coming out of Afghanistan, and hearing murmurs of an Iraq war. I decided to call the battalion adjutant and ask him for any news or issues before I officially checked in.

The adjutant knew precisely who I was and told me to come down to base to talk. He didn't want me to check in off leave but urged me to pick up a few things I would need.

Once I got there, the adjutant talked to me briefly, then ushered me in to see the executive officer, the XO. Centered in front of his desk, six inches away and standing at attention, I declared, "Sir, Second Lieutenant Angell reporting for duty."

Major Gentry, a bulky redhead from the East Coast, put me at ease and asked some relatively personal questions about family and where I was living. He then looked over at a white dry-erase board on his wall with a list of the four artillery firing batteries: Fox, Echo, Golf, and Kilo.

"Well, we're not sure where you're going," he said with his hands clasped together. "Golf Battery is headed towards Okinawa with the 31st MEU, Echo is returning from Okinawa soon, and Fox Battery just got tasked to head to Tajikistan with 1/5 and provide security for some airfield."

Tajikistan? *BINGO!* That was a combat deployment supporting operations in Afghanistan. I wanted in.

"Sir, does Fox Battery need any lieutenants?"

The major seemed surprised by my question.

"Actually, they do. You want to go with them?" he asked. "They are going as a provisional rifle company and not artillery."

I wanted to click my heels together and smack that major across his face in my excitement, but of course I stood there with no expression. I didn't join the Marine Corps to watch others fight, especially after the events of 9/11. My response was quick, strong, and without hesitation, typical of a cocky young officer.

"Yes sir. That's why I joined the Marine Corps."

He smiled. "All right, Angell. Fox it is."

As a testament to public school education in the US, the only thing I knew about Tajikistan was what was mentioned in the 1980s movie *Spies Like Us*, starring Dan Akroyd and Chevy Chase. In the movie, two half-wit CIA officers cross into the Soviet Union from Afghanistan but get compromised by border police along the highway to Dushanbe, the capital of the Soviet satellite state Tajikistan.

I walked to the dilapidated old building where Fox Battery had its headquarters. The marines had finished some small-arms training, and all the officers and staff noncommissioned officers (SNCOs) were drinking beer. I introduced myself. After some expected ribbing, they filled me in about the Tajikistan mission. We were going to be guarding an airfield north of the Afghan border, which would then be used as a staging point to enter Afghanistan. But the details boiled down to plenty of unknowns, questions, and directions to "stay flexible."

Two weeks later, the whole operation was scrubbed. I was disappointed to say the least, but I was glad I'd checked in early. Fox Battery, led by Captain John Orille, was a good unit filled with hard-charging marines and good SNCOs and officers. These formidable warriors manhandled the six 16,000-pound M198 towed artillery howitzers that provided support to Marine infantry battalions. I was humbled to be in their presence.

A little over a year later, in February 2003, after extensive training and preparation, we received orders to deploy to Kuwait for the invasion of Iraq. We had known this was coming, one way or the other. It was the storm on the horizon. I was lucky; I'd had a year to train with Fox Battery and with the unit I would be attached to for the war—Alpha Company, 1st Battalion, 5th Marines (1/5)—as a forward observer. I had been a rifleman with Alpha Company before being discharged for my previous injury while enlisted. This time in the field allowed me to create valuable relationships and build trust within the infantry company, whereas other young second lieutenants who showed up from artillery school got deployed immediately. Welcome to the Marine Corps.

Leaving for Kuwait was bittersweet. In September 2002, I ran into the lovely Joni once again, and we instantly hit it off. This time things were different. I was ready for a relationship, as was she. We got very serious very quickly, and I fell for her even faster. I took her to the Marine Corps ball in November. The following month, we took a quick trip to San Francisco, where she met some of my sisters. By the end of December, knowing that I'd be leaving on a deployment, I had moved out of my apartment and temporarily moved in with Joni.

On February 3, 2003, as the sun rose, Joni drove me down to Camp Pendleton and sent me off into the unknown. We had awoken at around 4:30 that morning. She cooked me breakfast while I took a shower. It was a solemn time. I had no idea when I would be coming back or when I would talk to her again. We would only be communicating through regular mail, as my grandfather and grandmother had done sixty years before during WWII and Korea.

That last morning together, we said little to each other. When we arrived at Camp Pendleton, I had her drop me off. I wanted to say our goodbyes with as much privacy and dignity as possible. With tears running down her cheeks, she drove away.

■ ■ ■

Six weeks later, I stood in the back of a Marine Corps amphibious assault vehicle (AAV) with other marines from Alpha Company in the northern desert of Kuwait. There the 1st Marine Division had amassed in assault positions, waiting to drive north into the heart of Saddam Hussein's army. We watched in awe as over fifty 155mm artillery guns from the 11th Marine Regiment (Reinforced) launched high-explosive rounds at various preplanned targets in Iraq over the course of a half hour. The artillery batteries lit up all around us, their guns roaring. On the horizon, the silent flashes as rounds exploded on targets looked like a distant thunderstorm.

Finally, our wait had ended. We were going in, crossing the huge border barriers between Iraq and Kuwait. As a badge of honor, 1st Battalion, 5th Marines was the first Marine battalion to cross into Iraq. It wasn't long before we briefly exchanged fire with Iraqi holdouts dug in on the opposite side of the border. For the next twelve hours, 1/5 went about attacking and clearing their initial objectives: oil and gas infrastructure held by Iraqi soldiers in the Rumaila oil fields.

Alpha Company was responsible for the last battalion objective. We hit the crude-oil pumping station as dawn approached. As the artillery forward observer, I called in numerous strikes around the objective while we advanced; Captain Lawler, the battalion's forward air controller (FAC, pronounced "fack"), directed air attacks.

Most of the Iraqis had been killed by the bombardment or had deserted. The remaining few were wounded. As the clearing continued, several SUVs sped towards us along a rough asphalt highway. Iraqi soldiers inside started shooting. The marines happily unleashed a barrage of deadly, accurate fire, halting the Iraqis' bizarre suicide assault. But the damage was done. We soon learned that one of the platoon commanders, First Lieutenant Shane Childers, had been shot in the gut below his body armor. He bled out right there and died on that desert floor, thousands of miles from his home. He was the first Marine KIA of the war.

This was obviously a shock to the company. Shaking his head, First Lieutenant Shull kept repeating, "He's dead. He's fuckin' dead." It was hard to believe. We had just shaken hands before loading into the AAVs prior to the breach. Now Shane was gone.

The mood changed. Captain Lawler was angry, shaking his head and claiming, "What a waste." Shull and I, as well as other marines, disagreed.

Besides tactical discussions, not much else was said. We were each forced to deal with our own mortality while mourning the loss of a brother. He wouldn't be the last.

For the next three weeks, we stormed north with the rest of the 1st Marine Division. We got into a few skirmishes and fights along the way, saw plenty of dead bodies, and received copious cheers from apparently grateful people—men, women, and children. It was surreal. We felt like liberators. Even dogs wagged their scruffy tails at us.

Things changed when we got to Baghdad.

Late in the afternoon of April 9, when the Western media was claiming that Baghdad had fallen, 1/5 entered Saddam City in the northern portion of Iraq's capital. Stopped on the side of a two-lane road among rows and rows of two- and three-story buildings, we watched looters ransack their neighborhood. People were celebrating. Cars were honking. Children were laughing. People were everywhere. To this day, I recall the screech of stolen rebar being dragged across the concrete.

Out of the jubilation and hysteria, I spotted something I still see to this day when I think of the invasion. From the back of the AAV that had been my home for weeks, I peered out into the crowd of Iraqis. There stood a man with a long, full beard, dressed in traditional Muslim garb, wearing sandals. He held no weapon; he wore no explosive vest. But when I looked at him, and he looked at me, I felt trapped by his anger and hate. He stood as still as a rock surrounded by churning waves. Disgust and fury simmered within this man, breaching the language barrier and the chaos of the crowd.

I broke his gaze and tried to point him out to another marine, but the man was gone. In my mind, he represented the seeds of the insurgency that would explode months later.

We were not simply there to witness Iraqis celebrate the demise of a tyrant. Alpha Company had been ordered to link up with a US Army Special Forces team to secure a palace on the banks of the Tigris River. I and other members of Alpha Company's FiST (fire support team) watched a couple of CIA paramilitary officers in baseball hats and tan cargo pants monitor the traffic as the sun started to fall. They were looking for something, not simply gazing around as we were. A car had been circling, showing signs of surveillance.

Shots rang out to my right. I dropped to one knee and repeated the call "Contact right," scanning for the threat, as did the other marines around me. We realized the rounds had been outgoing. The paramilitary officers were engaging a suspicious vehicle about 100 meters away. We swung our weapons to the right and started shooting, delivering multiple rounds through the windshield and into the engine block. Iraqi civilians screamed, dropped their loot, and fled. A neighborhood filled with the movement of thousands of human beings became a ghost town in seconds.

The encounter ended as soon as it had started, with screams of "Cease fire, cease fire!" The white four-door sedan caught fire and burned, and the man in the front passenger seat slumped out of the door as it opened. Only his torso made it out before he stopped moving.

Amazingly, Iraqi civilians quickly filled the streets again. They ignored the dead; they'd seen this before under the heavy fist of Saddam. A few hours later, we discovered that this car had a young child in it, along with a woman and another man. At the time I brushed it off as "War is hell," but after having children some years later, this memory resurfaced time and again. I recalled what my father had told me years before: "Nothing about war is fun." As usual, he was right.

Once the sun had set, Alpha Company moved towards the Al Adhamiyah palace in northern Baghdad with the rest of the battalion in trail. Our speed was slow and deliberate as we traveled west, deeper into the city. About two hours into the movement, the streets grew vacant. I noticed the first signs of an attack when I peered behind us with my NVGs and spotted tracer fire snapping out from buildings on both sides of the highway. I slapped a fellow marine on the shoulder and pointed it out. That's when we got hit.

Suddenly, there were fighters everywhere. RPGs, AK-47s, and RPKs belched flames from the darkness. Enemy bullets buzzed by our heads like angry hornets. A burst from automatic-weapons fire wracked the side of the AAV. Tracer rounds cracked between Lieutenant Shull and myself, hitting an antenna and showering us with bright sparks and embers. I briefly thought I was hit as sparks showered us. The marines around me were all engaged in their own battles.

Saddam's Fedayeen fighters appeared to be in almost every building, dug into every intersection we came across. Most of the movement through northern Baghdad was one big kill zone. Every marine in the AAVs was standing and returning fire as we pushed further into the streets. RPGs slammed into walls and vehicles. Automatic weapons strafed our AAV as the column roared down the dusty highway. The Fedayeen launched illuminating mortar rounds while we crossed major intersections, neutralizing our NVGs and increasing their ability to target us. We had no air cover and were moving too rapidly for artillery support.

As streaks of dawn split the eastern sky, we arrived at the palace.

It was vacant, but we were still being hit from outside the twelve-foot-high walls. Most of the battalion entered the compound as elements of 1/5's Weapons Company maintained positions outside. Bewildered, sweaty, and numb, we reloaded our magazines, drank water, smoked, and talked of our exploits. The marines were pumped up. Here we were fighting a ruthless dictator's henchmen in a pitched battle in the middle of a city founded in the eighth century.

"Man, that was fucking crazy."

"Those RPGs were everywhere."

"You see those SF boys lobbing grenades over the bridges?"

Then the men stopped talking. I turned and found out why. Standing beside the AAV was Alpha Company's first sergeant, First Sergeant Green. The veteran of Beirut was looking up at the company commander, Captain Sokol, and shaking his head.

"He's gone, sir. Gunny Bohr is gone," he told the CO.

It was a somber and gut-wrenching moment for the company and battalion. Tough but fair and with a fatherly edge to him, Gunny Bohr had been loved and respected by the marines. Of course, the larger-than-life veteran didn't go down without a fight.

The enemy had been targeting the unarmored HMMWVs, which presented softer targets than the monstrous tracked AAVs. Gunny Bohr's Humvee was riddled with bullets, but he and his marines kept returning fire. Eventually, Gunny was mortally wounded. He was thirty-nine years old.

Our fight was not over. The battalion received word of a Saddam sighting at the Abu Hanifa Mosque down the road. Alpha Company was given the task of securing the area and raiding the mosque. The AAVs belched black smoke and roared back to life. As we exited the large iron gates to the palace, Humvees from Weapons Company continued suppressing positions the Fedayeen had taken up in nearby buildings. A platoon of tanks accompanied us, and they weren't shy about shooting their 120mm main gun.

Heading west along a road paralleling the Tigris, we passed the

Al-Aimmah Bridge and turned north in the early-morning light. Fedayeen fighters shadowed our movement, using buildings as cover, while others waited, knowing Americans would eventually arrive. Just south of the bridge, we cut back east into the side roads and alleys leading to the mosque.

There was little room to breathe. The edges of our AAVs were inches away from building walls; the drivers crushed parked cars. Fighters shot at us from corners, windows, and bunkers built into the ground. Every vehicle was getting hit. Everyone was engaging the enemy. The double booms of RPGs went off in all directions, most going high as the fighters rushed their shots. The warheads slammed into walls, raining plaster and debris down on us.

As the company secured a perimeter, a platoon raided the mosque. Captain Lawler finally got some air support that would brave the intense fire. The Marine Cobras, our usual escorts, were forbidden from flying over the area until the enemy fire had died down, but that wasn't the case for the A-10 Warthogs. Piloted by Air National Guard officers, these beasts had no problem. Lawler directed them to make a few close gun runs, their legendary 30mm cannons spitting fire and hate. Marines cheered as rounds slammed into a nearby building.

The scene was chaotic. Rubble littered the streets, smoke wafted between our AAVs, and fires burned inside buildings. Our enemy would hide behind corners and jump into the open to unleash a barrage of fire, then scurry out of sight. The bodies of dead Fedayeen lay in the street where they were cut down, their weapons still in their grasps. Because the area was tight and cramped, some AAVs rolled over the dead or wounded enemy fighters. This was all-out war, a way of fighting that would be completely different when I returned to Iraq under battle-restrictive rules of engagement (ROE).

The raid eventually ended, and we returned to the palace under sporadic fire and without Saddam. We had plenty of wounded but thankfully no KIAs. The raid force had picked up a few detainees as well. Most of them were foreign fighters from Syria, Saudi Arabia, and other Middle Eastern countries. They came to Iraq to fight the infidel—to fight us.

■ ■ ■

With the invasion complete, 1/5 would leave that palace to the US Army as we started our retrograde back to Kuwait. By the end of May 2003, I was back on American soil with my girlfriend, the lovely Joni. During my thirty days of leave, we drove across the US—first to Texas, then to Colorado, and then back to Southern California via a brief stay in Las Vegas. I was glad to be alive, enjoying life with Joni and close friends.

Nine short months later, right before Christmas 2003, Joni and I said our goodbyes again. Such is the life of a marine. This time, I headed off to Okinawa, Japan, as a member of the 31st Marine Expeditionary Unit (MEU).

This deployment was utterly different from the previous. I spent my time living on amphibious ships such as the USS *Juneau* and in officer quarters aboard Camp Hansen on the island. When on ship, we made stops at exotic locations such as Singapore, Thailand, and Korea. Back on Okinawa, fellow officers and I took tours of WWII battle sites and enjoyed snorkeling among the reefs when we weren't training.

While on this deployment, I realized I was up for orders when I got back to CONUS (the continental United States, meaning the forty-eight connected states and DC). I had been with Fox Battery, 2nd Battalion, 11th Marines, including my time attached to 1/5 and the 31st MEU, since December 2001. It was now the summer of 2004.

My requests were simple. I wanted duty with ANGLICO, either 1st ANGLICO on the West Coast or 2nd ANGLICO on the East Coast. In typical fashion, I got neither. Major Orille, my former battery commander, was now the battalion executive officer. He called me to let me know that neither ANGLICO unit was in my future. I would be assigned as the targeting officer with the 1st Force Service Support Group (FSSG). Disappointment filled me.

I reported to the 1st FSSG in August 2004, about six weeks after I returned to Camp Pendleton from my seven months in the Western Pacific. It was as I had feared—full of staff officers, administrative clerks, and assorted rear-echelon types. These marines were all doing essential jobs, but these were jobs I didn't want to do. Technically my title was the targeting officer, but this unit didn't target anything. I was an assistant to the training officer, Major Maples. This infantry officer and I were the only combat arms officers in the building.

Major Maples was nearing retirement and had just returned from Iraq after seven months of watch duty aboard Camp Fallujah. Short and stocky with a nose as crooked as a politician, Major Maples was fun to be around. He was animated when he talked and held nothing back, especially when discussing politics. Besides his intellectual attributes, Major Maples was also an ultramarathoner—an endurance athlete who had been invited to run 135 miles in the Badwater Ultramarathon. He was also an ally to my cause.

Six weeks after reporting to the 1st FSSG, Major Orille called me.

"Angell, you still want to go to ANGLICO?" he asked, already knowing the answer.

"Yes sir."

"Well, they're expanding the companies," he explained, "and I know the new career monitor. I'll have him email you if you want."

Major Orille was a good leader. Though no longer in my chain of command, he was doing this for my benefit.

"That sounds great, sir. Thank you," I said.

About fifteen minutes after hanging up, I received an email. It explained that volunteering for ANGLICO would mean two more combat deployments to Iraq. I also had to get permission from Major Maples to transfer in the spring of '05, which was about six months away. The major agreed to the transfer if another lieutenant replaced me.

I was ecstatic. Knowing that I was going to join one of the Marine Corps' most misunderstood and intriguing units, as well as deploy to combat two more times, made my time with the FSSG easier. Within that period, I asked Joni to marry me. Two weeks after we tied the knot in April 2005, I reported to 1st Air Naval Gunfire Liaison Company (ANGLICO).

The next three years would be life changing, especially when I found myself in an Iraqi town by the name of Ramadi.

CHAPTER TWO:
HELLO, RAMADI

Ar Ramadi is the restive and violent capital of Al Anbar Province, Iraq. It is a place that I hate. It is a place I have feared. It is a place where I have killed. At the same time, it represents a period of my life that I cherish.

We lost fellow warriors there along the Euphrates River, watched them get wounded and killed. Some of these men I knew—most I didn't. In Ramadi, every pile of trash seemed to explode, every pothole hid an IED, and every dark window masked an insurgent. It is a place where young American marines and soldiers performed unselfish acts of bravery day in and day out. Ramadi is with me every single day. I can't shake it; there is no cure.

The first time I heard its name was in the spring of 2004. A ruthless insurgency had flared up and was engulfing Iraq, a country that some of us had departed under cheers from a seemingly grateful populace less than a year prior. Most of the news coverage concerned the fighting in Fallujah and Najaf. Ramadi was only briefly mentioned after a crack Marine infantry battalion suffered extensive casualties. As I watched the news, the city's name reminded me of the Ramada Inn hotel chain. I did not share that embarrassing and obscure thought as the brutality unfolded on the TV.

It is difficult for those who have never seen combat to understand, but a primitive urge deep within my soul burned in response to those images. I wanted to be there with my fellow marines. I wanted to feel the fear and adrenaline coursing through my veins. This odd sensation washes over me to this day when I see images of combat. It is raw and hard to suppress—a demon deep within my soul. I have learned to live with it over the years since I wiped the scourge of that city from my boots and brow for the last time.

Sixteen months after first hearing about Ramadi, I found myself gazing into the distance at this dusty city from the back of an armored seven-ton truck. As we sped down a remote Iraqi highway, Ramadi looked like any other Middle Eastern city: row after row of sand-colored buildings with flat, wall-lined roofs, interspersed with minarets, date palms, and the occasional water tower jutting up like a mushroom. Marines loaded down with body armor, M4 rifles, pistols, grenades, collapsible M249 Squad Automatic Weapons (SAWs), M203s, and ammunition squirmed and shuffled on the bench seat to get a better view as we inched closer to our destiny.

The city was built on violence and occupation. Located about seventy miles west of Baghdad, Ramadi was first established in the late 1860s by local rulers of the Ottoman Empire to control the regional tribes. It was positioned on key terrain where ancient trading routes spanned the Mediterranean, crossing the powerful Euphrates and Tigris Rivers to Baghdad and beyond. The rulers would change hands almost fifty years later when British forces pushed the last Ottoman elements out of the city in late 1917. During WWII, Ramadi was a bastion of anti-British beliefs, as was much of the region, becoming home to a regiment of forces loyal to Arab nationalists. An uprising ensued but was quickly beaten down by the British. Insurgency was in Ramadi's DNA.

As we approached from the west in late August 2005, we saw no explosions or burning buildings—nor were there any fierce firefights ongoing, at least that we could see. But we knew this whole area was violent and treacherous. We didn't need the endless intelligence briefings, situation reports, or repetitive news cycles to tell us the obvious. Well-trained and experienced marines needed only to observe the desolate, barren roadways and landscape to know how dangerous this place was as we made our way from Al Asad Airbase in northwest Iraq to Ramadi on the banks of the Euphrates, a three-to-four-hour drive.

Besides roads and the occasional dry riverbed, called a wadi, almost nothing lay between the old Iraqi airbase and the provincial capital of Al Anbar. It was a flat, dry, inhospitable moonscape to the Westerner, void of any redeeming characteristics. What we did see were burned-out shells of cars and trucks. Old Chevy Suburbans, small Toyota pickups, unidentifiable sedans, and even large eighteen-wheelers littered the roadway; all had been burned to the ground and pushed off the road. It was straight out of a Mad Max movie.

These carcasses were clearly the casualties of angry insurgents. Filling an old car with 155mm artillery shells and rigging them with some form of detonator that exploded as a convoy passed had become a common and deadly tactic. The vehicle-borne improvised explosive device (VBIED) was feared by all.

The highways and roads bore the scars of war. Most of the potholes the convoy swerved around were old IED craters. We scrutinized each hole we encountered and learned to turn away, close our eyes, and cover our ears as we passed, anticipating an explosion.

Heading east on Highway 10, designated by US forces as Route Mobile, the convoy slowed to exit. We made a right turn into Trooper Gate, the main gate to Camp Ramadi, coming to a slow roll as we departed the asphalt for the gravel and dirt. Conversation stopped; the back of the vehicle fell quiet. Fine, powdery dust with the consistency of flour filled the seven-ton truck. It hung in the air. The light-brown powder was difficult not to breathe in; it blanketed everything and everybody. Until the wet season arrived, this fine sand would be a constant companion, only to be replaced by mud.

We passed layers of concertina wire stacked atop one another, providing a lethal ring of steel around the base. This barrier was under observation by American sentries in guard towers. It was a fearsome obstacle for any jihadist contemplating the impossible.

We weaved through serpentine Jersey barriers meant to slow and channel vehicles, a method developed after the Marine barracks in Beirut, Lebanon, was destroyed by a suicide car bomb in 1983. A machine-gun bunker manned by soldiers from the National Guard had a commanding view of the entry point. As we passed the bunker, I strained to look inside. I saw only the barrel of an M2 .50 cal sticking out and the outline of a helmet worn by a soldier.

We stopped so the sentries could talk to the convoy commander, an officer from the headquarters platoon. A large, tracked monster roared to life, and we started moving again. Peering over my shoulder at the sound, I realized the Army was using a powerful M88 tank wrecker as the gate. It belched black smoke and roared again as it moved back into position, blocking the roadway into the camp once the last gun truck rolled past. The soldiers manning the entry point paid us little attention as they returned to smoking cigarettes, scanning the area, and talking amongst each other.

The convoy moved slowly along the narrow road, almost coming to a stop as we rolled over speed bumps made from deteriorating sandbags. The camp was lined with two- and three-story cinder block buildings, former Iraqi Army barracks built in the shade of palm groves. Soldiers went about their daily routine as we drove by. I overheard some of the teams who had been here eight short months ago pointing out changes and key features, such as the Army's tactical operations center (TOC), post exchange, and phone/internet center.

I noticed the amenities and marveled, *Laundry services? Internet and phone center?* There were even soldiers running in regular PT gear and tennis shoes. During the invasion, we had nothing. We lived out of our packs, sent and received snail mail, and ate MREs. That was it. Such luxury could make the time go by easier, but I worried it might distract my team from missions, a fear that later proved unfounded.

Before I knew it, we had pulled into an empty lot next to a one-story, U-shaped building and stopped.

"Dismount, Second Brigade," yelled one of the marines, followed by the sounds of gates and doors slamming open. This was home for the next seven months—or so we thought. Jammed into the seven-tons, we all grabbed our packs and weapons and shuffled towards the exit at the rear of the vehicle. I looked at my team chief, Corporal Anderson. "Well, here we go." A nonsensical comment.

His reply wasn't much better. "Yeah, here we go, sir."

What else are you going to say?

■ ■ ■

Our first day aboard Camp Ramadi consisted of meetings with the team leaders of 2nd ANGLICO. In typical Marine Corps fashion, we received the information at the rate and intensity of a fire hose. You swallowed what you could; the rest landed on the ground, wasted. The other team leaders and I listened, asking the occasional questions. New acronyms, one of the few things the Marine Corps is never in short supply of, were abundant. What the hell is a TIC or PID?

"Don't think you're gonna make these National Guard guys into marines," we were warned. "You're not going to drop a bomb here in Ramadi. After seven months, we've only had one."

"It sucks here," the officers proclaimed after ensuring none of the junior marines were around. The marines and officers from our sister company, 2nd ANGLICO, were professionals, but they were beaten down and jaded by constant attacks and ROEs imposed by leaders living in the safety of the green zone and Washington, DC.

My head was spinning from so much information, and much of it wasn't positive. It appeared that these teams hardly left their gun trucks and largely stayed on the road, which was of course where the IEDs were. The units they supported were reactive, unable to grab the initiative due to the lack of soldiers. Regardless, we would have to make the best of it and do what we could, a standing order when dealing with Major Grice, the 2nd Platoon commander.

I soon learned that my team was taking over for Gunnery Sergeant German, a team leader with 2nd ANGLICO, so I stayed close and listened to what he had to say. An outstanding marine, German was aggressive, knew his job, knew the area, and knew the units. He was well known in the ANGLICO community. He was also ready to head home.

"There's a possible mission tomorrow with one of the platoons from Bravo, 1st of the 109th. They're going into the Mike Charlie area north of the river," he told me while looking at satellite imagery called GRGs (gridded reference graphic).

"I'd like to go along on that," I replied, nodding. The gunny was hesitant.

"Are you sure, sir?"

"Yeah. I'd like to get out there with you to see how the soldiers work and how you operate with them. You guys are going to be gone in a couple days, and I won't get this chance again."

I could tell he wasn't ecstatic about it. Who could blame him? He and his team had endured seven months and come out virtually unscathed. Now he was going to risk his life, and the lives of his teammates, to go outside the wire one last time mere days before his journey home. But I had my team to think about, as well as the mission. I owed it to my marines—Corporals Anderson and Dyer and Lance Corporal Cureton—to learn as much as I could. Seven months later, I would feel the same as Gunnery Sergeant German— ready to go home.

"All right, sir. I'll talk to 'em," he replied. Once he found out the details and if it was still a go, he'd let me know.

An outstanding unit, 2nd ANGLICO was led by Lieutenant Colonel Campbell. An infantry officer with a strong reconnaissance background, having served with various recon battalions and Force Recon, he got orders to 2nd ANGLICO following a stint with Joint

Special Operations Command (JSOC). The unit's status of resources and training systems (SORTS) had been the lowest it could be when he checked in because the unit had recently been reactivated from the 2nd Marine Liaison Element (MLE) and expanded, but the lieutenant colonel got the unit up to speed and ready to deploy. They were now at the end of rotation and ready to head back to Camp Lejeune, North Carolina.

I spent the remainder of the afternoon in the officers' room, a two-room concrete space with some surprising amenities, like a refrigerator, television, DVD player, and an array of cheaply made bunk beds with paper-thin mattresses. Each room had a blacked-out window covered by tightly packed sandbags. Camp Ramadi received poorly aimed but dangerous rocket and mortar fire almost daily. The sandbags provided limited protection. After realizing the details of my new living arrangement were nothing but a distraction, I got back to the task at hand.

As dusk approached and the intense rays from the Iraqi sun loosened their grip, Gunnery Sergeant German found me talking with some of the other team leaders.

"Captain Angell?"

"Yeah, what's up, Gunny?" I asked, breaking away from the gaggle of officers.

He got straight to the point, a trait common to good staff NCOs. "That mission is a go for tomorrow morning."

A small boost of adrenaline shot through my system. I tried to conceal my excitement and replied, "Sounds good. What time you need me to be here, and what do I need?"

"Be here at around 0500, and we will head over to their company area. We haven't signed over the gear yet, so you can just ride with me and my team," he said unemotionally.

This was my first mission of the deployment—my first operation outside the wire and supporting another unit. I wanted to head out before my team and gather as much information as possible. The men had questions; I wanted to give them the truth so we were prepared. One thing the Marine Corps instills and absolutely requires of its officers is leadership by example. If I was going to require them to risk their lives for the next seven months, I would be the first outside the wire, the first through the door, and the first over the wall. I wouldn't be sitting in any COC/TOC or sending them out into the Wild Wild West as I "manned the radios" back on base.

"Roger that," I told Gunny before heading off to find Major Grice.

A couple of hours later, I found myself at the temporary transient quarters, a set of long, narrow wooden buildings used for units coming and going. We would be staying the night there before rotating with the outgoing 2nd ANGLICO marines.

Sitting on my bunk, I glanced around. Most of the other marines were at the chow hall or on a working party for the platoon sergeant, Gunnery Sergeant Jackson. Finally, I had a little peace and quiet to deflate and think. The air-conditioning unit over the door hummed in the background. Reaching into my right cargo pocket, I grabbed a can of chewing tobacco, took a large pinch, and stuffed it into my right cheek. I chuckled to myself, thinking of how my wife hated this habit.

Lying back on that bunk, I shifted as the wiry coils from the thin mattress jabbed and poked me. Although somewhat anxious about the unknown, I was excited about being in Ramadi and proud to be here as a team leader with 1st ANGLICO. I had been in awe of this unit, its mission, and the highly proficient marines. They had an outstanding and proud history and a unique mission, with roots dating back to the island-hopping campaign of the South Pacific during WWII.

■ ■ ■

Officially, ANGLICO's mission is to "provide Marine Air-Ground Task Force Commanders a liaison capability with foreign area expertise to plan, coordinate, employ and conduct terminal control of fires in support of joint, allied and coalition forces."

A simple translation: ANGLICO teams provide direct support to various allied, conventional, and special operations forces operating within Marine Corps–controlled areas of operations. ANGLICO teams specialize in providing, controlling, and coordinating close air support, artillery, rocket fire, and naval gunfire, more accurately called fire support. I recalled what that motivated corporal had told me when I was a young PFC at the School of Infantry—that ANGLICO was "not your average grunt shit." It truly wasn't.

Ramadi and its outlying rural farms and suburbs were "controlled" by the Pennsylvania National Guard's 2nd Brigade Combat Team, 28th Infantry Division (2-28 BCT), led by Colonel Jon Gronski. The BCT fell under the tactical control of the Marine Expeditionary Force (MEF). Air support, via helicopter gunships and jets, was provided by the Marine Corps. Traditionally, the US Air Force supports the Army, but since the BCT fell under the MEF, the Marine Corps would be providing the much-needed close air support. ANGLICO teams were tasked with supporting the BCT as the subject matter experts in directing air strikes.

At the time, 1st ANGLICO consisted of two brigade platoons and a headquarters platoon numbering about 200 men. The headquarters platoon was primarily responsible for two things: one, as a self-sustaining unit, they supported the brigade platoons by taking care of personnel, administrative, and logistical issues; and two, they were the liaison element at the division level.

As the name insinuates, brigade platoons support the brigade or regiment. In late August 2005, 2nd Platoon, led by Major Mike Grice, was assigned to 2-28 BCT in Ramadi. Within the platoon were HQ elements that worked with the headquarters of the Army brigade and the two supporting arms liaison teams (SALT) that supported the various battalions. Finally, within each SALT were two firepower control teams (FCT—pronounced "fict"). Doctrinally, the FCT is the team going out with the infantry companies and platoons. I was a FCT leader.

This is a simple explanation of ANGLICO, and I must stress that we did not operate by the book or by doctrine while in Ramadi. Marines assigned to the SALT and brigade platoons were organized into provisional FCTs and went outside the wire on missions, in addition to conducting their traditional mission of liaising and coordinating at the brigade or battalion level. Lieutenant Colonel Campbell, the commanding officer of 2nd ANGLICO, had developed the plan specifically to support the MEF. Because of ANGLICO's training and leadership, these provisional teams excelled at providing the MEF with much-needed support around Al Anbar Province.

ANGLICO marines worked in small teams, sometimes alone or miles from the nearest Marine unit. As such, they had to be mature, professional, and intelligent. The senior enlisted leadership within 1st ANGLICO expected a lot from the younger marines. They were given plenty of responsibility and in turn made the impossible possible. If you treat young marines like men, they act like men, usually. This was the philosophy ANGLICO practiced from the top down, although some marines might not agree.

Training back in the States had been intense and long. The daily PT was combat oriented and challenging. One of the first PT sessions I went on after joining ANGLICO was a ruck run with the marines. It was an enlisted-only run, but I tagged along to get a feel for the men. Wearing boots, camouflage pants, and green T-shirts, we grabbed our rucksacks with about forty-five pounds of gear and took off into the hills of Camp Pendleton. It was a challenge, but I enjoyed it.

Similar PT sessions in other units might be viewed as hazing. But like I said, ANGLICO is different. They have to be prepared to work with any unit, Special Forces or conventional, and the ANGLICO leadership understands that, as do the marines. We prided ourselves on our physical fitness. Mile after mile, hill after hill, we ran and ran hard during that run. A few marines fell back, but none fell out.

When a marine started losing steam, drifting towards the rear of the formation, his fellow marines would take his pack and keep going.

My team was interspersed within the run, but I kept an eye on them. Corporals Anderson and Dyer had no issues and were at the front of the run, not far from Gunnery Sergeant Jackson, their platoon sergeant. Lance Corporal Cureton struggled some, falling back towards the rear. I didn't intervene and instead watched these men take care of each other. The last thing they needed was some officer giving directions when the men were more than capable of handling these issues internally.

Before long, Cureton was back up with the rest of the marines. No one fell out. These men took care of their own, a philosophy drilled into them since the day they stood on the infamous yellow footprints at the Marine Corps Recruit Depot.

At one point during this grueling PT session, I saw a fireplug of a marine with a large amount of chewing tobacco in his cheek. This takes grit. I've tried it before and hated it. But here was Lance Corporal McKinney, a member of one of the other teams, about four miles into a ruck run and sucking on tobacco. These men were outstanding. I loved it. This was what I joined the Marine Corps for.

Within the brigade platoons, every marine, regardless of rank or MOS, was cross-trained on how to do each other's jobs. Lance corporals learned to direct air strikes while team leaders developed the technical skills of communications. Team communicators led patrols while team chiefs worked the M249 SAW. From fire and movement training, surveillance, small-team tactics, navigation, and Arabic-language classes to mortar and artillery fire support, the marines had extraordinary capabilities. While out training in the US Army's Yuma Proving Ground, Major Grice had young marines leading convoys and immediate actions in reaction to various situations. Every one of us learned and developed the unique skills required of the unit. It was impressive to see a lance corporal grab the radio, identify a target in the impact area, and direct an air strike. This built cohesion and made us a better fighting unit.

I had spent enough time as an artillery officer to know that often the forward air controller or forward observer treated their assigned communications marine as a man who only carried and fixed the radio. I disagreed with this. Calling them simply "radio operator" minimized their position and capabilities. They weren't just ROs; these marines were members of the team.

From the day I joined 1st ANGLICO, we were training. We were in the field almost every week as the clock ticked down to our deployment. We pushed the marines hard. We would conduct long patrols to the edge of impact areas, call in air strikes, and then patrol to a shooting range, where we would participate in a shooting package with our M4s, pistols, and various machine guns, like the M240G, .50 cal, or Mk-19 automatic grenade launcher. There were communication exercises, medical training, Arabic classes, patrolling, vehicle ops, more TACP (Tactical Air Control Party) shoots, visits to grenade ranges, and then we'd do it all over again. We went to the Yuma Proving Grounds every few weeks, it seemed. There we would increase the training intensity.

We cross-trained with the UK's Royal Marine Commandos and the Dutch Royal Marines. They gave us classes on building and operating out of a hide site in a rural environment, which would later help my team as we conducted counter-IED operations on the outskirts of Ramadi. We got tons of time to work with our teams. I wore the boys out with repeated immediate-action drills, night and day. Bounding forward, bounding back, shifting left, shifting right, cover and movement—these are all crucial drills for actions that need to be conducted without thinking. In my view, the 1st ANGLICO leadership really prepared the men for this deployment.

■ ■ ■

Anderson and Cureton entered the transient quarters. Getting rid of my tobacco in an empty water bottle, I sat up.

"Hey, sir. How's it going?" Anderson asked.

"Good. Just trying to relax. I'll be heading out with Gunnery Sergeant German tomorrow morning," I replied. "It's a short patrol. I should be back before lunch. What do you guys got going on?"

Anderson and Cureton were obviously curious about the upcoming patrol. Neither had seen combat yet. They were well trained, but you can never tell how someone will react during a firefight until they've been in one. The loud crack and snap of an AK-47 bullet screaming by your head as an insurgent tries to kill you is something you can't create in a training environment.

"Just got back from chow. Tomorrow we've got a working party with Staff Sergeant Ibanez for the turnover with 2nd ANGLICO," explained Corporal Anderson.

I asked about our communications chief: "Where's Dyer?"

Anderson thought he was at the phone center with some of the other marines.

"All right. When I get back tomorrow, I'd like to brief you and the team," I said before taking a pull from a warm bottle of water.

"Good to go, sir," they replied in unison. Lying back down on my bunk, I placed earbuds in my ears and listened to Blink-182. I thought about Firepower Control Team 7.

I don't think I could have picked a better team. Mike Anderson was considered an older corporal. He wasn't much younger than me, and at the time I was thirty-two. As a former member of the 82nd Airborne, he knew the games that came with military life and elected to be a marine even after the Corps informed him that he wouldn't retain his old Army rank of sergeant.

Mike was a Midwesterner, had married his high school sweetheart, and had a daughter and son attending an elementary school on Camp Pendleton. A consummate family man, he talked about them from time to time. I admired this about him but would not truly appreciate his sacrifice until I had children of my own. The more I worked with Anderson, the more I came to rely on his advice. He had a way of reading people and situations and had great instincts; this quality would later save lives, including mine.

Standing at about five foot ten with a powerful build, Anderson was well respected within the company for his experience and maturity. He was a true, quiet professional. Few marines made the mistake of challenging him, and he didn't take kindly to bullies.

Anderson was an expert scout observer. I can't remember a time when he didn't know an answer to a fire support question. In fact, after he had joined the unit and attended the ANGLICO basic course, he received almost perfect scores on the fire support tests. He was a solid performer in the field. When it came to weapons and tactics, he knew them well. As a former soldier, his liaison duties when dealing with the US Army were invaluable.

Corporal Chad Dyer, our communications chief, was another outstanding marine. ANGLICO relies heavily on communication. The teams need to talk to aircraft, artillery, mortars, TOCs, other ground units, and the list goes on. It's not unusual for a four-man team to contact a section of Cobra gunships, coordinate with a TOC, and request artillery simultaneously. This requires the use of several radios—all of which we carry on our backs and use even when we are directly engaging the enemy with our personal weapons. This in turn requires a marine who is an expert at using these radios: a communications chief.

Corporal Dyer was a Texas boy in his early twenties and had seen combat in the fall of 2004 during Operation Phantom Fury, the battle to retake Fallujah from Abu Musab Al-Zarqawi's insurgents. Not only had he slugged it out with hardened jihadists, but he did so as a member of ANGLICO. His previous team leader had been wounded in support of a US Navy SEAL detachment. Dyer was a true warrior, and it showed in the way he carried himself. He was quiet and confident. There wasn't a problem he couldn't fix when it came to radios and communication. I would quickly learn that he was indispensable.

The final marine on the team, although certainly not the least, was Lance Corporal Jon Cureton. Cureton was an intelligent young man from Las Vegas, Nevada. Graduating from a magnet school at age seventeen, he had to get his mother's signature to join the Marine Corps. Though he was the junior man on FCT-7, we treated him with the respect he deserved.

Cureton constantly fought to keep his weight within Marine Corps standards, but that didn't hold him back. As days became weeks and weeks became months, the team discovered that Cureton was a fighter. At times, Corporal Anderson had to rein him in. Cureton carried the compact M249 Squad Automatic Weapon (SAW), handling the beast like he'd been doing it for years. At one point, one of the other team leaders, an infantry officer, told me that Cureton was probably one of the best SAW gunners he had seen.

Cureton would prove himself as an aggressive urban street fighter, a quality overshadowed only by his knowledge of fire support, and he was solid with the radios. He was also the type of marine who cracked jokes during firefights and would fart during a mission brief and blame it on someone else. The team wouldn't have been the same without him.

As I listened to my music, I drifted off to sleep. My body was tired from a long day, and my mind was drained. I fell asleep in my boots, thinking of my wife.

Four hours later, I awoke from a deep sleep and sat up. It was pitch black except for a sliver of light coming from underneath the door. The rest of the marines had returned and turned off the lights. Nervous I might be late for my patrol, I squinted at my watch. It was only 0115. I still had a few more hours to rest. Then I realized why I had awakened.

The loud crack of outgoing artillery fire rumbled through the wood-framed building. I was initially unsure if it was outgoing or the dreaded incoming but soon realized it was ours. I took off my boots and lay back in the bunk, listening. The fire was constant, probably one round fired every twenty seconds. It lasted for about a minute, and it was strangely comforting. During the invasion of Iraq about two and a half years prior, the Marine artillery batteries were constantly firing as we pushed north. We learned to embrace the chaotic tune of the Marine cannoneers as they manhandled the M198 155mm howitzer.

About a quarter mile away, in a somewhat isolated part of Camp Ramadi, two US Army Paladin howitzers pumped 155mm high-explosive artillery shells onto some unknown target north of the city in the rural farmlands of the Euphrates. I listened to their melody and wondered what was on the receiving end of the barrage. *Good*, I thought. *A few less insurgents can make our lives a little easier.* I fell back asleep, fighting the growing weight on my shoulders.

The chime from my watch woke me at 0400. Rubbing my face and head, I stumbled through the darkness to my rucksack at the foot of my bunk. After brushing my teeth and shaving at the nearest bathroom trailer, which smelled of mildew and soap, I started my ten-minute walk to the 2nd ANGLICO compound. I could have used a cup of coffee.

Large generators hummed throughout Camp Ramadi. It was dark, the shadows even darker. The thought of jihadi infiltrators waiting to snatch an American marine popped into my mind, but I brushed it off. It was already ninety-one degrees; I was starting to sweat.

Strangely, motivation and pride engulfed me as I strode along the gravel road that early morning. This was where I wanted to be. I wanted to serve my country as a US Marine in combat. I'd been part of the original invasion force, but this was an entirely different mission. I was proud to be serving next to some of the best marines I would ever have the honor of knowing.

Approaching the ANGLICO compound, I expected to see Gunnery Sergeant German's marines prepping the gun truck for our mission. Instead, there was only silence. Of course, I was early by about half an hour, but still surprised. I removed my armor-plate carrier with all its attachments and laid it against the wall next to my helmet and rifle. Then I gulped down a large bottle of water, trying unsuccessfully to relax.

The one-story, U-shaped compound was shared by a Marine explosive ordnance disposal (EOD) unit, a canine team, a crash/fire rescue team, and a small US Army medical unit that dealt with psychological issues. ANGLICO took up about a third of the building; the other detachments occupied the rest. ANGLICO's four to five gun trucks were parked in the interior, with a small portion of the parking area hosting a couple of picnic tables, pull-up bars, and workout benches beneath a large camouflage netting for shade.

1st ANGLICO compound, Camp Ramadi

Before long, Gunnery Sergeant German came out of the team leader's room, wearing black running shorts and flip-flops and carrying his hygiene bag on the way to the shower trailer. The surprised marine spotted me.

"Morning, sir," he said, walking by. "You're here early."

"I didn't want you guys waiting on me" was my reply.

"We won't be long. My marines will have the vehicle ready soon," he assured me. Not that I needed assurance; I knew that he and his team were pros like the rest of 2nd ANGLICO.

Soon enough, the gun truck was ready. These marines had performed this dance for the last seven months, and they were ready to hand over the reins. Equipped with multiple radios and an M240G machine gun in the turret, we took the quick drive to the 1-109th Bravo Company office for an operations order.

Stepping into a large, open room on the ground floor of an old Iraqi barracks, Gunnery Sergeant German introduced me to a group of National Guard soldiers. I forgot their names almost as quickly as they offered them. A young soldier who looked tired but determined offered me a large bottle of water from a refrigerator. I eagerly accepted, feeling the cool water in my chest as I gulped it down.

The hulking platoon leader, a young second lieutenant from Pennsylvania, gave his patrol order. His platoon was going into Mike Charlie 3, also known as MC-3, a zone on the north side of the Euphrates River in the rural suburbs of the city. His company commander wanted him to conduct reconnaissance of a target building for an upcoming raid. Once that was complete, the platoon would pass out propaganda pamphlets and give candy and soccer balls to local children. We were to be inserted into the area via gun trucks and M113 armored personnel carriers, escorted by a Bradley Fighting Vehicle (BFV).

It seemed like a simple mission. The young leader was brief but to the point. He didn't give extensive operations orders; he didn't have to. His men knew their standard operating procedure (SOP). As an attachment, though, I was in the dark.

The previous day, the other ANGLICO team leaders had warned us that these units were not marines, so we shouldn't expect them to be. They appeared different by our standards, and they weren't going to change. However, these were the men getting blown up by IEDs and shot at daily as they patrolled the streets of this godforsaken city.

These men, along with other line companies, would later win the Battle of Ramadi. They deserved our esteem, and if we exhibited silly interservice rivalry, they wouldn't want our support, even though they might need it.

At the end of the mission brief, most of the soldiers went back outside to prep their respective vehicles. The lieutenant, Gunnery Sergeant German, and I stayed inside. Handing me a small, black handheld radio, the lieutenant asked if I had any questions.

"Yeah. What's your scheme of maneuver?" I replied. German stayed silent and stared at the lieutenant as I spoke. The young officer looked at me, then at the dry-erase board, and basically repeated what he had said during the brief.

The scheme of maneuver in a patrol is very important. Basically, I wanted to know how his squads were going to accomplish his intent—how the patrol was going to be conducted. I didn't know where Gunnery Sergeant German and I would be in the patrol. The lieutenant basically briefed us that we would go into MC-3 via vehicles, dismount, patrol around, look at a house, and return. Eventually, I would realize that his unit's SOP negated the requirement to brief order of movement.

Back outside in the heat, we waited to leave. Restocking my lip with fresh tobacco, I turned to Gunnery Sergeant German and shook my head.

"Is this how it always is?"

"More or less," he chuckled. "You kinda put that lieutenant on the spot."

"True," I said, slightly confused. "When lives are on the line, there are certain things we need to know." Truth be told, I felt guilty. Embarrassing the young officer was not my intent, but leaving the mission brief with unanswered questions would have been irresponsible.

We hadn't even left Camp Ramadi, and I was learning—not about the enemy's tactics but about the soldiers and their way of doing things. These were some of the soldiers we'd be working with directly and the types of missions we'd be going on. If things weren't as I expected, I needed to improvise, adapt, and overcome. This meant developing close working relationships with these units.

About twenty minutes later, the vehicles headed towards Camp Ramadi's front gate. Our gun truck was in the center of the patrol, behind an old M113. We were the only gun truck, a situation I didn't care for. One gun truck out of about eight tracked armored personnel carriers sticks out. We were an easy target. On the flip side, I didn't want to ride in the back of an M113, closed up in the dark and not knowing what was happening.

Just inside the gate, all the vehicles stopped. The soldiers and marines got out and loaded their weapons. Our gunner in the turret readied the machine gun. Marines and soldiers aren't supposed to have loaded weapons while on Camp Ramadi, or any other camp, for that matter. It's not needed, and it cuts down on negligent discharges. Every time a patrol returns from a mission, they unload their weapons.

Getting back into the gun truck, I muscled the door closed. The bolt-on armor made it feel like closing a bank vault. Armed, loaded, and strapped to the teeth, we were ready to go. With my satellite imagery map in one hand and my M4 between my legs, I couldn't help but smile. I soaked up the adrenaline and the fear. It had been two years since I last felt this, and it was intoxicating.

The large M88 tank wrecker moved back, and we rolled out towards the north. Dirt churned up as the tracked M113 in front of us tore through the parched earth. Turning east on the paved highway called Route Mobile, we picked up speed and started scanning the roadways for signs of possible IEDs. I regularly peeked down at my map as Gunnery Sergeant German pointed out various areas of interest, though he had to yell over the high-pitched roar of the M113. Once again, I tried to take it in and remember what I could:

"That's 'Low-Water Bridge' and OP-1, manned by some artillery guys from the 222nd."

"See that scorched mark on the asphalt? Well, that was where two soldiers were killed last week from an IED. One of them burned to death."

"That road there, the one that parallels the river and leads to Camp Blue Diamond—their main gate got hit by a suicide VBIED not long ago."

This wasn't like the invasion at all. I had a lot to learn in a very short period.

North of Route Mobile lay nothing but an endless expanse of flat desert all the way to Turkey. To the south of the highway, along the river, were lush green farm fields, dirt roads, date palm groves, and multistory houses. We crossed the mighty Euphrates River, its cool water rushing south.

The patrol slowed minutes after leaving Camp Ramadi as we approached a freeway overpass attached to a cloverleaf interchange. The intimidating BFV, with its 25mm cannon, took up a position on the overpass to cover us. The gun truck slowed even further as we rolled over a curb and into a litter-infested field next to a row of houses south of Route Mobile. In what appeared to be no particular order, the M113s stopped.

We peered out of our windows, still looking for IEDs. Our vehicle stopped amid an assortment of garbage. There could have been ten IEDs around us, and I wouldn't have known. It took experience operating in the area to learn how to identify them. Regardless, I searched for wires and anything suspicious.

The gunny reminded his marines to stay with the vehicles, and we would link up with them at another location. Where? He didn't precisely know, hence my original question to the lieutenant regarding the scheme of maneuver.

To be a US Marine on an ANGLICO team, you must think on your feet and adapt to any situation. Every single member of a team, regardless of rank, must be prepared to make quick and tactically sound decisions without the luxury of asking for guidance. Gunnery

Sergeant German's marines had to be able to operate without him. This was an issue I would bring up with my team. It was important to remind them and reinforce the need to be independent thinkers as well as team players.

Dismounting the gun truck, I moved to the back of the vehicle and faced outward, searching for threats. On the street about 100 meters away, Iraqis went about their daily lives. Some stared, while others ignored our presence. I watched their hands and eyes. My heart rate increased as reality set in. I told myself to relax. Before long, my breathing and pulse had settled.

The gunnery sergeant took up a position on the other side of the gun truck with his PRC-117 radio on his back. That radio was our lifeline in the event we got hit by insurgents, our sole reason for being there. One quick call to the ANGLICO representatives in the brigade TOC, and we could have gunships or jets overhead, suppressing any real attack.

"ANGLICO, you with us?" squawked the radio the lieutenant had given me at the patrol brief.

"Affirm. We're at our vehicle," I replied.

"Okay, just meet me over at the lead M113."

I glanced over at the gunny. He had his M4's ACOG (Advanced Combat Optical Gunsight) scope against his eye.

"He wants us over at the lead vehicle," I said, standing and adjusting my body armor. With my M4 held close to my chest, we passed through the soldiers preparing to step off on patrol. The lieutenant was easy to find. At six foot three inches tall and weighing about 215 pounds, he stood out. This young man was a former football player for a small college in Vermont who joined the National Guard after the events of 9/11. He was calm as he led his men through the heat and stress of the mission.

Motioning to his lead squad leader, the lieutenant ordered the patrol to move south down a small dirt path. The soldiers simply stood around as they waited for the column to stretch out and create dispersion, so I bent down on a knee to present a smaller target. Peering over my left shoulder, I waited until the lieutenant and I were a good five meters apart before standing back up.

The pace was slow as we moved parallel to a cinder block wall. Every few steps, I turned around to ensure that German and the remainder of the patrol were behind me. Studying the fields and houses, I looked for signs of danger. If an Iraqi woman hung her laundry on a rooftop, it got passed down the line. When soldiers saw an old man plowing his field, they pointed it out. Even a young boy herding his goats was scrutinized. Everything and everyone were a potential threat.

As we patrolled, I kept tabs on our location. *Okay, that was about a hundred meters south; then we went west for another hundred meters.* Our location was tracked on the GRG, and occasionally I'd look at the GPS in my pocket. Technology is a great tool, but it wasn't my primary means of navigation. Batteries go dead, buildings interrupt satellite signals, and bullets shatter plastic. It was a great backup, though. I noted navigational markers and monitored our pace count.

As we patrolled through the area, I tried to think about my reaction to certain situations. *If we take fire from that palm grove, the roofs of those houses would be a great position to direct an air strike from. If an insurgent engages us from that house, the ditch over there would provide a good spot to return fire from and react to the ambush.* My mind was going a hundred miles an hour, but I still had my rifle up, maintaining awareness of my surroundings. You learn to multitask quickly; it keeps you alive.

The loud, sharp clap of a lone gunshot came from behind us. Instinctively, I fell to the ground in the prone position, facing north towards the sound with my M4 pointed out. The majority of the soldiers, skittish and jumpy, did the same, although some continued to stand. The lieutenant yelled for a report. Everyone wanted to know what was going on.

I fought the urge to direct these soldiers into maneuvering on the enemy. This was the lieutenant's patrol—not mine. I waited to hear the screams "Medic up," meaning we had suffered a casualty. Thankfully, the call never came. Then a soldier at the rear of the patrol yelled that he'd seen a MAM (military-aged male) running away but the man was unarmed. Unsure whether this was the shooter, they let him go. Chances were the young man had fired a rifle and dropped it in the ditch or bushes. The enemy knew we needed positive identification (PID) before we shot.

Shaking his head with a quick smirk, Gunnery Sergeant German stood up. I followed suit, slightly embarrassed but unsure why. Less than a week ago, I was in safe, sunny Southern California. Now I was in one of the most dangerous cities in the world. My anxiety was extremely high, my heart pounding. The thought of my beautiful young wife getting a knock on the door from men wearing Marine Corps dress blues saturated my brain. I shook off the paralyzing thought and promised myself I wouldn't think of my wife while outside the base on operations.

For German, this was his last patrol. The idea of getting killed on the final combat mission has plagued marines since the branch was established in 1775.

Continuing south, the path opened and cut through a pasture, then through a small neighborhood tucked into the shade of palm trees. The locals stared. Unemployed young men squatted in their yards, drinking chai and smoking cigarettes. As the patrol meandered through their neighborhood, these men glared at us. The women, clad in all black except for their faces, peeked outside doors and around corners before rushing back to their duties. When children approached us, old men shooed them away. It was painfully obvious that we weren't welcome here.

For the next two hours, we sweated in the desert heat and patrolled the northwest portion of MC-3. The mixture of farmland adjacent to tightly clustered homes required continual adjustments in our movement. Occasionally, we'd stop to talk to locals. The lieutenant and his soldiers would ask about insurgent activity. Of course, no one knew anything.

"No Ali Baba, no Ali Baba," they'd say. It was a scene common to counterinsurgency movements all over the world.

As the powerful Iraqi sun rose high in the noon sky, the M113s and lone gun truck pulled up alongside us. In a flash, we were back on Route Mobile, heading for Camp Ramadi. I sucked down a bottle of water with little effort. In the back of my mind, I considered what I had learned.

As far as ANGLICO teams were concerned, I didn't believe such operations were an effective use of an FCT team, which could summon and direct air strikes. Going on everyday-presence patrols with the regular infantry didn't appear to produce results, although I would later realize I was wrong. Yes, if attacked, and if an FCT was with the patrol, close air support could be used. But 2nd ANGLICO had made things clear: no one was dropping bombs in Ramadi.

■ ■ ■

Gone are the days when a marine under attack from the Viet Cong or NVA could grab a radio off his dead lieutenant and call in the "fast movers" for an air strike. That is now reserved for the realm of Hollywood, not reality. The powers that be within the military bureaucracy decided at some point that a specially trained individual must be on-site, or at least within radio contact, for bombs to be dropped within proximity to friendly forces. For the Marine Corps, only forward air controllers or joint terminal attack controllers (JTAC) could control air strikes.

Designated Marine Corps pilots and combat-arms staff NCOs and officers are trained in the lethal art of close air support (CAS) during a roughly three-week course. During two weeks in the classroom and one in the field, they learn the basic technical skills of controlling an air strike safely and effectively from the ground.

It wasn't a challenging course compared to others, but it was required, and there were few openings. Once certified, Marine pilots became FACs, and the ground marines became JTACs. I became a JTAC.

■ ■ ■

When we made it back to Camp Ramadi twenty minutes later, I was still disheartened by the patrol. I sat under the shade of camouflage netting at the ANGLICO compound and reflected. Was this what FCT-7's next seven months were going to be like? All that training, skill, and physical fitness going to waste as we stumbled around IED-infested streets, getting shot at by cowards who rarely stood and fought? There had to be a more effective way for my team and me to be utilized. We would have to use our imaginations.

CHAPTER THREE:
OPERATION SAND EEL

About a week after arriving at Camp Ramadi, I was in the 2-28 BCT TOC, perusing intelligence and incident reports while on duty. ANGLICO had to maintain a twenty-four seven presence in the operations center. It was my turn to monitor the radios and request immediate air support from the MEF if it was needed somewhere in the AO. All officers and SNCOs had this duty for a four-hour block every few days or so.

At around 0800, Major Gordon, the brigade air officer, came into the TOC and sat next to me. After he asked if we had any air on-station, meaning any fixed-wing aircraft or gunships over Ramadi, he wanted to know what I was looking at. One of the computer screens in front of me displayed imagery of an isolated road south of the city called Route Long Island. I must have piqued the major's interest, because he didn't shut down my research.

An air officer with the North Carolina–based 118th Air Support Operations Squadron (118th ASOS), Major Andy Gordon and his airmen were attached to the 2-28 BCT to provide tactical command and control of air support. The scholarly-looking, bald major from Dillsboro, Indiana, was well liked and respected by those of us who had a chance to work with him. He wasn't tied down by risk aversion and had a bias for action when it came to going after insurgents with air power.

Route Long Island was a two-lane highway that served as a detour around the notorious Route Michigan, which ran from Baghdad to the Syrian border and, more significantly, cut directly through Fallujah and Ramadi. IED and insurgent attacks on convoys traveling down Route Michigan between Ramadi and Fallujah had gotten so bad, and so deadly, that the MEF mostly forbade the practice. Only mission-essential and combat patrols were authorized. This required most convoys to travel on Route Long Island, which added more than two hours to the convoy and took them south around Lake Habbaniyah. Insurgent forces had recognized this and started planting IEDs accordingly.

Major Gordon and I started talking about these IED attacks and how to kill the insurgents planting them. One of my suggestions was to insert a few small teams into covert observation posts for a few days to observe portions of the road where IEDs were consistently hitting convoys. Surprised, he told me he would bring it up with the brigade operations officer.

I saw Major Gordon again the next day. In a nonchalant manner, he gave me a very brief warning order for a mission.

"We're a go for the counter-IED ops along Route Long Island. From the seventh through the ninth of September, you're going to establish an OP and watch for insurgents emplacing IEDs. We are going to get you some air support as well."

Surprised about the mission, my mind went into planning mode.

"How are we going to get out there, sir?"

The major replied, "The Triple Deuce has an overt OP in the area. When they rotate out platoons, you and your team, along with two snipers, will ride with them. Then, if need be, they can insert you via gun truck, or you can just walk off the OP at night; your choice."

"Snipers, sir?" I asked, writing in my little green notebook.

"Yup, contact Major Cody Marsh. He will give you the information for the sniper team leader. The operation is called Sand Eel. Write up your CONOPS [concept of operations] and scheme of maneuver, and brief me and Major Grice tomorrow morning."

With that, I left the TOC and headed to the ANGLICO command post to see my team. This was a great opportunity. We had participated in a few missions since arriving on Camp Ramadi, one of which was relatively big, but they were otherwise uneventful except for IEDs, a constant nuisance. This operation could be a step in the right direction.

■ ■ ■

Forty-eight hours later, my team—call sign Wild Eagle Two-Seven—plus two snipers were sitting in the back of three gun trucks, waiting to be inserted. Earlier in the day, we had hitched a ride with a platoon from the 222nd Field Artillery Battalion of the PA National Guard from Camp Ramadi to a small, isolated outpost called OP-2. Lovingly called the Triple Deuce, these men were tasked with providing security for a key intersection along Route Long Island. Now they were going to insert us into the desert so we could conduct a patrol and set up our covert OP. These men would also serve as our quick reaction force (QRF) if things got interesting and we needed support or emergency extraction. It was reassuring to know they were located only a few miles from our proposed hide site.

The men of the Triple Deuce who secured and manned this remote outpost were older compared to the marines. As National Guard soldiers, they likely had years of service with minimal promotions or had prior service and switched over in the hopes of earning a Reserve retirement pension. To us, they were good soldiers doing a thankless but necessary job. The moment we stepped into their gun trucks, we felt like part of the team. There was no ego and no confrontation, only eagerness to support and accomplish the mission. These men knew this AO inside out, so I picked their brains for intelligence. They were more than happy to support us in any way possible.

Crammed into the back left seat of the lead gun truck, I looked down at my watch. It read September 7; the time was 2300 hours.

"All right, move out," I told the driver. Next to me, between two heavy rucksacks, Corporal Dyer sat quietly, looking out the window into the darkness as we started down a small hill towards Route Long Island. The vehicle behind me held Corporal Anderson and Lance Corporal Cureton. The rear gun truck held the two snipers, Corporals Johnson and Smith.

I watched the GPS in my left hand as we drove through the darkness. The first checkpoint soon came into view.

"All right. Stop up here," I said, breaking the silence. The gun truck's engine whined. It was a false stop, a technique originally used in the jungles of Southeast Asia during the Vietnam War. The idea behind false stops or insertions is simple: confuse the enemy. Helicopters are loud, attracting unwanted attention. When small teams were inserted into the jungles, the communist forces knew the Americans were in the area and would commence hunting them. To throw off the enemy, American pilots and reconnaissance teams would land and take off at various LZs while the recon element stayed in the bird. This would happen a few times before the team disembarked. The intent was to conceal where the recon team had been inserted. I used the same general idea here but with gun trucks.

As ANGLICO, we had the option of being inserted by helos, but my team chief agreed with me that it would attract too much attention, whereas these gun trucks traveled up and down Route Long Island all the time. The insurgents had grown accustomed to their presence. Using them helped avoid unwanted attention during the more vulnerable stage of our insertion.

After two false stops, we came to our actual insert point. My heart pounded as the gun truck slowed and stopped in a depression, which provided some concealment from the small village about three kilometers away. I pushed open the heavy armored door, stumbled out with my weapon up, and lumbered to the side of the road. The rucksack hanging on one arm acted like an anchor, slowing my movement. Out of the corner of my eye, I saw Corporal Anderson and one of the snipers exit. Dyer, Cureton, and the other sniper climbed out on the other side of the road. The drivers and assistant drivers in the passenger seats climbed out with their weapons for cover, then hurriedly got back in.

Taking a knee, I looked over my shoulder at the turret gunner on the lead gun truck. I gave him a thumbs-up. As instructed, he scanned behind him to ensure my team was clear of the vehicles. He briefly disappeared into the turret before popping back into view with a thumbs-up; they sped off, the engines struggling under the weight of the armor.

Anderson counted everyone to make sure no one had been left behind. It was an easy count to six. We quickly shuffled north about twenty meters and got into a tight circle, lying in the prone position beside our rucksacks. Everyone faced out with their weapons up and ready. Using our NVGs to cut through the darkness, we searched for enemy movement and listened for anything that could be a threat. The rumble of the gun trucks faded as the vehicles continued north, and then there was silence. We stayed motionless, trying to forget about the equipment and body armor digging into our necks.

At this point, we waited, conducting a security halt. We needed our eyes and other senses to acclimate to our surroundings. Lying in the sand and dirt for about fifteen minutes, we strained to pick up manmade noises. But all we saw was an empty desert with small, rolling hills overshadowed by a sky that seemed to explode with stars. All we heard were the distant noises of life in a third-world country.

After a few minutes, I double-checked my map and GPS to reorient myself. Our primary planned OP was only about three clicks to our northwest.

Satisfied we hadn't been compromised, I rose on one knee, and the team followed my lead. To cover each other's movement, we threw our rucksacks on our backs one at a time, always maintaining 360 degrees of security. Each of us was weighed down, but what we carried was necessary.

Death and survival were the two commodities our ANGLICO teams dealt in. We didn't train to hand out leaflets or candy and soccer balls to local children. We specialized in what the American military has relied on for decades: overwhelming firepower. This firepower is more restrained but also more precise in our modern world, and this specialty requires unique equipment.

Of course, our lifeline and modus operandi revolved around communications. If we wanted to blow something up with a bomb, we needed a radio. If we needed to call in artillery, we needed radios. If we needed an emergency extract, we needed radios. If we had to report intelligence information, guess what we needed.

For this mission, we had four radios. Corporal Dyer carried the two large PRC-117s, and two of the smaller PRC-148s went with Anderson and me. Both versions could communicate via satellite, VHF, and UHF. We also needed plenty of batteries, which were cumbersome and hefty, although we'd only be utilizing one or two at a time. We all carried the batteries, not to mention copious amounts of water, ammunition, and small portions of food that consisted primarily of granola and power bars.

More specialized equipment was included as well. Anderson had a shovel with most of the handle sawed off, plus a thermal night sight called a See-Spot. I carried binoculars, a spotting scope, and the Infrared Zoom Laser Illuminator Designator (IZLID), which was a device about the size of a flashlight that beamed an infrared laser only visible through NVGs. We used it to point out targets for attack aircraft. The snipers had their own equipment, although they didn't have radios; that was our job.

Lance Corporal Cureton was our de facto weapons man. He was humping the SAW, which had a relatively short barrel and collapsible buttstock. This beast eats up ammunition, so he carried boxes of belted 5.56mm. Besides ammo, Cureton was hauling a few other surprises, such as multiple fragmentation grenades and our trip-wire flash bang grenades we planned to deploy along approach to our OP.

Set and ready to move out, I motioned to Corporal Johnson, one of the snipers, and pointed in the direction of movement with my left hand. The soldier nodded and stood up. His dark silhouette slowly and deliberately moved towards the northwest and into the low desert hills. Behind him was Cureton with the SAW. If we got ambushed, I wanted him to put down maximum firepower in the direction of the enemy as we either broke contact or transitioned into attack mode.

Behind Cureton and in front of me was the sniper with the M14 scoped rifle, Corporal Smith. Corporal Dyer was behind me. He had one of the PRC-117s up and running, with a handset tucked between his head and helmet. Crackling in his ear was the radio frequency monitored by the soldiers who had dropped us off. If something went down, he would report it to our QRF. Finally came Corporal Anderson. As my team chief, he protected our rear, a vital and weighty responsibility. While Dyer could have performed this function, I needed my communications chief close by.

Ambient light came from the stars and the sliver of moon. We relied on our NVGs. They would give us the edge should insurgents lay hidden in the dunes and dry wadis ahead. Through the monocular headsets, the darkness became shimmering shades of green. But this wasn't the only advantage we had over our enemy.

In the distance, I heard the low *thump-thump-thump* of Marine Corps AH-1 Cobra attack helicopters thundering over the dark landscape. The pilot's voice hissed through the earpiece attached to my radio: "Wild Eagle Two-Seven from Tyrant."

Still moving methodically towards our primary OP, weapons facing in alternating directions, I used my left hand to key the transmit button on my plate carrier.

"Tyrant, this is Wild Eagle Two-Seven. Go with your check-in." I placed my hand back on my M4 as the pilot briefed me on his weapons, loadout capabilities, and time on-station.

The day prior to this mission, Majors Gordon and Grice had informed me that they requested several sorties of air support for this operation and every request was approved. This was good news. Increasing our capabilities, the aircraft would conduct intelligence, surveillance, and reconnaissance (ISR) of the area while we were out there. They could help us identify any insurgents bold enough to come out of hiding.

This operation held plenty of risk. About five weeks earlier, seven Marine snipers had been conducting operations in the vast desert around the Haditha Damn, about 125 miles west of Baghdad, when they were ambushed by insurgents. Six were killed by small-arms fire. The seventh was reportedly chased down and killed, his body later found a couple of kilometers away from the ambush site. Insurgents filmed the attack and bragged about it online.

During my mission briefing, I mentioned this incident to impress upon my marines the seriousness of the situation. "Keep your heads on a swivel, boys."

We continued towards the OP as I listened to the Cobra pilots.

"Wild Eagle Two-Seven copies your check-in," I reported in a hushed whisper after the pilot had finished. "Tyrant from Wild Eagle Two-Seven, I need you to get eyes on my primary and secondary planned OP. Look for anything suspicious, any movement, anything out of the ordinary."

I cringed at that last sentence. *Out of the ordinary? Anything suspicious?* This was Al Anbar Province; everything was out of the ordinary and suspicious. Regardless, these pilots had been flying these missions for the last five months and understood my concern.

"Tyrant copies" was the reply.

I continued, "My team and I are on foot and located about seven hundred fifty meters southeast of the primary OP. We've got IR strobes flashing. Let me know when you have a visual on our position."

About thirty seconds later, he came back on the net. "Tyrant is visual your location, Wild Eagle."

As the Cobras covered my small team of six, we closed in on our OP. We had seen no activity or movement in the area since our insertion, but that didn't mean there was none. We remained extremely cautious.

About 100 meters from the OP, I raised my left hand, signaling team to halt. It was repeated down the line. Instinctively the men bent to one knee, faced out, and ensured we had all-around security. I joined Corporal Smith, who was steadily scanning our front.

As per my plan, the sniper and I dropped our packs. With our weapons up, we made a purposeful movement to the base of the small hill I'd planned to make our home for the next couple of nights. The remainder of the team stayed with our packs, covering our recon, while the Cobras kept an eye out.

Despite all our planning and preparation, Murphy's Law would have a say. As we attempted to ascend the rolling hills, we were bogged down in the fine, dirt-like sand. The harder we tried, the more we slid back, the walls of the dune gradually collapsing at our feet.

"Fuck, we can't make it up on this side. We're going to have to go around to the east and then north and give it a try before moving on to our alternate OP," I whispered to the soldier.

He agreed. Our two National Guard soldiers were not your average citizen warriors. They were both former US Army Rangers and had various patches or tabs on their shoulders to prove it. I trusted their judgment.

We made our way back to the rest of the team, hefted our packs, and headed out. The other side of the OP was only an extra few hundred meters away. As we turned north, we entered a C-shaped opening to the rolling hills. The open part faced more dunes and a wadi—not Route Long Island, which was good.

Corporal Smith and I stopped and dropped our packs once again. Thankfully, the ground was much more stable, allowing Smith and I to ascend to the military crest of the hill.

This was a dangerous point in our mission. If I could see the road and believed this to be a decent observation post, the insurgents might have come to the same conclusion. Although we were almost certain we would have spotted any insurgents already had they been there, and the Cobras would have also, the threat at this point was IEDs or mines.

About a month later, during intense fighting around Al Qa'im, Iraq, a five-man ANGLICO team led by Captain Mike Hays and Sergeant Brian Coulter were operating with Marine snipers when they tried to establish an OP overlooking the city on the Syrian border. Insurgents had recognized the area as prime real estate for observation and emplaced several IEDs triggered by pressure plates. Someone tripped a device, detonating the explosives and wounding several marines. The threat for us was very real.

Staying as low as possible, the sniper and I peered towards Route Long Island to the northeast. There, through our NVGs, we viewed the two-lane road jutting from the northwest to the southeast, making the occasional slight turn and bend. We saw roughly eight kilometers of road, although there were undoubtedly dead spots we could not observe. At more extended distances, we were unable to detect human movement.

Brushing dirt off my face, I turned towards the sniper.

"Well, it could be worse."

He agreed, keeping his eyes on the road.

"All right. I'm going to make sure that we can communicate with the BCT and QRF from here before making the call," I said before sliding down the dune towards Dyer and his radio.

Anderson and the rest of the team provided security at the bottom of the hill, oriented to the north and northwest. I had Dyer make a few radio checks with the QRF and Iron Xray, the 2-28 BCT call sign. Before setting up, we had to be able to talk to an assortment of units.

Meanwhile, I pressed the radio transmit button on my body armor. "Tyrant from Wild Eagle, we've made it to our primary OP, and looks like we might be setting up here. Can you look north along Route Long Island?"

The pilot replied, "Tyrant copies, and be advised we've got about five minutes time on-station left." It didn't seem like an hour and a half had passed. The perception of time had become distorted, and we hadn't even fired a shot.

About thirty minutes later, we were set. Corporal Dyer had communicated back to the BCT and QRF, so I made the decision to occupy the OP. Corporal Anderson and I had needed to adjust to a few changes, but we made it happen. Improvise, adapt, overcome.

Because of the terrain, the only way to access our position was from the north, which was covered by the three marines and former Ranger concealed in the hide site below. They had dug about three feet into the soft earth and covered their position with camouflage netting. All equipment and packs were hidden. They could only be identified if someone walked right up to them, but we would see them coming long before that happened.

The team at the harbor site monitored and conducted hourly radio checks, rested, ate, and provided security for the observation site. They were bored but dealt with it by assigning specific duties and timelines. The distortion of time now headed in the opposite direction.

Up in the observation site, Corporal Johnson and I were hidden as well. Similarly tucked under camouflage netting and dug into the side of the dune, we blended in perfectly, especially at night.

We were about 300 meters west of Route Long Island, but my main concern wasn't necessarily insurgent attacks from the road. The itchy trigger fingers of fellow Americans was equally worrying. Blue-on-blue incidents were a significant risk that I had to address.

Throughout our planning, we notified other units, especially the BCT, of where we would be and why. Artillery, mortars, air support, convoy units, the QRF—everyone with the ability to shoot or bomb in that area was warned. Iron Xray was supposed to establish a no fire area (NFA) around our location, thereby restricting the use of air-delivered ordnance, artillery, or rocket fire once we had sent in our

OP grid. But it would only take one young soldier in the turret of a gun truck to notice us and unleash a wall of lead. Though in theory that soldier should have been told of friendly units, it didn't mean that he was paying attention or the information was passed along.

Once we were all set up, the main business of our presence commenced: the long, intensive observation of Route Long Island. We knew it was a long shot to catch a lone insurgent or two somewhere on eight kilometers of Iraqi highway, but it was worth taking the chance. I preferred being proactive in attempting to trip up IED emplacers. And I wasn't the only one undertaking these operations. Gunnery Sergeant Jackson, Major Grice's platoon sergeant, was conducting them as well.

I switched back and forth from my thermal optics to my night vision goggles. Johnson did the same. We were constantly communicating, pointing out suspicious areas and further examining them. An immense, dark landscape spread before us, and we sought movement of any kind.

Around 0115, my eyes were drawn towards the horizon. Straining to figure out what I was looking at, I asked Jones, "Look at the road where it disappears over the horizon. Are those lights or something?"

"Yeah. I think you're right," he replied. "Those are lights."

We realized what it was as a pair of vehicle lights crested the horizon, then another and another. It was an American convoy, and it was long. We counted about thirty tractor trailers and gun trucks snaking down the narrow road.

Using the intersquad radio, I contacted Anderson and told him to notify the soldiers on OP-2. He swiftly replied that the convoy commander had already been informed of our location. The 222nd boys were watching our backs; they were impressive. We continued monitoring the light show through our NVGs.

The ensuing silent explosion resembled Fourth of July fireworks that had mistakenly burst on the ground. Sparks flew up, out, and down in slow motion. The distance was deceptive. In an odd way, the display was almost beautiful, but I knew that wasn't the case for the vehicles that got hit.

About ten seconds later, the low rumble of the detonation reached us.

Down the hill, Corporal Anderson notified OP-2 and Iron Xray.

"Sir, the BCT is sending us some Harriers," Anderson reported. "They should be arriving in the next ten minutes." Whoever was working in the BCT TOC that night hadn't been sleeping on the clock.

The sniper and I remained still, eyeing the area surrounding the convoy. Figures moved about the vehicles as they treated the wounded and prepared the disabled gun truck to be towed.

My earpiece crackled: "Wild Eagle Two-Seven from Pack Five-Five on Cyan Two-Nine." These were the jets Anderson had told me about. I skipped the usual pleasantries, wanting to help the convoy out as much as possible.

"Pack Five-Five from Wild Eagle Two-Seven. We just observed an IED attack on a US convoy traveling southeast on Route Long Island. Um, are you familiar with that road?" I said before asking what ordnance he and his wingman had on their aircraft.

"Affirmative, Wild Eagle Two-Seven. We are familiar with that area," he replied.

I requested that the AV-8B Harriers scan the vicinity around the convoy for the triggerman or other possible insurgents waiting to attack. However, chances were this IED had been set in place right after sundown. If the insurgents hadn't used the IED detonation to initiate a complex attack, they probably wouldn't be attacking at all.

High-resolution forward-looking infrared (FLIR) sensors display an image in the cockpits of Harriers. This allows pilots flying at about 15,000 feet to see what is happening on the ground in significant detail through close coordination with the team.

For the American convoy, the jets could peer into the dunes and wadis past the hard, cracked surface of roads. After about twenty minutes, the convoy started moving again, gradually heading south down the road towards us, the headlights growing larger. The closer they got, the lower Corporal Johnson and I shrank into our position. I kept glancing back at our IR strobe to ensure it was still blinking. The rattled soldiers in the convoy never fired on us.

With the convoy gone, I had the Harriers continue observing the highway and adjacent desert. They soon left for Al Asad Airbase or some C-130 tanker to refuel. Their high-pitched rumble grew fainter and fainter, leaving us in eerie silence.

The next battle would be boredom. During the hours of darkness, I sat in the observation site while the lead sniper watched for insurgent activity. This was hunting, plain and simple. To hunt requires patience, persistence, and extreme focus. Being in the same position at night plays games with your mind. Small bushes become crouching men waiting to attack. As the breeze ebbs and flows, natural noises tell your instincts a patrol is approaching. The snap of a small branch can sound like a rifle being loaded. Reality and perception become one.

The BCT staff had briefed me that things were different out here. If the opportunity arose, and if the situation dictated, I could direct an air strike, use artillery based out of Camp Habbaniyah, or simply engage the insurgents in an ambush. Unlike downtown Ramadi, there was almost nothing around here but this road and the desert. If vehicles were out on the road after the coalition-instituted curfew, the occupants were considered insurgents.

Route Long Island was deemed a "rat trail" used by foreign fighters coming east into Iraq from Syria to fight the "crusading infidels." Intel was that Routes Mobile and Michigan had too many American checkpoints for these jihadists' tastes. Just as the American logistic convoys wanted to avoid the hotly contested area between Ramadi and Fallujah, so did many of these foreign fighters.

Besides trying to take out insurgent IED teams, we were also here to neutralize those foreign fighters. Simple enough. If they were planting IEDs, we were to kill them or report their position. If a vehicle passed through the area after curfew, Major Gordon made it clear that I was authorized to use deadly force. But all of this was nothing but theory until insurgents were found.

At around 0430, we started hearing human noises in the distance. Across the desert, past the road and on the banks of Lake Habbaniyah about 1,800 meters away, a small Iraqi fishing village was awakening. Old cars started, and dogs barked. Then the drawn-out, rhythmic melody of the *adhan*, the Muslim call to prayer, began. In Arabic, the word "adhan" means "to listen." The ritual serves as a statement of shared belief and faith for Muslims. It also serves as a warning that prayers will begin shortly inside the mosque.

Echoing across the desert floor, the muezzin's song erupted from speakers attached to an ancient minaret on the village mosque. We listened, wondering how long that village had been there.

Fed by the Euphrates, Lake Habbaniyah is vast by Middle Eastern standards, covering over 140 square kilometers. Locals use it to fish and for recreation. When the British occupied the area in the 1930s and '40s, they used it as a refueling point for flying boats traveling to and from India. But to my team and me, the lake was simply a large object that dominated part of our view as we sat and watched the endless roadway.

A warm breeze came off the lake, carrying the haunting sound of the adhan under the blanket of a now moonless sky.

About an hour later, streaks of light appeared to the east, across Lake Habbaniyah and over Ramadi on the horizon. It was time to switch out the observers, and I wanted to do it before sunrise. I keyed the transmit button on my intersquad radio.

"Anderson, we're going to switch out soon. You and Corporal Smith need to grab what you need for the day and come on up."

"Copy that" was the quick reply.

Once Anderson and the other sniper had replaced us, I kept low and slid down the hill, squeezing into the tight quarters under the camouflage netting. The heat quickly became oppressive; the camouflage netting provided minimal relief from the powerful sun. Anderson and Smith scrutinized the civilian traffic up in the observation site, looking for anything suspicious. Vehicles stopping on the road were a red flag, but there were few of those. This was a waiting game.

At around 0930, Lance Corporal Cureton nudged my shoulder. He'd been on radio watch.

"They just saw a MAM in a civilian vehicle with an AK-47," he whispered in a matter-of-fact tone.

I grabbed the radio. "Anderson, what do you got?"

He repeated what they had seen.

A convoy of civilian vehicles was traveling south on Route Long Island. In one of the lead cars, they'd spotted a weapon and MAM hanging out the window. Normally this would have evoked an immediate response in the form of a direct fire attack. But something bothered Anderson and Smith about it.

We contacted the soldiers at OP-2 and let them know what we saw. Apparently, the man with a weapon was an Iraqi security contractor providing support to a civilian convoy. Such incidents are great examples of why having mature, independent thinkers on your team is imperative. We didn't shoot first and ask questions later. We used our minds and discipline to make sound judgments.

The remainder of the day was uneventful. We battled only the heat and a fast-dwindling water supply. The hot liquid was far from refreshing, but we drank it faster than anticipated, causing our stomachs to bloat. Sweat stung our eyes. The breeze off Lake Habbaniyah became positively fiery. Short, powerful gusts hit us like a hair dryer, pelting our faces with billions upon billions of grains of sand and draining us of moisture.

Relief came only when the sun dipped below the horizon. Anderson and I switched positions again while Cureton and Dyer maintained security and monitored the radios within the harbor site. I'm sure they hated it, but these men dealt with it like pros—though I'm sure Anderson got an earful.

The time was 2032. We had eight more hours until our extraction. Until then, we were to maintain observation of this long road. In about an hour and a half, a section of Marine Corps Harriers would arrive overhead to help detect insurgent activity.

Time crept by. Long, slow military convoys came and went, headlights weaving along the road. Our eyes were occasionally drawn to the northeast by silent flashes of explosions in Ramadi. The power in that city soon flickered off, and the horizon went dark. The cogs of war kept spinning. Still, we saw no sign of the enemy.

Around 2200, the two Harriers arrived; they would be with us for the next three hours. That's a long time to have two multimillion-dollar jets loiter overhead. But if it could save one life, I was all for it. This was part of what my small ANGLICO team brought to the fight, and I was more than willing to contend with boredom and monotony for a chance at hitting the elusive insurgents.

"Wild Eagle Two-Seven from Pack Four-Eight. Looks like I might have identified some activity," reported one of the Harriers sometime later. I heard the excitement in his voice. The lead pilot, Pack Four-Seven, had departed the airspace to refuel with a C-130 tanker over western Iraq after about an hour and ten minutes. He'd return shortly, and then Pack Four-Eight would depart to refuel. But for now, it was just the junior pilot and my team. Using his targeting pod, he had noticed movement around what appeared to be a vehicle, although he wasn't certain.

"Pack Four-Eight, can you give me the grid to that location?" I said, switching the volume on my radio so the sniper and I could both hear the pilot.

The grid point showed that the activity was about four kilometers away, a couple hundred meters off the road and in the same general location as where the IED had hit the convoy the night prior. It could be a position used by insurgents to watch for coalition forces traveling down Route Long Island and to stage IEDS for attacks.

The pilot seemed certain it wasn't a house. He kept seeing movement. Reflecting on my orders via the BCT, I radioed Anderson.

"I need you to come up here. The Harriers have identified a possible target close to where the IED hit the convoy last night," I said into the PRR. Anderson wasted no time.

"On my way."

I contacted Dyer and had him radio OP-2 to confirm it wasn't their men out there. Additionally, I needed them to stay at OP-2 so they didn't scare anyone off.

"Pack from Wild Eagle Two-Seven. Can you shine your IR light on what you see? I want to get a better look from my position," I asked.

"Pack copies. Sparkle on," came the response, using the brevity code indicating that the pilot had turned on the IR light and pointed it at the target.

Anderson, Johnson, and I all stared up into the sky. Through our NVGs, a greenish light appeared, as if God had turned on a flashlight only we could see. The beam gradually enlarged as it got closer to the ground. We followed it. There we faintly discerned what appeared to be a vehicle, but at over four kilometers away, it was hard to get details. Corporal Anderson grabbed the thermal sight.

The flight leader returned. Pack Four-Eight had briefed his wingman on the situation. He could see what we'd found but wasn't sure precisely what it was either. There was no more movement.

Without PID, a requirement before I could directly control an air strike onto the target, there would be no attack. But to be sure, we contacted the BCT and informed them of the situation. Because the distance from Ramadi was so far, we couldn't talk directly to the BCT without breaking out the satellite antenna; I requested that the aircraft relay the information. The targeting pods transmitted their live view to those with the equipment to pick it up and view it.

The verdict from Iron Xray was in: no attack.

I was fine with the answer, although the team and I, along with the pilots, felt some disappointment; I heard it in their voices. But the last thing any of us wanted to do was wound or kill innocent people. It was a huge weight off my shoulders. This situation reached the cusp of the directive I'd been given by the BCT. If it had clearly been identified as a vehicle, with it being out past the coalition-mandated curfew and near a historical IED spot, I would have gone ahead with the air strike.

Before long, the two Harriers said goodbye, wished us luck, and left us to the desert as they flew back to Al Asad. It was about one in the morning. Anderson slid back down into the harbor site to prepare for our exfil in three hours. Meanwhile, Johnson and I continued monitoring the road for activity, but the night was quiet and still. There were no more convoys.

At 0330, we contacted Iron Xray via satellite and informed them we were preparing to depart our OP. The sniper and I returned to the deconstructed harbor site. The camouflage netting had been taken down, the hole was filled with dirt, and our trash and debris was cleaned up and tucked into our packs. We were to leave nothing. Anderson rapidly had the team in a defensive posture, ready to throw on their packs and move out as soon as I gave the word. It was difficult to tell we had even been there.

The exfil could be a dangerous part of a mission. Rather than attacking us in our OP, where a defender generally holds the advantage, the insurgents could have been waiting to ambush us as we left, when we were most vulnerable. Unlike during our infiltration, we had no air support. The team and I were on our own—at least until the boys from the 222nd came screaming down the road.

Before shouldering my pack, I pulled out my notebook and checked my information under the dim illumination of a red-lensed flashlight. We were supposed to rendezvous with the gun trucks from OP-2 about one kilometer northeast of our OP, along Route Long Island. We got inserted south of our current position, but the rule is you don't insert and exfil from the same spot in case the enemy spotted you and set up an ambush or an IED.

Anderson and I conferred on our data and direction, and I shuffled up to my point man, one of the snipers.

"Listen, go slow, and take your time," I said softly. "There's no hurry."

Satisfied we were ready, I gave the signal to move out. The sniper stood, inconspicuously adjusted his rucksack, and began the push northeast. As soon as he'd covered a reasonable distance, Cureton and his SAW went next. The rest of us followed in trail.

Our movement was measured as we assessed every shadow and odd-shaped mound. Halfway to our rendezvous point, I stopped for a short security halt. We all faced out and rested on one knee, listening and scanning. Satisfied that we weren't being shadowed, we continued the rest of the distance without incident.

About 100 meters from the road, we stopped again. Anderson came abreast of me as I looked to our southeast. We heard the high-pitched engines of the gun trucks. Then they slowed.

The black outline of a Humvee slowly crested a small hill.

"Three, two, one, right?" Anderson asked to reassure himself.

"Check," I confirmed in a whisper without taking my eyes off the Humvee. The signal was simple, but the consequences could be dangerous. Using a small red LED, Anderson sent three long flashes towards the gun truck. Two long flashes from a red-lensed flashlight answered from within the vehicle. Anderson replied with one flash.

With that final signal, the gun truck revved its engines and sped towards us. They were followed by two more gun trucks. As soon as they stopped, the drivers and soldiers in the front seats opened their doors and stepped out to provide security while we threw our packs in the vehicles and got in. Dyer and I jumped in the lead vehicle.

"Don't leave until the others have confirmed that everyone is in and ready," I told the driver. About thirty seconds later, everyone was good to go. The drive to OP-2 only took about fifteen minutes.

We wouldn't be heading back to Camp Ramadi until midday, after this platoon was relieved. All of us felt tired and drained. As I was sitting on my pack, drinking water under the dark early-morning sky, Anderson approached me.

By the way he shook his head and laughed, I knew he had something to tell me.

"What's up, Sergeant Anderson?" I asked.

"Hey, sir. Cureton and I had to ride on the back of the Humvee," he told me.

"What?"

"Yup, we opened the doors to that last Humvee, and there were soldiers in all the seats," he explained. "They said that's how the other ANGLICO guys did it. I didn't want to stand there much longer, so we gave 'em our packs and got on."

I walked up to the platoon leader, a tall, skinny kid who immediately pointed the finger at his platoon sergeant.

"Sorry, sir. Sergeant First Class Howes said that's how you guys usually get picked up," he sheepishly explained.

"Lieutenant, I've never been out here before, and I would never, ever agree to such a thing unless absolutely necessary," I quickly informed him. The young Army National Guard officer obviously wasn't running things, so I found the platoon sergeant.

After apologizing, the large NCO explained that this was how they inserted and extracted Major Jacques Pelletier's team, a brigade platoon commander for 2nd ANGLICO. He figured we worked the same way. The slightly embarrassed NCO explained further that Major Pelletier and his team often came out here to hunt insurgents using air support and small-team tactics.

"We'd just drop them off after the sun went down, and they'd call us to pick them up before the sun came up. We never knew what they were doing, although they always informed us of their location throughout the night," he said.

I had met Major Pelletier when we first arrived at Camp Ramadi. He was a stocky, shaven-headed, unconventional leader who didn't mind getting his hands dirty while working outside the box—and outside of doctrine—if it meant taking out bad guys and saving lives. The few times I'd talked to him, he was confident and relaxed, much like Major Grice, and always had a pair of Oakley sunglasses atop his head. With a thick, bushy mustache and shirt sleeves rolled up his forearms, he must have drawn the ire of the gunnery sergeants who walked around Camp Ramadi targeting soldiers and marines who appeared out of uniform.

I met back up with Major Pelletier a year later when I was in Baghdad leading a personal security detail (PSD). At the time he had retired and was a security contractor for DynCorp International.

I told the NCO that the next time we were out here, we'd be getting into the vehicles, not on them. Truth be told, I wasn't upset, but I didn't like being surprised. The soldiers thought they were doing the right thing. In the end, this was my responsibility. I just never thought to ask if the Army expected us to ride on top of the gun trucks or in them. Lesson learned.

The next afternoon, we returned to Camp Ramadi. Dirty and exhausted, we bid goodbye to the sniper team, who seemed eager to work with us again.

"We never get to do this type of stuff, sir," they explained. "Our command puts us with the quick reaction force, and that's not how we should be used."

I agreed and told them we'd like to work with them again. They were experts, and they too were fighting a reactive war and not operating to their full potential.

CHAPTER FOUR:
TAMIM

During September, my team settled into a rough routine, as did the rest of Major Grice's platoon. Every few days, each team was assigned QRF (quick reaction force) duties. On other days, the team leaders and chiefs were assigned four-hour watches in the brigade TOC. The rest of the time, we were either on a mission or preparing for or returning from operations. To the ire of my guys, I had them up early almost every morning when we weren't on operations for PT runs within the perimeter of Camp Ramadi.

The large chow hall was a favorite, providing almost anything we wanted. From water to energy drinks, there was an unlimited assortment of beverages for the marines to take advantage of. Cureton and Anderson would stock up on Red Bull prior to going out in the gun truck. The food was also great on Camp Ramadi. Many combat outposts didn't have it so good.

No one enjoyed being assigned to QRF. I must admit that when I first heard of the QRF requirement, I was excited. Images of reinforcing fellow Americans under attack popped into my mind. However, most QRF missions were nothing like that. Ninety percent of the time, QRF was called out because some unit had discovered an IED and needed EOD support.

The brigade QRF consisted of a National Guard platoon in five or seven gun trucks. EOD brought their vehicle with all their equipment, and ANGLICO brought another gun truck. Once QRF was requested, the brigade would call down to the ANGLICO command post and dispatch the duty team to link up with QRF staged outside of the brigade TOC.

Once dispatched, we would drive to the incident location and wait for EOD to disable or destroy the IED. ANGLICO was there in the event air support was needed. We were the hammer. These were usually long, boring missions laced with stress. We rarely encountered direct fire or sustained firefights. By their very nature, these missions were reactive.

During downtime, the marines worked out, watched DVDs, went to the small store, or called home at the call center or internet café. In the evenings, some of the other officers and I would view DVDs in our room—usually *Chappelle's Show* over and over. There was a volleyball court near the small trauma center, Charlie-Med. Some of the marines would play games with soldiers and nurses. It was a great way to reduce the constant tension. But we could never escape it for long.

During one warm evening, a large IED detonated on a Marine patrol. The word came down to Charlie-Med of a mass casualty event. Seven wounded marines showed up in a couple of gun trucks. Anderson and Cureton, who had been playing volleyball, grabbed stretchers and went to help.

When the wounded marines arrived, they were bleeding and bandaged up, some wearing tourniquets to stop the flow of blood. Once the wounded were in Charlie-Med, another vehicle pulled up. It had gotten dark, so the gunner in the vehicle motioned to Cureton and Anderson, and the two men ran to the rear left door and opened it. They found a marine lying in the back, his right leg gone below the knee. They grabbed him by the belt and pulled him out, taking him into the aid station. The expression of shock and fear on the young man's face would stay with Cureton for years to come.

In early September, half of Major Grice's platoon went to Camp Corregidor to support the 2nd Battalion, 69th Armored. Captain

Mike Carroll and his team, Staff Sergeant Ibanez's team, and Captain Elward, the air officer, rode down Route Michigan to support the fight to the east. There was a significant difference between our AO and theirs in eastern Ramadi. Those teams were fighting day in and day out. Not only were they dealing with IEDs, but the insurgents to the east would stay and fight. Captain Carroll's gun truck was hit. He was wounded, but his hard-charging marines pulled him out of the vehicle before it was engulfed in flames.

As days became weeks, I gravitated towards one specific unit: Alpha Company, 3rd Battalion, 172nd Infantry—call sign Catamount. The first time I visited their CP to discuss a mission, I ran into Lieutenant Mark Dooley. A tall, light-haired police officer from Vermont, Mark was a calm professional. I imagined the rest of the company was similar. Unfortunately, I wasn't able to conduct many missions with Mark. He was killed a few weeks later in an IED attack. But like this young officer, many of the soldiers from Catamount were squared away. My petty prejudice against the National Guard had almost completely vanished.

Catamount's AO was larger than they could effectively control. From the sky, the green water of the Euphrates River flowing west to east dominates the city. Feeding off the river is a large canal that flows southeast into Lake Habbaniyah. This canal and river cuts the city into thirds. The southwest portion of Ramadi is the Tamim district. At the time, it was extremely poor and made up of densely clustered buildings, including the University of Al Anbar, a large grain-processing plant, a glass factory, industrial areas, a former Republican Guard barracks, and a slum called 5K or Five Kilo. All were part of Catamount's responsibility.

It was daunting, to say the least. Most places were left untouched and thus became the territory of insurgents. Catamount attempted to control key roadways and intersections by conducting patrols and establishing overt OPs. Like the rest of the US Army and Marine Corps elements in Ramadi, they were holding on by their fingernails.

Based out of Jericho, Vermont, the company and its attachments were led by a short, stout major with a thick mustache who carried the weight of his responsibility well. His executive officer, a former marine, knew about ANGLICO and wanted our help. The company was full of men who wanted to serve their country, do their time, and go home. Like the rest of the BCT, Catamount had arrived in Ramadi in July after six months of training in Mississippi.

One thing I liked about Catamount was that the leaders were open to operating outside the box. On one of our first missions with the company, a raid, the CO had ordered the men from the long-range reconnaissance patrol (LRRP) platoon to insert the night prior and conduct reconnaissance of the objective. Right off, he asked if my team and I wanted to insert with the recon element. Unfamiliar with the company and the men from the LRRP section, I declined in favor of inserting with the raid force. But the gesture showed that the company was willing to use their imagination to reduce insurgent activity in their zone.

My team supported Catamount on numerous occasions during September and October.

On September 19, we had a preplanned mission with a platoon from Catamount. We were supposed to conduct a foot patrol into Five Kilo, just outside Camp Ramadi's eastern gate in the Tamim district. Except for Operation Sand Eel and a few minor patrols, most of our missions revolved around gun trucks. That was simply the way many of these units worked. Catamount, on the other hand, had shown interest in working without vehicles.

As Anderson and the team were gearing up for that patrol, I called down to Catamount's CP to check on any changes to the mission. Within seconds of talking with their XO, I could tell something had happened. Two IEDs had detonated on a couple of their vehicles. There were casualties, possibly KIAs, and they wanted my team out in-sector with them.

I hung up and ran out to the courtyard to find Anderson.

"The patrol is scrapped," I told him as I threw on my equipment. "Get the truck ready. We've got to head down to Catamount's CP before heading out into Tamim; they've been hit hard."

The marines shifted gears and prepped the gun truck. It didn't take long. Although we'd only been in-country about three weeks, the marines had the routine down pat.

About ten minutes later, we arrived at Catamount's CP. I jumped out and ran to talk with the XO. Soldiers outside the TOC were smoking and obviously upset. Wasting no time, the XO gave me a few radio frequencies and briefed me on the situation. IEDs had hit a gun truck and Bradley Fighting Vehicle in the vicinity of Route Jones and Carter, two main roads through the Tamim neighborhood. The brigade QRF and EOD were out in the city with them. Their CO couldn't get to the attack site until his area had been cleared of IEDs. They had at least two KIAs and half a dozen wounded soldiers.

I asked about the enemy situation. Had they been taking any small-arms fire? What about RPGs? The XO informed me that there was some small-arms fire, but the main threat, as usual, was IEDs. Putting my notebook in my cargo pocket, I ran back out to my gun truck. Anderson was driving, Cureton was on the gun, and Dyer was in the back seat.

"Head to Ogden gate," I told Anderson as I got in, putting on my helmet.

A Catamount gun truck was there waiting for us. Before I could ensure it was them, an older Army staff sergeant climbed out to give us a thumbs-up, then took off towards Route Michigan. Anderson slammed down on the gas pedal and followed. Cureton loaded our machine gun as Dyer slapped a magazine into his M4 and pulled back the charging handle. The rest of us followed suit.

From the guard post at Ogden Gate, we flew down a narrow dirt road bordered by a large concrete wall to the north. The escort vehicle in front of us was almost invisible as we drove through their thick dust cloud. Approaching the infamous Route Michigan, both of our vehicles slowed, making visibility slightly better. The city was unnervingly calm. The only sounds were the roar of the engine and the unrelenting squeaks and rattles of the vehicle.

As we pulled onto Route Michigan, we were immediately engaged with small-arms fire from the southeast. The burst pelted the asphalt between us and the other gun truck. Scanning for the attacker, we saw only row after row of buildings. Clearly shot in haste by nervous insurgents, the rounds kicked up dirt and chipped at the pavement. Neither we nor the Catamount truck returned fire; none of us could see the shooter. Cureton was frustrated up in the turret. He wanted to pull that trigger and unleash a barrage of 7.62mm against the enemy. I sympathized with his plight.

We quickly picked up speed on the paved road. As usual, we stuck to the center. The farther from the shoulder, the better. We swerved and dodged piles of trash and potholes formed by previous IED blasts, never knowing if they'd been reseeded with more explosives. Before long, we turned off the main thoroughfare and zigzagged through the small alleys and side roads within the urban jungle that comprised most of Ramadi. Goats, children, and scruffy dogs jumped out of the way as we flew through the courtyard-lined neighborhood. Adults glared in defiance. They were obviously not accustomed to seeing Americans this deep in the backstreets of Tamim.

Clearing the buildings, we drove down a path cutting through a dirt field where trash and sand danced in the wind. Straightaway we saw Americans nervously checking the area for the telltale signs of hidden IEDs.

My team gazed in befuddlement at a twenty-seven-ton BFV lying on its side. This behemoth, originally designed to fight Soviet armor on the plains of Europe, had been toppled by an enemy that dared not show his face. I peered through the transparent armored glass of our gun truck at the multitude of homes and buildings bordering the field. Out there somewhere, hidden in the shadows, was an insurgent waiting for the chance to detonate another IED. That was why no one was near the Bradley. It hadn't yet been cleared.

I spotted the lieutenant running the QRF.

"Let's head over there," I told Corporal Anderson.

Corporal Dyer and I got out of the vehicle and made our way to the lieutenant, who was talking to one of the Marine EOD techs. The tension was thick; the soldiers were nervous about stepping off the road.

"Hey, Lieutenant, what's up?" I asked the young officer as we approached. Dyer kept his distance. It was a sound tactical decision on his part. Why should he risk being hit as the lieutenant and I formed a juicy target for some innovative and observant insurgent? The lieutenant grinned at me.

"Sir, glad to see ANGLICO's out here."

"Wouldn't miss it," I said before getting down to business. I asked for the CO of Catamount company. "Have you seen Cat-6?"

The lieutenant nodded to the south. "He's on the other side of the railroad tracks and can't get over here until EOD clears the area. There are IEDs everywhere. Try not to step off the pavement."

"Copy that," I agreed while visually inspecting the ground around me. "I'm gonna set up down that road in a blocking position. The brigade is supposed to be sending me some birds."

Dyer was about ten meters away now, keeping an eye on the buildings in the near distance and an EOD tech standing in a four-foot crater. I started back to our gun truck. Just as I turned and glanced over my left shoulder, the EOD marine yelled for everyone to move back. He'd found something.

When an EOD tech tells you to move back, you move back without asking questions.

At about the same moment Dyer and I slammed our doors shut, we were rocked by a large explosion. It felt like getting hit in the gut with a sledgehammer. My ears were ringing. My body ached. A thick layer of dirt surrounded the area thrown up by the explosion. Immediately, I grabbed Cureton's leg.

"You okay, Cureton? You good?" I shouted, blinking and coughing. Up in the turret behind the machine gun, he was the most at risk. He yelled some colorful words back, but he was okay. The rest of us were shaken up but fine.

My mind flashed to that EOD marine standing in the hole. Shaking my head, I looked over at Anderson. "That EOD gunny was standing in that crater."

Anderson shook his head in disgust.

"He's dead. He's fucking dead," I said. *There is no way he is alive.*

After ensuring my team was good, I jumped out of the vehicle to see if the QRF needed help. Anderson reported the IED attack back to the brigade while he and the guys scanned the area for signs of the triggerman. Amazingly, the EOD marine was on the ground in what appeared to be one piece! He was moving as the Army medics attended to his injuries.

Explosions from hidden IEDs—that was our enemy. The shadowy insurgents didn't show themselves; they didn't give us an opportunity to respond and fight back. They lay hidden, watching from a distance, waiting for one of us to venture close so they could push a button on some ingenious remote-control device while yelling, "*Allahu Akbar.*" Chances are they were videotaping the whole thing. Oh, how they loved to upload footage of Americans getting killed and maimed.

I returned to the vehicle and had Anderson reposition the gun truck to a location we could fight from if the insurgents instigated a more direct attack. As the gun truck moved slowly to the south, I looked back through my window at the QRF. To my astonishment, Gunnery Sergeant Michael Burghardt was not only alive, he was standing, albeit with no pants and only his boots, skivvy underwear, body armor, and cammie top. He made a one-finger gesture to the insurgents in the shadows. This scene would later become famous as a civilian photographer from the *Omaha World-Herald* was there to capture the image.

Gunnery Sergeant Michael Burghardt.
Photo: *Omaha World Herald*

Something was wrong with my communications. I tried to contact the Cobra and Huey that had arrived overhead but got nothing but static. Thankfully, someone in the QRF threw a red-smoke grenade, signaling the gunship to land for an emergency medivac of Gunny Burghardt. Soon after the marine was evacuated, we were tasked to support the ground evacuation of a wounded soldier. The gunner of the Catamount gun truck we had followed earlier had received a concussion from the explosion and blacked out. We had to get him to Charlie-Med on Camp Ramadi as soon as possible.

After we escorted them back to Camp Ramadi, we linked up with a few other gun trucks from Catamount and returned to the city. Cat-6 wanted as much firepower in the area as he could muster. To support his company, we established ourselves at one of their overt OPs—OP Jones, located at the intersection of Route Michigan and Jones Road—as the sun dipped below the buildings.

We were one of three gun trucks positioned at the OP. Anderson oriented the vehicle south so we could watch portions of Route Michigan and a section of an old industrial area. To our west, across

Route Michigan, was the ghetto of Five Kilo, and to the north were more apartments, markets, and homes sprinkled with trash and debris. The other two gun trucks pointed north and east. This was a key location with good standoff from the buildings, homes, and civilian traffic. We sat and listened to the radios, waiting for something to happen. That was what I didn't care for: we were merely reacting.

As the sunlight slipped beneath the horizon, we snapped our NVGs onto our helmets. Cureton connected night optics to the M240 machine gun. Now an odd greenish world appeared before us.

Around this same time, we started to receive highly inaccurate machine-gun fire from the southeast. The rounds cracked over Cureton's head, and Anderson instructed him to stay low in the turret. Without PID, we didn't return fire, and neither did the two Catamount gun trucks. We searched for the source, but as usual, the insurgents had disappeared. Shoot and move, shoot and move—sound tactics given our strengths compared to their weaknesses.

Two Marine Corps Harriers circled over the city, conducting ISR. We needed their support, so I got on the gun truck's radio and called the TOC. After a brief situation report with the ANGLICO representative, they pushed the birds to me. Pack Four-One and Four-Two turned their targeting pods towards our position. I briefed them on what had happened earlier to set the tone so these pilots understood our frame of mind. It had been a tough day for the Catamount soldiers; we wanted to support them. The Harriers searched for about ten minutes before the brigade took them away to support activity on the eastern side of Ramadi. Something was always happening over there.

"I've got movement 'bout 150 meters to the south," reported Corporal Cureton, in the same tone another man his age would use to order dinner. Through the thermal scope he could detect the heat signatures given off by humans, something our NVGs couldn't do. As soon as he reported the activity, the rest of us leaned slightly forward, as if that would help. The industrial area was pitch black; we saw nothing.

"What do you see, bud?" asked Anderson. "I can't see anything."

"Neither can I," announced Dyer.

"You see that low wall about a hundred fifty meters in front of us?" asked Cureton.

"Yeah," we replied almost in unison, "we see that."

"Three Iraqis keep peeking over at us," he reported calmly. Cureton, like Anderson and Dyer, always impressed me. He was eighteen years old. Most other men his age were still in high school, playing video games.

"Keep watching, dude," I ordered, grabbing the radio handset. "If you even think they pose a threat, go ahead and fire."

Once I reported the situation to Catamount, I got clearance to engage—not that I was asking or needed their approval.

Up on the machine gun, Cureton abruptly unleashed short eight-to-ten-round bursts at the insurgents. They hadn't started shooting yet, but we didn't want to give them a chance to put an RPG in our front windshield. The loud claps from the M240G reverberated through the vehicle as spent links and cartridges rained down around Cureton's feet.

With the thermals up on the gun, he could see clearly. The rest of us had a one-sided show and could do nothing but watch as Lance Corporal Cureton enthusiastically pumped rounds at the heat signature given off by the enemy fighters, hampering their ability to maneuver on our position.

After a few bursts, the insurgents either scurried away or were bleeding to death on the ground. Either way, we wouldn't find out. We didn't go looking for dead bodies or a blood trail. Shortly after our quick engagement, we jumped into a convoy headed back to Camp Ramadi. Most of the recovery operations for the IED attacks had already ended. While we celebrated our quick engagement with an enemy we barely saw, Catamount was mourning the deaths of their brothers.

Back at the ANGLICO compound, I got the team together for a quick debrief. We discussed the evening's actions.

Dyer explained that we most likely hadn't been able to communicate with the helos before the EOD marine got hit because we were surrounded by the different electronic warfare equipment in the gun trucks. These devices deliberately scramble certain radio frequencies, such as those used by insurgents to remotely detonate IEDs. Sometimes this would degrade our ability to communicate. I reiterated another point with my team, a point I had originally explained to them back in the States.

"Remember," I said, looking around at these three warriors, "you do not have to ask permission to engage the *muj* if you can later verbally explain to me why you engaged. I will back you up one hundred percent if questions arise, but be aware that you must have a reason. Be able to explain the threat and what was going through your mind. I'll support you."

"Check, sir," they replied.

I left to see Major Grice as the team made sure we had all our weapons and equipment.

He asked a few questions, wanting to know how the marines were and how Catamount was doing. He listened intently to the issues, asked who was in the turret when we engaged, and talked about the EOD team.

"All right, Captain Angell. Good job," he said genuinely. "Oh, and I need your AAR [after-action report] on this by tomorrow evening."

Combat or not, we had to feed the bureaucracy.

"Roger that, sir," I said. Major Grice was a good man to work for because he let you do your job.

About an hour later, I was sitting at a picnic table outside my room in the dark, warm evening, staring up at the stars and smoking. I tried to relax but kept thinking about the mission. To be honest, it wasn't intense combat. We arrived on-site after the soldiers from Catamount had been killed. The IED that almost killed Gunnery Sergeant Burghardt mere feet from our gun truck, not to mention an exchange of gunfire, shook us up, but in the grand scheme of things, these were minor. For Catamount, this was a different story, of course.

This was a good learning experience for my team. The men were honing the skills that would serve them until the end of the deployment. Within our first few weeks in Ramadi, we'd been subject to numerous IED attacks, rockets, mortars, and a few small-arms exchanges. As expected, the marines did great. They fell back on their training and the aggressive mentality instilled by the Marine Corps ethos.

So far, our experiences in the city of Ramadi had not been ideal— if there is such a thing in war and combat. Waiting to be attacked or blown up by someone or something we couldn't see was a horrible way to fight. During the invasion, we had a clear enemy and objective. Now it wasn't so black and white. The ambiguity can cause hesitation. Hesitation can get you killed.

We wanted to stand toe to toe with these jihadists and slug it out. I knew our ANGLICO team held the advantage if we could at least see the enemy and fix them in a position, but the enemy did everything in their power to ensure we could not use our strengths. Whether we liked it or not, the enemy always gets a say.

This was a devastating day for our Army National Guard brothers in western Ramadi. First Lieutenant Mark H. Dooley, Sergeant Michael Egan, Specialist William Evans, and Specialist William Fernandez were all killed by the IEDs. We'd worked with these soldiers previously. Now their young lives had been snuffed out thousands of miles from their families. It was a tough pill to swallow.

Another issue popped into my mind, something I couldn't shake. How had the EOD tech survived that blast? Gunnery Sergeant Burghardt was right on top of those artillery shells when the IED exploded, his face mere feet away. I'm not one to believe in miracles, but my team and I might have witnessed one on that scorching, dusty day.

I looked up and away from my smoke and saw Gunnery Sergeant Jackson standing nearby. It was easy to make out his silhouette in the darkness.

"Evening, Gunny," I said, surprised.

"Hey, sir. Feels crazy, huh?" he asked. He had seen plenty of combat in Afghanistan.

"Yeah," I said. "Just trying to relax a little."

I flicked the ash off my smoke, kind of embarrassed. Officers with bad habits were supposed to be discreet, as I thought I was being. Gunnery Sergeant Jackson was among the many outstanding SNCOs within the ANGLICO community. I respected his opinion and advice.

He said something else before walking away, leaving me with my thoughts. About twenty minutes later I went to the phone center and called my wife. I didn't mention the day's events. I just wanted to hear her voice.

■ ■ ■

Around the beginning of October, after Anderson and Dyer were promoted to sergeant and Cureton was promoted to corporal, the commanding officer of Catamount approached me about an upcoming operation. The Iraqis were set to vote on a permanent constitution. Catamount had been tasked to secure a polling site east of Route Michigan in the Tamim district with the Iraqi Police.

This was to be a five-to-six-day operation. Their first task was to secure the polling site, then secure and hold adjacent buildings to provide some standoff. Once this was accomplished, engineers would erect barriers around the site during the hours of darkness. With everything secure and in place, Catamount would back off so the Iraqi Police could provide direct security.

Cat-6's question for me and my team was simple: "Do you want to be a part of this?"

Of course I did. This vote was a massive step for the people of Iraq, and at the time I was still under the illusion that a democratic Iraq had something to do with individual liberty within the United States. Besides, Major Grice had informed the team leaders that all

FCTs needed to be out in the city during this sensitive time. Military intel believed insurgents would attempt to disrupt and interfere with the voting. The enemy had already been circulating threats that Iraqis caught voting would be struck down by jihad. They might come out of hiding and fight—something we yearned for.

Dyer, Anderson, Cureton, and I were not in Ramadi to absorb random IED blasts while we followed National Guard soldiers around streets that smelled of burnt diesel and sewage. It was October, and most of the fighting we had seen was quick and sporadic. Gone were the days of hate-filled jihadists running into the street and spraying an Abrams main battle tank with an AK-47. Natural selection had eliminated those geniuses long ago, and the insurgents who remained were more cunning. Any situation that might draw them out from the cracks and crevices held promise.

Instantly, I knew where my team should be: the grain silo. This roughly ten-story building dominated Tamim. It was 400 meters east of Route Michigan, across from the Five Kilo ghetto. There was plenty of standoff from other buildings, plus a wall around the compound. It overlooked OP Jones about 500 meters to the north and the proposed polling site about 200 meters to the west. We would be able to observe a considerable length of Route Michigan, some streets, and multiple buildings. This was key terrain.

Cat-6 agreed with my proposed location. He planned on putting the LRRP platoon and their snipers in there as well.

LRRPs, pronounced "lurp," were made famous in the jungles of Vietnam. These highly skilled four-to-six-man teams conducted reconnaissance deep in enemy-held territory. In Ramadi, these teams mostly performed conventional operations with the occasional small-team mission. I was happy to work with these men.

The six-day operation started off smoothly. The soldiers from Catamount secured their objectives with no resistance. The only issue my team or the LRRP soldiers confronted when we first entered the grain silo was carrying our gear up the ten flights of stairs in darkness. We swiftly forgot this minor discomfort once we reached the top floor.

On the north side of the building, we found a doorway to a small walled-off patio. The view was better than we had expected. Large stretches of Route Jones and Route Michigan lay before us. Places that went largely unseen during everyday missions became visible. We now had the ability to observe activity from great distances. With devilish grins, we whispered together, pointing out areas of interest, such as those usually dominated by insurgent activity. The position gave us front-row seats. Everyone tried to hide their excitement.

Automatic-weapons fire from the north interrupted our jovial discussion. Rounds slammed into the concrete wall behind us. Instinctively, the team and I dropped down. Sergeant Anderson and I looked at each other and laughed as we tried to become one with the floor; we were in the odd zone where the absurd and dangerous become hysterical. Laughing at death, or the potential for death, helped us deal with the stress and uncertainty.

Plaster and bits of concrete showered us as the enemy machine gun tore up the wall. As quickly as we had dodged his bullets, we were back up, but as usual the phantom had disappeared into the shadows.

My team stayed on the northern patio as half of the LRRP element disappeared into the building, searching for different vantage points. The remainder of the soldiers stayed with us to scan the concrete jungle to the north. The excitement of the enemy fire wore off rapidly, as did the whispered chatter. Our devoted companion, boredom, had returned. Unfortunately, he would be staying awhile.

At this time of night, around 0130, civilian movement was rare. Sergeant Anderson and Corporal Cureton had taken out the thermal scope while Dyer and I used our NVGs. Next to us, the radio squawked with the typical tactical conversations. I listened to an Air Force F-16 pilot and Captain Rard, an ANGLICO air officer in the TOC who went by the call sign Shrek, talk to each other about past

IED locations and MAMs on rooftops. Captain Garrick Rard was on his short FAC tour. A large outdoorsman from Oregon and an AV-8B Harrier pilot by trade, he was an interesting individual.

■ ■ ■

Back in the States, Rard had seemed annoyed with being away from his duties as a pilot and unconcerned with training unless it involved dropping bombs and controlling close air support. Before we deployed, when I was attending TACP school on Coronado Island to get my certification as a JTAC, the men of SALT Delta were out training in the hills of Camp Pendleton, inserted by a CH-46. They had to conduct a patrol from the LZ to an OP.

The marines were loaded down with gear, enough for a few days in the field. One of the marines started falling behind, slowing the patrol. Captain Rard, as the senior man on the operation, made the call to go "administrative," meaning the men were no longer tactical; they simply walked to the OP. This was a big faux pas. The correct decision would have been to spread the load and continue with the mission in a tactical manner. In combat, you can't go administrative. When the 1st ANGLICO leadership found out about this, they weren't happy. Most of us ground officers just chuckled at the behavior, chalking it up to Rard being a pilot.

Once we deployed, my view of Captain Rard started to change. He was aggressive when it came to killing insurgents and supporting ANGLICO teams out in the city. For whatever reason, he always held the late shift in the 2-28 BCT TOC. He didn't go outside the wire like the rest of us, and he wasn't a team leader, but he was good at using the technical capabilities of attack aircraft in conjunction with the capabilities and limitations of a FAC in a TOC. This was one reason pilots in the Marine Corps conducted ground tours as FACs. Silly call signs aside, these experts knew everything about close air support. They were integral to combined arms operations.

All fixed-wing aircraft in Iraq carried the Litening targeting pod. This device dramatically enhances an aircraft's ability to support warfighters on the ground regardless of weather or time of day. The system displays an image to the pilots and aircrew. This image can be transmitted in real time to TOCs that have a receiver called a ROVER (Remotely Operated Video Enhanced Receiver), like the 2-28 BCT TOC. When fixed-wing aircraft were flying over Ramadi, supporting the various units, whatever the targeting pod looked at would be displayed on a large flat-screen television in the TOC.

Sitting at the ANGLICO desk with a series of radios and computers next to him, Captain Rard worked the jets, directing them up and down the roads, alleys, and highways. When they noticed something suspicious, they'd scrutinize it. Most units had this capability, but for whatever reason, Captain Rard was a genius at persuading the various Army officers in the TOC to attack the enemy with the use of close air support as opposed to dispatching a patrol to investigate.

Most fixed-wing attack aircraft over Ramadi supporting the Marine Corps and Army were either F-18 Hornets or AV-8B Harriers from various Marine squadrons. The occasional Air Force F-16 or F-15 would show up, and even the rare British RAF Tornado, but normally it was the US Marines. It was a safe bet that almost all these aircraft were armed with some form of cannon and carrying a 500-pound laser-guided bomb (LGB), an AGM-65 Maverick missile, and rockets or some combination thereof. However, Ramadi being the provincial capital of Al Anbar, the media, politicians, and military leadership analyzed everything occurring here and weighed the potential political blowback. This meant that dropping a 500-pound bomb required approval from God—but in the Marine Corps, a general would do just fine.

To get release authority for a very precise and accurate bomb in Ramadi, a unit needed to be attacked and maintain contact with the enemy while some officer in a TOC notified and briefed the BCT commander and ultimately the commanding general of the division. Once the general officer was happy that all pertinent boxes had been checked, permission would be granted to use a 500-pound LGB. Now, we are not the Russians, and Ramadi is not the capital of Chechnya. Americans don't summarily carpet-bomb and conduct air raids—at least, not anymore; but this process was very difficult for the troops patrolling the deadly streets of the city. Captain Rard helped develop an informal way around the red tape. Improvise, adapt, and overcome.

The Maverick is an air-to-ground missile specifically designed for close air support and has been used since Vietnam in some form or another. The variant used throughout Iraq was the laser-guided Maverick missile (LMAV). Initially designed to take out armor and other hardened targets, ANGLICO in Ramadi started using the LMAV against insurgents rather than seeking approval for an actual bomb. It was as accurate as the 500-pound LGB but had less destructive power, making it eminently suitable for the urban environment. Captain Rard explained the relevant details about this weapons system to the 2-28 BCT staff, who increasingly allowed us to use it.

As the insurgent attacks escalated in the fall of 2005, Rard mounted an impressive number of enemy KIA via air strikes. Every three or four nights, Rard and the supporting aircraft would find insurgents digging IED holes along the various roads, and the BCT was allowing the jets to take them out. A couple of his air strikes even attracted media attention.

Late one evening in October, two jets spotted insurgent activity. Under the direction of Captain Rard, the aircraft followed a group of Iraqis to a house in the rural suburbs north of the Euphrates River. The black-and-white infrared video showed a large group standing around with weapons. They were unaware that the jets flying at about 18,000 feet were watching them. Soon after, a bomb exploded in the middle of the group. This was one of the few occasions we used an actual bomb near the city. Days later, CNN reported that according to local insurgent groups, dozens of civilians had been killed. Amazingly, attacks briefly declined after this air strike. We can only speculate how many American or innocent Iraqi lives this saved.

"Captain Rard got another control," I'd hear after returning from a mission or upon waking in the morning. Personally, I liked his bold attitude. Even the Army brigade we were supporting loved him. Many of us secretly laughed because we knew the ANGLICO leaders back on Al Asad were skeptical of Rard.

■ ■ ■

In the darkness, atop that grain factory, we searched the rooftops, alleyways, and roads. The enemy attacked once again that first evening. Past Route Jones, in a back alley hidden by countless two- to three-story buildings, we witnessed a huge explosion. Sparks and debris flew up and descended in an arc. The flash was blinding. Only about 1,200 meters away, the low crack and thud of the detonation reached us after a brief pause. We all cursed the IED aloud—except for Sergeant Anderson; he wasn't one to use profanity.

"I hope no one's hurt," he whispered, shaking his head. He didn't allow the bravado and calculated hysteria of combat to change him.

Sergeant Dyer handed me the handset to the radio. The LRRP soldiers were already reporting the explosion to the Catamount TOC. I stopped whispering once the shooting started. A gun truck from the patrol had been hit and was now firing at something. The rapid *boom-boom-boom* of the M2 .50 cal machine gun echoed through the city.

Captain Rard quickly tasked the F-16s to support us once I notified him of the IED attack. I had the F-16s—call sign Reece Five-Three—scan the area, but they found no other movement besides the soldiers on the ground. Doing what I could, I requested that the jets perform a show of force, a low but fast flyby to dissuade further activity by insurgents. Sometimes it worked; sometimes it didn't. I set them up on a run from the southeast to the northwest. Blazing as low as 1,000 feet above the buildings, they banked and dropped a few flares, hitting their afterburners as they shot back into the sky to avoid the risk of surface-to-air missiles (SAM).

That was it. That was all we could do for the men out on that patrol. The LRRP soldiers enjoyed the show, but they too felt helpless. Their sniper rifles were silent. There was no target for any of us. Thankfully, the patrol only had a few wounded and no KIAs.

Until the sixteenth of October, the mission remained relatively quiet. We got harassed by the occasional sniper, and we even fired at a couple of suspected VBIEDs, but it was calm for Ramadi. For the first days, we stayed inside the building with the LRRP teams, watching from the shadows behind the mosquito netting over the windows. When darkness fell, we climbed to the top of the silo. It was probably the best observation point in western Ramadi, but it was obvious we were there, so insurgent activity decreased in the Tamim district during this operation.

View of the Tamim district, Ramadi, from atop the grain silo.
The Glass Factory and Route Michigan looking north.

The Iraqis came out to vote on October 15. They were not allowed to drive on the roads for fear of VBIEDs, so they had to walk. At first, only one or two Iraqis seemed willing to venture out near our polling station. But soon we witnessed long lines of Iraqis winding towards the voting booths. A cool breeze whipped across the desert as the sun warmed our faces. The new practitioners of democracy below us enjoyed the cooler temperatures of fall weather breaking the summer heat.

Al Anbar Province was Sunni dominated, and they held an advantage while Saddam was in power. But now the tables had turned in this country where the Shiites outnumbered the Sunnis and Kurds. After all the votes were tallied, although Al Anbar Province had voted over 90 percent against the new constitution, the Shiites voted for it. The constitution would be approved.

Our area was quiet during the constitutional referendum, but other parts of the city were not so lucky. Five soldiers from the 2nd Battalion, 69th Armor Regiment, operating out of Camp Corregidor in eastern Ramadi, were killed when an enormous IED detonated near their BFV on October 15. The IED had struck again.

The insurgents in Ramadi were ingenious at making an IED look like anything but. The smarter insurgents would assemble an IED, cover it with molding plaster in the shape of a curb, then paint it gray. Another insurgent would take the risk of placing it along a curb. Or they would hide them in the dead animals littering the roadsides, inside trash and tires, attached to guardrails, and the list goes on.

Some of the insurgents' vehicles were equipped with false floors. Pulling up to an old crater, they could open the false floor, drop the IED, and drive away. One resourceful insurgent even attached an IED to a donkey. Thankfully, the marines dispatched the animal before it killed anyone.

When it came to their weapon of choice, Ali Baba had their act together. Marines and soldiers were forced to deal with this ingenuity.

The violence escalated during the last half of October, and most attacks came from IEDs. In Ramadi during that month, all American KIAs resulted from IED attacks except for when a lone marine from the 3rd Battalion, 7th Marine Regiment, was shot. These IEDs started to rob us of our initiative and warrior spirit.

It's difficult to explain, but imagine walking through a crowd and getting punched. You turn around to confront who hit you, but no one is there. Then you get punched again, and again. You keep looking around, but the phantom has disappeared. In Iraq, instead of punches, we got 100-pound artillery shells and tank mines. It put us on edge, made us angry. And when you're angry and on edge, you make mistakes. Mistakes get you killed. We had to learn to control our frustration.

After the referendum vote, we departed the grain silo, handing it back over to some Iraqi caretaker. The operation was successful but not what we had expected.

■ ■ ■

One way to lower the risk of IED attack was to stay off the roads and kill those emplacing the IEDs. Taking out these cunning insurgents required small, clandestine teams in covert positions waiting around for enemy activity, such as Operation Sand Eel, the ANGLICO/ sniper operation we'd conducted in early September.

My team and I repeated this mission with a different sniper team towards the end of October. Once again, we left empty handed, but it was a valid way of operating if you had the time and patience. Route Long Island was still plagued with IEDs but not as many as the actual city or its rural suburbs. So, I brought up the idea of more operations of this type with fellow FCT leader Captain Shane Murray.

Instead of using one team, Murray and I discussed two teams mutually supporting each other while observing different areas of interest. I briefed a couple of the units I supported, and all seemed very interested. But before Captain Murray and I could continue planning, I was notified that my team and I would be leaving Ramadi and heading towards Al Hit.

CHAPTER FIVE:
AL HIT, PART I

On the morning of October 30, 2005, the team and I said goodbye to the marines of 1st ANGLICO in Ramadi and departed for the small city of Hit. Our gun truck was packed tight with an assortment of gear and equipment as we headed off to the convoy staging area. The light from the powerful rising sun dominated the blue desert sky. From horizon to horizon, there wasn't a cloud in sight; the cool fall air hid the reality of where we were. I could have closed my eyes and been back in Southern California.

Sergeant Anderson pulled the gun truck alongside several other vehicles and logistical tractor trailers. The larger supply trucks looked like iron-wheeled monsters from the old Mad Max movies—not the first time I'd made that association in-country. Sheets of metal and steel used for armor plating were welded on at strange angles and had turned a dark, rusty orange. Some showed signs of IED blasts and small-arms attacks, scars from traveling the dangerous Iraqi roads.

The soldiers were milling about, joking with one another in small groups and smoking cigarettes, drinking coffee; some were reading magazines. I jumped out of the vehicle to find the convoy commander. Anderson turned off the engine as Corporal Cureton prepped our M240 machine gun up in the turret. Sergeant Dyer, the consummate quiet professional, sat in the back left seat, chewing Copenhagen tobacco as he worked on our communications equipment and dusted off his rifle. As usual, Anderson and Cureton traded banter. I laughed to myself as I approached a cluster of soldiers. Although apprehensive about our move, we all were in good spirits.

"Is this the convoy headed towards Al Asad?" I asked a short, stubby Army specialist.

"Yes sir, it is. The lieutenant is over there," he replied after breaking his attention away from the anatomy of a young woman in a magazine.

A tall, thin Army lieutenant with a young face was leaning against the hood of a gun truck, reading something out of a small notebook. Noticing me, he stood and took off his sunglasses. In stark contrast to the baby face, dark rings circled squinting, sunken eyes that had seen things they wished they hadn't. The lieutenant appeared tired but steadfast in his duties. Traveling across Iraq's highways, escorting supply convoys for months on end, had put him and his soldiers on the receiving end of countless attacks and limited rest.

This soldier's job wasn't "high speed, low drag," but it was the meat and potatoes of the Iraq war. He wasn't a Special Forces operator taking down high-value targets (HVT) while wearing the latest gear. The media wasn't writing glitzy profiles on him or his soldiers. In the end, he had a demanding job moving equipment where it needed to be—one of the toughest and most thankless job in this war. He got hit by IEDs almost daily and rarely had the satisfaction of returning fire.

The lieutenant forced a grin.

"Mornin', sir. You ANGLICO?" he asked, shaking my hand.

"Yes, I am, along with three other marines in that gun truck," I said, pointing at my vehicle. I handed him a small roster with our information regarding weapons and marines.

"Glad to have you guys along. Ya never know when the muj are goin' ta hit ya," he said, taking my paper. "It's always nice ta have mo' trigga pullas and bomb droppas with us when we're out thar 'lone and afraid."

While I couldn't place his accent, I was surprised he knew what ANGLICO was.

"Whatcha headed up ta Al Asad for?" the lieutenant asked as he put his sunglasses back on.

I took out a can of tobacco from my left shoulder pocket. "Actually, we're going to a city called Hit, by way of Al Asad."

He was quick to give his opinion.

"Dat place sucks, sir. Dangerous as all hell. The two times we drove up da road that parallels da city and Euphrates—I forget da name . . . Route Bronze or somethin'—we got nailed. Da first time, we were just south of some FOB when da muj attacked us hard after one of my trucks ran over a fuckin' mine. Must'a been about ten muj bastards hidin' in a palm grove spraying small-arms fire and using RPGs. Before we could really react, they broke contact and fled across da river. Didn't even give us a chance."

I listened intently; the team would want to hear this. The soldier continued.

"I lost a couple of my guys that day," he explained. "'Bout a week later we cam' back through dat area and got hit again with a daisy chain IED. It didn't kill anyone, but we sure as hell got shook up."

The young officer brought out a cigarette and started smoking. He didn't say much after that. Nor did I.

Twenty-five minutes later, after a quick brief, the convoy headed west along Route Mobile, the large, knobby tires making that familiar whirring sound on the asphalt. I sipped on warm coffee and shared the few details I had learned about the city of Hit.

■ ■ ■

Located eighty-five miles west of Baghdad and thirty miles northwest of Ramadi, the city of Hit—sometimes called Heet—lies on the northwestern banks of the Euphrates River, east of Highway 12. The population runs about 150,000, and almost every citizen is a Sunni Arab. Unbeknownst to me at the time, Hit sits on the ruins of the ancient Mesopotamian city of Id, or Is.

Around 4,500 BC, Id became famous for its abundance of bitumen, a thick, black petroleum substance used for everything from binding objects together to art and early roads, along with various other uses. This natural asphalt became extremely important to the people of Mesopotamia, and the bitumen gurgling from the ground around Id was used extensively in Babylon. It was the first petroleum product ever used by man. The substance was so crucial to the kingdom of Babylon and so synonymous with Id, or Hit, that the ancient name for bitumen was simply Iddu, which literally translates to "product from Id."

Besides its unique and interesting history, Hit was another stopping point for foreign fighters from Syria. It had been a thorn in the side of the Marine Corps ever since the green machine took over responsibility of Al Anbar Province in March 2004. Because of its isolation and relatively small size, Hit was never part of the major rotation of occupying US forces; however, its location on the Euphrates and possession of a large bridge made it relatively important ground.

Units were usually only assigned there for short-duration deployments. That the coalition leadership appeared to view Hit as some sideshow doesn't mean that this restive city was absent of violence—far from it. The new and unproven foreign fighters on their way to Ramadi, Fallujah, and Baghdad often felt the urge to prove their ferocity and so tested their skills in this speck of a town. Attacks were a way of life in Hit, just as the young lieutenant alluded to.

To make matters more difficult, when the intense fighting flared up in Fallujah in the spring of 2004, the few marines who did operate in the city were pulled and sent to support that operation. It happened again in the fall of 2004 when Fallujah was finally cleared. During the marines' absence, the insurgency grew powerful and very deadly back in Hit.

■ ■ ■

The convoy slowed and exited Route Mobile before heading north. Gun trucks turned and swerved around the countless potholes and craters. The tractor trailers avoided what they could, their loads swaying as they rolled down the highway. Done with my coffee, I grabbed a Red Bull energy drink. I marveled at the design of the thin can as I popped the top open and took a sip, cringing at the odd mixture of bitter and sweet. We'd helped ourselves to a litany of drinks from the dining facility (DFAC) during breakfast before we left.

"Hey, sir, can you get me one of those out of my bag?" asked Anderson as he studied the bumpy road ahead. The gun truck squeaked and creaked.

"Sure, man," I said, balancing my drink as I reached over and got him one.

Anderson leaned back a little and yelled up to Cureton behind the machine gun, "Cureton, you need something to drink, man?"

"No, I got some water," he replied.

"Now, what was the name of that unit in Hit, sir?" Anderson asked. He never took his eyes off the road.

The 2nd Battalion, 114th Field Artillery, was a Mississippi National Guard unit operating as a provisional infantry battalion. Originally a member of the 155 BCT, they had been in Iraq for about ten months but only took control of Hit six weeks prior. The battalion headquartered at FOB Hit, about five miles north of the city proper. Inside Hit itself was Firm Base 1 (FOB-1), which sat on the northwest corner between Highway 12 and the town. Then there was Firm Base 2 (FOB-2) at an old youth center in the middle of the city. Finally, Combat Outpost 3 (COP-3) was located along the banks of the Euphrates in a gaudy vacation home once owned by a wealthy Sunni Arab from Baghdad. The soldiers called it the Pink Palace.

The 503rd Iraqi National Guard (ING) battalion was based out of FOB Hit and worked throughout the countryside. The irony of this unit was that it was primarily composed of Shiites from central Iraq, a sensitive subject for the Sunni population. An Army Special Forces

A-team led by a young captain named Brent was there as well, helping train the Iraqis and conduct other operations against insurgent forces. A Marine Corps 6th Civil Affairs Group (CAG) detachment was located at FOB-1. My team was tasked to support all these units in any way I deemed fit.

We reached Al Asad Airbase in the late morning. The base was alive with activity. Helicopters, jets, and C-130 cargo planes flew out and arrived constantly. The team and I jealously looked down our noses at the array of service members going about life as if they were not in a war zone. All the amenities an American would have back in the States were available here at Al Asad—except sex, but I'm sure that was still going on as well. There was a bus service, swimming pool, movie theater, fast food served out of small trailers, educational classes, and the list went on. It was a different world.

Al Asad was also home to 1st ANGLICO's headquarters platoon and command element. Besides figuring out the information about our next convoy, etiquette required that I pay my respects to the company leadership. So, without delay, we broke off from the convoy and made our way to Camp Ripper, a Marine compound within the sprawling airbase.

Anderson parked the gun truck next to a set of pull-up bars outside ANGLICO's building and turned off the engine. The quiet was deafening. For over three hours, we had been inundated with the high-pitched rumble of the gun truck and the whirring of its tires against the asphalt. Now there was nothing but the distant sounds of helicopters and jets coming and going at the airfield about a mile away.

Climbing out of the gun truck, we stretched and looked around. Cureton started laughing. Curiously, I glanced over to find the team staring at the Regimental Combat Team 2 (RCT-2) command building. In typical Marine fashion, a colorful display of painted rocks spelled out *RCT-2* beside the flagpole. At some point, a marine had been ordered to paint these rocks.

Throwing my helmet and body armor in the gun truck, I grabbed my M4 rifle and headed off to the CP, leaving the marines to discuss who would watch the vehicle.

On Camp Ripper, 1st ANGLICO shared a building with 2nd Force Reconnaissance Company. Walking into the ANGLICO side, I made a right and immediately came across the company XO, Major Stohs. He rose from his computer and swiftly greeted me, asking how my team was doing. The major obviously cared about the men.

Major Stohs was a calm, quiet leader, never raising his voice, losing his temper, or showing much of a sense of humor. He was also very intelligent, with an engineering degree from the Naval Academy, and fluent in Turkish. When he spoke, he was quiet but deliberate. An F/A-18 pilot by trade, the XO had been with ANGLICO back in the early '90s as a lieutenant.

Eight hours later, accompanying a convoy from the Mississippi National Guard on Highway 12, the team and I approached FOB Hit in darkness. The convoy slowed, making a left onto a narrow, rutted road, and slowly headed east. Everything appeared in tones of green through the NVGs.

The convoy slowed to a stop. Looking ahead, we saw a small, sandbagged bunker with the barrel of a M2 .50-caliber heavy machine gun poking out of the guard shack. The convoy commander and sentry were having a brief discussion.

The marines and I didn't say much. It was kind of a culture shock. Everything was dark and silent except for the constant hum of the large diesel generators. A pleasant, crisp fall breeze blew across the land. To the north, we saw the silhouette of a few two-story buildings. Absolutely no lights were visible. It seemed like the power was out, but it wasn't. The FOB was practicing light discipline, a technique Camp Ramadi ignored.

The convoy rolled on a little further before everyone got out and unloaded their weapons. Corporal Cureton commented that the base was quiet, dark, small, and creepy. Anderson agreed, and Dyer merely chuckled. Though we had only just made it through the gate, we were convinced that our time in Hit was going to be very different. The unknown and darkness increased our unease. To reduce our apprehension, the team made jokes and smart-ass comments.

The final stop with the convoy was in front of the TOC, on the northeastern corner of a building. I noted the small assortment of unit flags outside the TOC door. The night was moonless, and the stars gave little ambient light. We could barely see the soldiers walking about. Few turned on flashlights, and those who did used red lenses. It was easy to get disoriented.

I told Sergeant Anderson I was going to find out where we were billeted and asked him not to move the gun truck; when I came out, I wanted to be able to find him. He didn't plan on going anywhere.

Walking into the TOC, I was greeted with bright lights, the smell of stale coffee, and the sounds of military chatter from multiple radios. It was typical of most TOCs: busy, with maps on the walls and computers and radios manned by various soldiers and officers. No one noticed me at first, but when I spotted the familiar face of Captain Blalock, he was grinning—signifying amusement rather than a hearty welcome. I quickly found out why: he was leaving first thing in the morning to return to the comforts of Al Asad.

I didn't know Captain Blalock very well. He had joined ANGLICO just prior to our deployment. After graduating from some captain-level career course, he was assigned to the company as opposed to heading off to an artillery battalion to command a firing battery. He wasn't a team leader or even in a brigade platoon but rather a member of the headquarters platoon. This meant he was under the constant eye of 1st ANGLICO's commanding officer. I should have been the one grinning with amusement.

With our pleasantries over, Captain Blalock introduced me to some of the staff. One individual I'd be working with was the officer in charge of TOC operations, Captain Morgigno. The vice principal of a Mississippi school, Raymond Morgigno was on the shorter side, with light hair and a big smile. As the battle captain, he would be the officer requesting air support for me and my team while we were out in the little town. He had been in-country for ten months and knew how to request air, which would make my life easier and our operations more efficient.

Before getting too in-depth with introductions, I asked where my marines and I would stay. The team was still waiting outside in our gun truck. Blalock agreed to run out and show them to our room.

As Captain Morgigno and I talked, an older gentleman approached.

"Good evening, sir," I said smartly, noticing his rank: lieutenant colonel.

He shook my hand with a warm smile. "How ya doin', Captain?"

Morgigno introduced us. Lieutenant Colonel Gary Huffman looked more like a grandfather than he did an infantry battalion commander in combat. He had gray hair, a matching mustache, a round face, glasses, and a slight belly. His Southern accent wasn't as thick as some of the other Mississippi soldiers; he might have lost it sometime between earning a bachelor's and a master's degree. The lieutenant colonel was educated and intelligent, as are many of his rank. However, he lacked an abrasive know-it-all attitude and gave off an aura of dignity and competence.

I stood next to a large map board as Captain Morgigno and LTC Huffman discussed the AO with me. It was around this point that we were hit.

The two mortar rounds detonated right outside the building. The power in the TOC blinked on and off, and the thundering *kurump-kurump* echoed throughout the FOB as the 120mm high-explosive rounds dug out chunks of concrete from the building's exterior.

For a few seconds, everyone in the TOC was silent—waiting. Two more hit north of the previous barrage. *Kurump! Kurump!* These two were a little further away, a sure sign of a hastily emplaced mortar tube and baseplate. This time they landed right where my team's gun truck had previously been parked.

The radios in the TOC lit up with activity. The counterbattery radar (CBR) identified the point of origin (POO) for the mortar. Soldiers from COP-3, down by the river, also identified the mortar position and started engaging with a .50 cal machine gun. Within less than a minute of being hit by the mortars, two 155mm Paladin guns retaliated in anger with four rounds of their own high explosives.

Boom . . . boom.

Boom . . . boom.

The deep crack of outgoing artillery fire reverberated through the FOB. I stood there smiling as the chorus of warfare played out around me, the primeval urge within me longing to once again fight. This was nothing new, although there was something different about the soldiers and their determination. They weren't messing around.

"Captain Angell, I just contacted the RCT and declared a TIC [troops in contact]. They're sending you some Cobras," announced Morgigno, as if proclaiming I was up to bat. Looking down at his computer, he inquired about my call sign. Captain Blalock pointed me towards the radio they used to communicate with aircraft. Almost as soon as we switched the radio on, it came to life with the eager voices of Marine pilots.

A voice squawked from the radio: "Wild Eagle Two-Seven from Vendetta Four-Seven."

Studying the map of friendly units and reported enemy position, I answered, "Vendetta Four-Seven from Wild Eagle Two-Seven, go with your check-in."

Immediately, I briefed the Cobra and Huey gunships on the enemy and friendly situation. Lieutenant Colonel Huffman didn't want to destroy the mortar tube. He hoped the insurgents would return to retrieve their precious weapon. In the meantime, the gunships flew about like angry wasps, searching for the enemy. The soldiers at COP-3 reported that the insurgents had vanished in the cool evening air. This was starting to play out like Ramadi in that the commander was being cautious as the insurgents fled and melted back into the civilian population.

After twenty minutes, the Marine gunships informed me that they only had thirty minutes left before returning to Al Asad to refuel.

"Okay, Captain Angell. Have 'em destroy the mortar tube," the CO announced after I informed him of the birds' impending departure.

With a smile, I responded, "Roger that, sir."

I swiftly worked up an attack plan—a "six-line"—for the gunships. I briefed them on the nearest friendly units, how their position was identified (in this case, an IR strobe light), the direction and distance from friendly element to target, what the target was, and how we were going to mark the target for the gunships. Within minutes, the birds were set up for their attack and bearing down, coming in from the west towards the river over the city's outskirts, their rotor blades giving off that distinctive repetitive thumping noise. Relaying through Captain Morgigno, I had the .50 cal gunner start shooting at the mortar tube position.

From the gunship's view, they saw the rapid flashes of orange tracers snap across the river and slam into the target beneath the date palms.

"Vendetta from Wild Eagle Two-Seven, we're marking the target," I announced.

"Vendetta is visual the mark, tally the target, and we are wings level" was the reply. Using standard CAS jargon, the pilot announced he'd seen the mark, spotted the target, and was in a level flight pointed at the target.

"Vendetta Four-Seven, you are cleared hot; guns only." As the JTAC, I gave him clearance to attack and a restriction to cannon fire only. The loud, excited voices of the soldiers at COP-3 blared from Captain Morgigno's radio, reporting that the gunship's fire was off by about sixty meters. I relayed the correction to the aircraft. For the next five minutes, I ran the gunships up and down the target. Before

I knew it, Vendetta declared they were "bingo"—out of fuel—and headed back to Al Asad.

The TOC was in good spirits at that point, and Huffman appeared pleased. Setting down the handset to the radio, I felt uneasy about the whole thing. Yes, I got a few controls, and hopefully we'd killed some bad guys, thus saving the lives of soldiers, marines, and civilians. But my hesitation wasn't about the attack; it was about the method.

As a FCT leader, I felt I could best direct lethal fires against insurgents by being up close and personal with the enemy. That meant my team and I had to be outside the wire, finding the enemy, identifying him with our own eyes, and attacking him with whatever we had available—either our personal weapons, artillery, mortars, or attack aircraft, all of which we had at our disposal. When I briefed a gunship or jet on the nearest friendly unit to the enemy, I wanted me and my team to be that unit. That way, I could almost ensure that we weren't going to get other Americans killed with blue-on-blue fratricide. This is how FCTs are supposed to operate, in my view—not out of a TOC.

Of course, controlling CAS from the TOC has its place, especially when fixed-wing aircraft utilize the Litening targeting pod and the TOC is equipped with a ROVER. Captain Rard, among others, had proved this tactic to be very successful. I'd personally helped destroy an artillery piece from the TOC while in Ramadi back in September. But to be honest, I didn't like it. It was impersonal and full of potential for mistakes.

Back at COP-3, a small patrol came under fire from a building across the river about ten minutes later. The soldiers returned fire and displaced back to the hardened Pink Palace. Known as building 239 from its designation on maps and GRGs, the insurgents' hideout lay directly across the river from the palace.

Once the reports came to the TOC back at FOB Hit, Captain Morgigno declared a TIC again and requested more gunships from RCT-2. Still apprehensive about not being on-site, I grabbed the radio in anticipation of air support. The gunships arriving from the northwest reported they had "eyes on" the firefight.

Directing this attack was relatively simple. Both friendly locations were on the northwest side of the river, while the enemy location was on the opposite side of the Euphrates. The birds could clearly see the exchange of gunfire. I set them up for an attack, allowing them to engage with both rockets and cannon fire.

The view from the different fighting positions at COP-3 must have been surreal. The gunships unleashed their 2.75-inch rockets on building 239, followed by cannon fire. The rockets slammed into the building and threw off a shower of shrapnel. In a futile attempt to fight back, the outgunned insurgents turned their AK-47s and RPKs towards the gunships. The Huey door gunner responded with a steady stream of 7.62mm rounds from a GAU-17 minigun, spewing hate and discontent at a rate of 2,000 to 6,000 rounds a minute. We heard the soldiers cheer over the radio. COP-3 reported continued sporadic small-arms fire from the building. Lieutenant Colonel Huffman looked at me.

"Sir, I can have the aircraft put a Hellfire missile in a window," I advised with the radio handset to my ear. Without much hesitation, the grandfatherly officer agreed with my recommendation. I turned my attention to the radio and GRG, reanalyzing the friendly location in relation to the enemy position. Then I briefed the pilots and set them up for their attack, having them launch the AGM-114 Hellfire—heliborne, laser, fire and forget missile—west of the city so the missile wouldn't go over the heads of the soldiers.

A few minutes later, the pilot announced his heading and that his wings were level. Comfortable that the attack angle was safe and within my restrictions, I gave the gunships the "cleared hot" authorization. The hundred-pound laser-guided missile designed to defeat tanks slammed into building 239. The firefight was instantly over. The soldiers at COP-3 reported several secondary explosions.

With the TIC concluded, Vendetta Four-Five departed Hit, flying off to points unknown to support someone else against the ever-increasing insurgency. I laid the handset down and turned off the radio. Huffman stayed in the TOC a little while longer, talking to his staff, before eventually leaving. Captain Morgigno and I conversed for another hour about the city and employing me and my team. I made it a point to explain that this was not the best way to use us. In my opinion, it was unsafe and less efficient. We needed to be out in-sector, in the fight, as much as possible.

Captain Morgigno and I started to wrap up. Before I said goodbye for the evening, he told me that Lieutenant Colonel Huffman was leaving with some soldiers tomorrow to tour the area as usual and maybe tag along on an operation with the local Iraqi soldiers. I got the impression that the CO left the relative safety of the FOB quite often, a sign of a good leader in my view. Eager to see my new AO, I told the captain that my team and I would like to accompany the CO. He agreed and told me to be outside and ready to depart at 0800. Grabbing my rifle, I left the TOC.

Outside, I was hit with pure darkness. With no natural light, my eyes had difficulty adjusting. I couldn't see the wall, dirt path, vehicles—nothing. I waited. Finally, my eyes started to adjust. I made out silhouettes of gun trucks and a building. Inching along, I thought of the air strikes tonight. It had been way too impersonal. I lacked any real feeling of accomplishment or even revenge. One thing I was satisfied with was the 2-114th Mississippi National Guard. They hadn't come here to play; they meant business.

■ ■ ■

The following day, the team and I jumped in on a patrol with the battalion commander and a Special Forces detachment herding a group of Iraqi soldiers. It was quiet and uneventful, but it gave us a chance to see the outskirts, which consisted of date palm groves, small villages, and farms. We didn't go into the city. That would be next.

When we got back to FOB Hit, I entered the TOC to check my

classified email account and talk with Captain Morgigno.

"So where do you think you and your team should be?" Captain Morgigno asked as we studied a large map of the city.

I answered with a question of my own: "Well, where do you get attacked the most?"

The Army officer didn't hesitate. "COP-3."

■ ■ ■

A day or two later, the team and I jumped into a patrol and headed to COP-3 for a few days to see if we could get into a fight. This was our first time entering the city proper. Making a left off Highway 12, also known as Route Bronze, we headed south for a quick stop at FOB-1. This compound was dominated by an old four-story schoolhouse transformed into a sandbagged fortress. Huge strands of chain-link fence hung from the roof, a defense against RPGs. Every window was filled with green sandbags, the glass long removed or blown out. A good portion of the area lay under two or three inches of sewage-infested water. A trash pile at the southeast corner burned continuously. The combined smells permeated the area. It was sickening, but the scent was familiar to the boys and me. The place smelled like Ramadi.

After about fifteen minutes, the patrol left FOB-1 and headed north. We quickly reached the powerful Euphrates and made a right into the COP-3 area. I peered out the window at the lone Iraqi soldier guarding the entrance. Cureton, up in the turret, commented about "security" or lack thereof. For a place that was constantly under attack, the lone Iraqi sentry with an AK-47 didn't fill us with hope and confidence. As was our team's standard operating procedure, we would be securing ourselves and watching our own backs.

Anderson stopped the gun truck next to a row of large barriers. The other vehicles in the patrol did the same. Easing out, I looked around. The sky was strikingly blue, and the crisp morning air was starting to warm up.

Dividing us and the Euphrates River was a row of HESCO barriers topped with poorly laid concertina wire. On the other side of the street stood a row of abandoned and demolished houses and stores at the base of a hill. Most of the abandoned houses were occupied by American and Iraqi soldiers. COP-3's "secured" area was only about 300 meters long, starting at the point where the lone sentry was half-awake all the way to the southern side of the Hit Bridge. The gaudy Pink Palace was the command center for the local soldiers. Behind that, a house atop the hill with a dominant view of the area held a small contingent of soldiers.

"Where do you want to set up, sir?" asked Sergeant Anderson. I gazed up a set of stairs leading between the decrepit two-story homes. A couple of soldiers were walking down.

"If the Army's got a post up there, we might get pretty good observation of the area," I said, rubbing my head as I removed my helmet. Anderson grabbed Corporal Cureton, and they headed up the old staircase. Sergeant Dyer and I waited at the gun truck.

A few minutes later, Anderson and Cureton returned. The position looked good, albeit overt.

"All right, let's grab our gear and head up," I told the team. We only took what we needed: our weapons, radios, some water, and chow. We also grabbed the M240 machine gun out of the turret. You can never have too much firepower. Cureton grinned as Anderson threw the machine gun on his shoulder and started up the stairs.

Sergeant Anderson had found a position along the wall-lined roof of the relatively extravagant home, which appeared to be stuck in 1970s America. There was fake gold trim on all doorknobs and hinges, a large glass chandelier, ugly wood furniture, marble floors, shag carpet, and large, thick drapes over windows. Soldiers not on patrol or sentry duty slept on the sofa and floor, the homeowners long gone.

Breaking away from our amazement, we nodded at the National Guard troops, who stared curiously at the rough, dusty marines wandering around with radios and a machine gun.

FCT-7's view of the Pink Palace and Euphrates River
from OP at COP-3.

Anderson was right. We had decent observation and fields of fire to our north and northeast from this position. The Army had a few soldiers on watch but hadn't taken advantage of the elevated position by building a machine-gun bunker. The OP would overlook the Pink House, the bridge that crossed the Euphrates, building 239, and much more. To our north and across the green-flowing Euphrates, beautiful, thick groves of date palms stretched along the banks, moving deep inland. Past the vegetation spread ancient, barren desert.

The infamous building 239 taunted the National Guard soldiers. Only nights before, we had pounded this house and the land around it with rocket and cannons from Marine gunships. It looked untouched amid the foliage. The bridge was the only one for miles. Civilians crossed back and forth on foot as if there were no war going on. Vehicles were no longer allowed on it after a VBIED blew it apart a couple years prior; it had since been repaired. In the middle of the Euphrates was a large island infested with overgrown, dust-covered shrubs and reeds.

The wall of our new position was three and a half feet of brick and plaster. Spaced evenly were decorative iron grates that gave the roof a little decoration and style only the 1970s could appreciate. Anderson, Dyer, and Cureton created a small, rudimentary machine-gun position with sandbags against the wall facing the river. As always, Sergeant Dyer had our communications up and running almost perfectly.

We gathered a few chairs to sit low behind the wall and watched over the area through the iron grates. Basically, we were still waiting on the enemy. Like the National Guard soldiers, we were in a reactive state. The OP was overt, and we would see no insurgent shenanigans they didn't want us to see. But if COP-3 was where the battalion got hit the most, this was where my ANGLICO team belonged.

When the sun fell below the western horizon, we stayed in position. Daylight was replaced by a brisk November breeze and darkness. Dyer had the radio hooked to a small military speaker, allowing us to listen as the Army went about its business. The battalion CO wanted us to monitor it in case something came up, but to us it was a standard procedure whenever we worked in someone's AO.

Around 2100 hours, after listening to the eerie sounds of the Islamic evening prayers, we started a sleeping shift, two on and two off. The soldiers on the roof said little to us. Anderson and Dyer went to sleep first, leaving me and Cureton up to watch for signs of an attack and listen to the radio traffic.

Cureton and I chatted as we scanned the area with our NVGs and the thermal scope. A sound on the island in the middle of the river drew our attention. It was a donkey; we had no idea how it got out there. Everything about this place was odd. We could hardly fathom the history of the area. Next to us stood an old minaret connected to a crumbling mosque that was no longer used. We didn't realize that this minaret was a 4,000-year-old tower originally used to watch for invaders of the ancient fort city of Id. In fact, the hill under this house held the old ruins of the city's center, mixed in with "newer" construction. When Muslims under the second caliph took over the area in 640 AD, they built a mosque around the old tower. So here we were, beneath an unimaginable number of stars, positioned next to ruins that predated the Marine Corps by over a thousand years.

The night was long, cold, and quiet. A section of Harriers flew overhead around midnight, sticking around for an hour and fifteen minutes. Cureton and I had them search the area for insurgent activity. The pilots, as bored as we were, spotted some dogs eating a corpse across the river. That wasn't enemy activity unless you were the corpse. The two jets then flew off to points unknown.

Every few hours, Cureton and I switched out with Anderson and Dyer. It was peaceful. Gazing up at the small sliver of a moon, I wondered what my wife was doing back in Newport Beach, California.

The next day was more of the same. We waited, glassing the area with our optics countless times as we listened to the radio traffic from the National Guard. Minor skirmishes erupted and dissipated throughout the city. Insurgents would unleash a quick burst of automatic-weapons fire and run off. A patrol would detonate an IED from time to time. The distant attacks were quick and violent but usually ineffective.

Always yearning to battle it out, Cureton kept remarking that the National Guard had "lied" to us about COP-3.

"Man, this is bullshit," he would say with a mock frown. Rubbing his M249 SAW, he bragged about his ability to handle the flip-flop-wearing insurgents. His antics always made us laugh. Sometimes he'd go too far, and Sergeant Anderson would have to step in.

At around 1530, a four-vehicle patrol from the National Guard was hit along Route Bronze. As soon as an IED exploded on the second vehicle, insurgents unleashed a barrage of AK-47 fire along with RPGs. From our position, we heard the detonation followed by the firefight. Our radio exploded to life as the patrol leader reported the attack to the battalion. Anderson grabbed the GRG and followed along. The firefight stopped abruptly.

As the patrol leader reported minor casualties to the battalion, we noticed two small boats making their way towards the far side of the river. They were about 1,100 meters away but in the general vicinity of where the attack had occurred.

Dyer immediately relayed the information to the Army.

"Dragon TOC, this is Wild Eagle Two-Seven. Be advised we see two boats with about five to six MAMs moving across the river away from where the attack on the COLT [Combat Observation Lasing Team] element took place."

We soon spotted another boat with two more men going across the river. With no hesitation, the Army relayed that those individuals were insurgents escaping across the Euphrates River towards the relative sanctuary of the far side. The battalion didn't debate the issue; they were decisive and made a call that necessitated action. It was impressive.

Our ANGLICO instincts kicked in, as did our adrenaline. I turned to the boys.

"Let's get a fire mission worked up and hit 'em with some artillery."

Anderson wordlessly pulled a six-digit grid from the GRG imagery. We'd all trained for this scenario consistently as a team. Dyer had his M4 with ACOG scope up, watching the insurgents paddle for their lives. Cureton used our binos to glass the activity. These insurgents were out of the effective range of our personal weapons, with the exception of the M240G. Showing their professionalism and discipline, the team held their fire without me saying anything. The reality was that without a tripod and a T&E (terrain and elevation), at that range, it didn't look good. We needed artillery. It's hard to fight the raw power of a few 155mm shells exploding around you.

Anderson contacted the Dragon TOC and requested a fire mission. Usually there is a separate frequency for such requests, called a conduct of fire net, or COF. But here the National Guard was operating outside the norm. They didn't hesitate to approve the request, and within about twenty seconds, we heard the "shot over" call from the artillery battery at FOB Hit. We saw the puff of smoke on somewhat elevated terrain about four miles northwest as the

155mm self-propelled Paladin howitzer launched the high-explosive shells, followed by a low thud as the round exploded in the dense palm grove.

Just then, one of the boats finally made it across. An insurgent jumped into the knee-deep water before the boat touched the riverbank, knowing his life depended on it. Fifty-caliber machine-gun fire from the opposite side of the river opened up on the fleeing fighters.

"He's dead. He just fuckin' dropped," proclaimed Cureton and Dyer. I was jealous I hadn't seen it.

Anderson made a quick adjustment to the artillery and sent it back to the National Guard: "Direction two-seven-five, drop five-zero, fire for effect, over."

The rest of us observed the activity. The patrol that had been hit arrived on the riverbank and engaged the insurgents fleeing for their lives. Machine-gun fire wracked the boats, but some of the insurgents still escaped the river. Anderson's artillery fire exploded further inland to hit those seeking refuge in the vegetation.

As the last boat landed, artillery fire detonated in the air thanks to the variable time (VT) fuse. It was in a perfect position. White-hot splinters of steel rained down on the insurgents; the next round promptly followed and exploded on the ground. At this point, we saw no more activity. But to be sure, Sergeant Anderson sent the National Guard the command to repeat the artillery mission. A couple more shells landed and exploded with unknown results. Our cohorts down the river from the patrol stopped firing. The artillery strike had done its job, at least by our estimates.

We kept watch of the area. Two of the small canoes drifted downriver towards us. From our position, we saw a few dead bodies in them, struck down by accurate machine-gun fire. Down below us in the Pink Palace, a Mk-19 automatic grenade launcher propelled 40mm grenades at the boats as they drifted ever closer. Better safe than sorry.

We held our fire. Oddly, the scene reminded me of when I was a kid. Down by a bayou, I'd shoot my BB gun at tree limbs drifting in the water. But like all things in combat, this event centered on the dead, the dying, and the bored. I didn't think about it at the time, but our respect for life had been altered. As the canoes coasted down the river, we joked about the sideshow. We made dark comments that only men in combat can appreciate.

The next day, while perched atop our OP around noon, we were once again listening to the National Guard's radio traffic when an odd request came over the net. Down at the bridge, about 150 meters away, an Iraqi approached one of the National Guard interpreters. This elderly man wearing a white robe was requesting permission to carry four bodies across the bridge to a cemetery. They had been killed during our engagement. About twenty people carried and accompanied the white-cloth-wrapped bodies solemnly across that bridge. The sun was high in the desert sky.

One of the marines, probably Cureton, noted that the National Guard should detain all those people as insurgents. We all agreed. The air was tense, at least to me, even though we were a good distance away from those Iraqis on the bridge. Skeptical and wary, we discussed the possibility that those bodies were foreign fighters trying to enter the city disguised as the dead—not a far-fetched claim considering that male insurgents had disguised themselves in women's clothing in the past, but our cynical skepticism stayed between us.

That was the beauty of being in ANGLICO: the day-to-day duties of occupying a city were left to other units. We came in to help them with kinetic operations, operations that dealt with killing the enemy, and then we left. We were, at times, the hammer to their anvil. To be honest, it was exciting, and I loved every minute of it. After three days and two nights, we packed up, left COP-3, and headed back to FOB Hit to rearm, eat some food, send a few emails, and see what else this city had in store. It turned out to be an interesting time.

CHAPTER SIX:
AL HIT, PART II

The November weather in Hit was pleasant. The evenings were cold, and the days were crisp. It was a nice change considering that six weeks prior, the average temperature had been in the triple digits and the evenings sank only to a sweltering ninety-five degrees. This made life slightly more tolerable. But with more enjoyable weather came increased attacks.

The boys and I engaged in a rough operational tempo. We would head over to COP-3 for a few days, come back to FOB Hit for a couple of nights and go on patrol with the battalion CO or the Special Forces detachment, then head back to COP-3. I didn't want to get too complacent, so I kept us moving as much as possible. There was always something to do. We were able to pick and choose which missions to go on.

Lieutenant Colonel Huffman seemed to like having us around. Most of all, he trusted us. He assigned our gun truck as rear security when he was out on patrol.

One day near the middle of November, a couple of Marine officers from the 13th MEU arrived to tour the area. The 2-114 was due to rotate back to the States soon, and the MEU would take over the AO at the end of the month. While giving the tour, we were driving down Route Cherry towards COP-3 when the five-vehicle patrol stopped. The CO had received word about insurgents in a black sedan, and we'd just passed one. Over the radio, he tasked my team and me to approach the vehicle and search it.

Without hesitation, Anderson moved the gun truck closer to the target. Up in the turret behind the M240 gun, Dyer reoriented towards the threat. Cureton and I exited the vehicle with a purpose. He covered me with his SAW.

I offset myself from the gun truck so that Dyer had a clear line of fire in case things went south. All the Iraqis in the area had stopped to watch. The occupants in the black Opel froze. They probably didn't realize that I was nervous as well. No one wanted to get killed by a suicide bomber. I hid it behind years of training in the Marine Corps.

When I approached the vehicle, I tried to push this thought out of my mind. It was tough to do. I investigated the old dust-covered car through the smeared windows and saw a nervous, plump Iraqi man driving. Beside him was a young boy in a dark tracksuit. In the back of the vehicle stood a couple of goats. This was normal for Iraq. The Iraqis were scared—I could practically smell it—but didn't show the nervous contempt usually found in fighters with their backs against the wall. Cureton and I bounded back to the gun truck and got in. We continued with the patrol.

In and of itself, this little event meant nothing, but within the ANGLICO community, at least back in 2005 and 2006, such actions had become an issue. Many team leaders, including leadership within the company, didn't want us to do such things. It wasn't our "job." But ANGLICO is supposed to be a force multiplier whose mission partly includes the big "L" in ANGLICO: liaison. We had to sell our services to some of the units we worked with. We had to build relationships that increased our ability to support the various commands. Units who legitimately needed us wouldn't want us if we did nothing but tell commanders no. Plus, I wanted to be an asset to these soldiers and help them however I could.

Now, I wouldn't accept "checkpoint" duty, but I would help in these instances. Additionally, there was no way I was going to tell the Army ground commander "no" when we were driving around with the operations officer for the 13th MEU.

Within the Marine Corps, ANGLICO holds an odd reputation as prima donnas and wannabe Special Forces. There is some legitimacy to this claim. A significant number of senior marines and officers are known as the anti-ANGLICO mafia. The last thing I wanted to do was feed into that stereotype by claiming my team and I were too good to do a basic tactical task.

Later that evening, when a lieutenant colonel from the 13th MEU approached me, I was sure I was going to get my ass chewed for something. I cursed myself for not shaving that morning. With a stern, emotionless expression, he told me he wanted to talk. Moving away from the National Guard soldiers, I was ready for it.

"You with 1st ANGLICO, Captain Angell?" he asked.

Increasing the formality, I shifted my stance.

"Yes sir, I am. My team and I arrived here in Hit a couple weeks ago."

This marine was tough to read. "Who's your CO?"

I gave him the name of our CO while trying to remove any expression from my face.

"Well, I just wanted to let you know that the National Guard here thinks highly of your team." Finally, his face softened. "They've told me you and your marines are aggressive and outstanding representatives of the Marine Corps. From what I've seen, I'd have to agree."

I exhaled in relief, hoping he didn't notice.

"Is that right, sir?" I said, slightly surprised. "I appreciate it." I paused. "I'll relay this to my marines; it's due to their hard work."

He shook my hand and walked away after some small talk. I stood for a moment, thinking about what he had said. To be honest, I felt silly and embarrassed for appreciating the compliment, but in a world full of egos, compliments are not easy to come by. The lieutenant colonel could have easily ignored this young captain, but he took a few minutes to tell me, "Good job."

On November 14, the team and I set up at COP-3 again. As usual, we waited for an attack. We passed the time by meticulously searching the area across the river with our optics. Every few hours, a section of Harriers or Cobras would arrive overhead to support us. We'd task them to scan areas previously used to launch mortar and rocket attacks against the National Guard, then have them sweep the riverbanks a click in both directions. For anything suspicious, I'd report the details back to Dragon TOC.

The night was again spent working in two-man shifts so we could get some sleep. Boredom was our ever-present friend. We talked about everything: our families, the Marine Corps, our plans when we got back to the States—anything to pass the time. Occasionally, one of the National Guard soldiers posted near our position would come over to chat. A dog might bark in the distance, drawing our attention, or the donkey on that miniature island would let out a loud bray.

Around 1030 the next morning, we received a call on the radio. The Iraqi Army (IA) down the road had observed insurgents setting up a mortar tube across the river. The team and I immediately grabbed our gear and made our way to the IA position about 100 meters away, atop a four-story building adjacent to the bridge. There the half dozen Iraqi soldiers were pointing and watching a thick palm grove across the river. Sergeant Anderson worked his magic with the Iraqi lieutenant in very broken Arabic. It became apparent that the Iraqi soldiers could no longer see the insurgents or the mortar tube.

Back at Camp Hit, Captain Morgigno had requested air support when the Iraqis reported the incident. The team and I waited for the birds to arrive as we knelt behind the rooftop wall, searching the palm grove for movement. It was a beautiful day. Strangely, Iraqi civilians were nowhere to be seen.

The team had weapons up, looking for targets, when we started to receive sporadic fire from multiple AK-47s. The fire was coming from across the river, in the thick palm grove, but we couldn't see the insurgents. No one returned fire. Before long, the slapdash attack stopped. I didn't have positive identification, but in retrospect we should have shelled the palm grove with artillery or mortar fire— although that might have been denied.

My earpiece came alive as the two Cobra gunships approached the city from the west. As usual, I briefed the birds on the situation. We were becoming very familiar with the various pilots. They knew my call sign and where the team and I worked, so we occasionally exchanged small talk. They too had found nothing. Before long, I sent them back to Al Asad to support someone in actual need.

After the situation died down, we jumped into a patrol and headed back to Camp Hit; two hours later, we found ourselves back at COP-3. ScanEagle, a small unmanned aerial vehicle (UAV), had identified a mortar tube atop building 239. We found ourselves behind HESCO barriers and concertina wire beside the Pink Palace. Lieutenant Colonel Huffman stood beside me as we monitored the house and waited for the Harriers to arrive. There was no movement or activity; it was too quiet.

Once the Harriers—call sign Pack Two-Two—arrived, I got Huffman's approval to use an LMAV. He'd had enough of building 239; insurgents had used it to stage attack after attack on his soldiers. Now he had a perfect excuse to destroy it, and I was more than happy to help. I had already created a nine-line for it.

The abbreviated nine-line is a set of information that the controller on the ground provides the aircrew, also known as the CAS brief. Set in a specific sequence, the information is used by the aircrew to attack a target effectively and safely with bombs, rockets, and cannon fire.

After a few relevant changes, Anderson speedily double-checked my work. This was a sensitive situation, considering that the target was only 250 meters away. The close distance required Huffman's initials. The requirement was instituted because such proximity—called "danger close"—to friendly forces was inherently risky, and he would need to take full responsibility. I passed the attack information to the pilots. As one Harrier circled high above, painting the target with a laser designator, the other aircraft headed northwest about eleven miles before turning around for the attack.

Anticipation hung in the air. Everyone was quiet, even Cureton. I started getting nervous when I didn't hear from the Harriers. Anderson was right next to me.

"I hope we haven't lost comm," I said quietly. He shook his head and continued watching the building.

"Pack Two-Two in-heading one-zero-one," announced the pilot. Instinctively, the team and I looked to the northwest.

I gave the final approval for the strike. "Pack Two-Two, cleared hot."

In the sky to the west, the sun reflected off the aircraft. We were lucky; AV-8B Harriers are notoriously difficult to see.

"Here it comes," I reported to Lieutenant Colonel Huffman. "Stand by. Here it comes," I warned the small group gathered behind us.

A loud boom came from the northwest as the LMAV missile was released and its propulsion system kicked in. Behind the team and me, Iraqi soldiers started pointing and hollering as the vapor streaked from the missile.

"There it goes," Anderson announced.

As the missile ripped through the sky towards building 239, I yelled to those around us, "Stand by!"

Everyone crouched in anticipation. The missile impacted towards the middle of the house; a dark-gray bloom of smoke shot into the sky. Dust and debris billowed around the building. The explosion, a low thud only 250 meters away, wasn't very impressive, but the boys and I were excited. Soldiers cheered as we waited for the smoke to dissipate. A mild breeze from the north pushed the smoke down the Euphrates. Part of building 239 had collapsed. I got back on the radio and informed the Harrier pilots what the building looked like from the ground.

"Okay, sir, the Harriers have a five-hundred-pound bomb, a GBU-12, if you want to use it to take out the rest of the building," I said, turning to the lieutenant colonel.

"Captain Angell," he said without turning his gaze, "I'm tired of dealing with it. Let's do it."

Anderson and I smiled at each other as I briefed the birds, and I handed Anderson the radio handset. This would be his control. Anderson was the team chief, and he needed this, although he wasn't a JTAC. Every single member of this team was vital. Years later, when I looked back at this time, I realized how significant these men were to me. As an officer, I couldn't acknowledge this outwardly, but I could show that I completely trusted each one of them. I had told them—and we had trained this way—that if I were killed in combat, they would need to be able to grab this radio and do what needed to be done. Silly bureaucratic nonsense like JTAC certifications were meaningless when lives were on the line.

Anderson conveyed the pertinent information such as attack headings, restrictions, and friendly locations relative to the target. Before long, he had cleared the birds hot for their attack, requesting a delay so the bomb would penetrate before exploding. We wanted to cause maximum damage to this building that had been giving the National Guard such trouble.

The bomb utterly demolished the insurgent hideout across the Euphrates.

Signal intelligence later reported that the insurgents had planned to attack that night with heavy mortars and RPGs in retaliation for our use of artillery on their fighters crossing the river a few days ago. An eye for an eye, a tooth for a tooth. We got lucky when a young Iraqi soldier spotted the insurgents moving the mortar tube through the palm grove earlier in the day. Once we were fixated on the palm grove, the insurgents diverted us with AK-47 fire and snuck the mortar tube to the roof of building 239. Thankfully, UAV operators had noticed the 120mm mortar during a routine patrol.

I was impressed by the muj's use of diversionary tactics. They fooled us—I'll give them that.

■ ■ ■

For a few days after we destroyed the building, things in the city were quiet. We took this time to squeeze in some training and a little rest. Camp Hit had a crude weapons range surrounded by dirt berms and trash. We did some fire-and-movement and immediate-action drills. Up and down the range and back again, the team blew through ammo. Dyer and Anderson would move forward while Cureton and I engaged targets. Once they were set, they'd fire while we moved up. Anderson switched the order around, and we kept going; then we would break contact under covering fire. They were good basic drills to keep us sharp and maintain proficiency.

In the late afternoon of November 18, the team and I did a short independent patrol about a mile west of Camp Hit on a terrain-denial mission. We left through a small break in the wire along the south side of the base, moving through the various wadis for concealment. Basically, terrain-denial missions involved random targeting of empty fields. The idea was to identify locations the insurgents used and shoot artillery or drop bombs on these locations at random times. It was supposed to deter insurgents; I'm not sure how productive they were. However, I'd been tasked by higher-ups to develop the target package and observe the impact area for the JDAM strike.

We kept our movement slow and methodical, stopping occasionally to listen for anyone moving in on our location. About forty minutes later, we reached a spot where I felt we could observe the strike and stay safely out of view. We called back to Camp Hit, gave them our position, and waited for the birds.

For whatever reason, Iraq was never short on random piles of dirt. Almost everywhere you looked, it was like a dump truck had dropped off more dirt. I took advantage of this and set up between three large piles about head height. They gave us some cover, but we still felt naked and exposed in the daylight. In a 360 defensive position, we leaned against the mounds and scanned for trouble.

A farmer about 500 meters to the southwest was tending to his field. Sergeant Dyer had noticed him while filling his cheek with fresh tobacco. Luckily the Iraqi didn't have any dogs with him; dogs could be a pain in the ass. Anderson tried to stay still, but leaning against loose dirt and keeping tactical isn't easy. Cureton had his SAW at his shoulder, waiting to use it. Once again, boredom was tapping on our shoulders.

About fifteen minutes later, at around 1745, the small earpiece connected to my radio crackled: "Wild Eagle Two-Seven, this is Dealer Six-Seven."

Finally, I thought. *Let's get this over with.*

"Dealer Six-Seven, go with your check-in."

The F-18 pilot had already been briefed on this mission. He was to drop a 500-pound GPS-guided JDAM. We confirmed that the target area was clear of civilians. He double-checked this by using his targeting pod. From my position, the target area lay just beyond some palm trees on the bank of the Euphrates, about 600 meters to the west.

I didn't even see or hear the F-18; he simply pushed a button at around 30,000 feet and went back to Al Asad. The bomb exploded where it was supposed to. We left as the sun was going down.

The next day, November 19, was a little more eventful. Around 0800, I entered the TOC to get some coffee and check my secure email account to see if ANGLICO command had news for me. Sitting at the dusty desk, I sipped my burnt coffee, waiting for the computer to turn on. Around this time, the Special Forces ODA captain, Brent, joined me.

Brent was a character with a permanent smile, a thick blond mustache, and shaggy brown hair. As usual, we joked around and teased each other about the usual interservice rivalry, but he soon got down to business. He and his A-team had to visit some intel contacts in town. For whatever reason, they wanted more firepower, and who better to ask than a team of marines aching to slug it out with the muj?

Back in the team room, the boys were sleeping. If they got their business done with no issues, I didn't care if they slept in. Besides, when we were out on operations, we didn't get much rest.

Within ten minutes, the team was up, vehicle prepped, weapons ready, communications functioning, and we all had a nice cold Red Bull in hand.

Over at the Special Forces compound, we linked up with Brent and his team. This mission consisted of one SF vehicle, one IA vehicle, and our ANGLICO gun truck. The plan was simple: depart Camp Hit, head southeast down Route Bronze and into the old Pepsi factory, and talk to some Iraqis about insurgent activity. Of course, we weren't going to talk to the Iraqis. We didn't know the first thing about running intelligence assets in a combat zone. However, when a team of Green Berets asks if you and your marines, along with your machine gun, want to go after some insurgents, you say hell yes.

Our gun truck jumped in behind the SF vehicle and provided rear security. Dyer weaved and dodged old IED craters and piles of trash. It was a quick drive down Route Bronze to the old factory. We pulled into the gravel parking lot and oriented towards the main threat: the roads and palm grove across the street. Dyer was behind the wheel while Anderson stood behind our M240 in the turret. Cureton and I got out to help provide security under the shade of a eucalyptus tree.

A convoy of Iraqi Army "Bongo" trucks with a couple Mississippi National Guard vehicles for security was making its way down Route Bronze. I was putting my Copenhagen back into my cargo pocket, laughing with Cureton, when we were rocked by an explosion on the highway. I instantly spun towards the gun truck and used the intersquad radio to contact Anderson.

"You guys good?"

"Check, we're good to go. Looks like the Iraqis got hit, though," Anderson said calmly.

He was leaning into the M240, straining to see what was going on. Cureton had his SAW against his shoulder. The distinct clatter of AK-47 fire erupted to our northwest, in the palm grove across the street. This was followed by the double boom of an RPG. We weren't the target. Peering over the hood of our vehicle, I saw that about 300 meters down Route Bronze, a white IA Bongo truck was on fire. Black smoke roiled in the air, carried north with the breeze. Iraqi soldiers scrambled about in confusion. The enemy fire stopped as quickly as it had started.

"Get in the vehicle. We're going to head over there to help," I told Cureton as I turned to find Brent. "Brent," I yelled, adjusting my body armor, "we're going to help those guys out. You okay?" As usual, Brent gave me the thumbs-up and a smile, his mustache failing to hide his reaction. One of the other A-team operators good-naturedly flipped us off. I shook my head and laughed.

The moment I got into the gun truck, Dyer informed me that 2-114 had called over the radio. A TIC had been declared, and air support was requested; they wanted us to link up with the convoy. "I told them we are aware of the whole thing and on our way," he said as he sat with his left hand resting on top of the steering wheel.

I adjusted the tobacco in my cheek and replied, "Roger that. Let's go."

We made the quick drive down Route Bronze, thankful we hadn't been blown up as we passed through the kill zone. Parking next to an Army gun truck, Cureton and I got out to talk to the convoy commander, a big Army staff sergeant. Before I could shake his hand, a scratchy radio transmission in my earpiece drew my attention. Cureton took over talking to the soldier.

"Wild Eagle Two-Seven from Dread Six-One" echoed in my ear. It was a couple of US Air Force F-16s flying at around 20,000 feet—or, as pilots like to say, "angels twenty." I informed them of what had transpired with the IED and small-arms attack and tasked them to use their sensors to find these bastards hiding or maneuvering on our position. I noted the ten-digit grid on my GPS and sent them the coordinates.

For whatever reason, the "fighter jocks," as they like to be called, wanted it in latitude and longitude as opposed to the usual military grid reference system (MGRS). I smirked at Cureton.

"What's up?"

"They want the coordinates in lat-long," I replied, shaking my head.

Cureton laughed. "Of course they do."

Almost every time I talked to an Air Force pilot, they gave me a hard time. They are outstanding at what they do but are considered by some to be high maintenance. I told the pilot I couldn't do that. He'd have to scroll through his onboard computer screen and change it himself. They didn't like that but acquiesced nonetheless. These were good men; they just had a different method.

Sometime later, I brought this up with one of the air officers serving with 1st ANGLICO. Captain Elward, a studious F-18 pilot who was back in Ramadi, told me that it's easy for them to switch to and from MGRS on their onboard computers. The pilot simply didn't want to.

This certainly wasn't the first time I had butted heads with the Air Force. Not long before, when the team and I were on foot patrol in the urban jungle of Ramadi, some F-16s showed up to support us. The Pennsylvania National Guard unit we were with had been hit by another IED. As the medics worked on a wounded soldier, we established ourselves near an intersection to a road, Route Duster, that paralleled the northern banks of the Euphrates. Everyone was out in the open, trying to help this young soldier—prime targets for a well-placed RPG or sniper attack.

According to the pilots, their sensors were having a difficulty picking up much detail from 20,000. I asked if they could descend to the 15,000- or 16,000-foot altitude the Marine Corps F-18s and Harriers usually flew when above the city. After a long pause, the pilot committed to berating me about how expensive his jet was and how he wasn't going to risk his aircraft. Cureton and Dyer were close enough to hear the pilot's transmission. They both wore big fat grins. I just shook my head as we knelt on the ground, surrounded by IED blast craters in 110-degree heat and the smell of sewage and burning garbage. I told the pilot to contact Iron Xray, the brigade air officer, for further tasking. The insanity and egos were almost as frustrating as the insurgents in that war.

Besides the lat-long pushback, Dread Six-One was affable and proficient. They were quick to get our position and started scanning outward, searching for the usual insurgent activity. I put another lip-full of tobacco in and tried not to stare at the pool of bright-red blood mere feet away. The dead Iraqi soldiers were already heading towards Camp Hit for evac to the morgue. The F-16s couldn't find anything unusual, so I had one of them come down and do a show of force with flares and ear-piercing afterburners. We could only hope that it caused the jihadist to hesitate, thus possibly saving some American or Iraqi soldier's life.

As the F-16s returned to altitude, Lieutenant Colonel Huffman pulled up next to us in his gun truck. I greeted him but was distracted by the arrival of two Cobras. I had the birds check along the river, the same location the National Guard patrol had been hit during our first operation at COP-3 where we ended up smoking the insurgents. Sure enough, the Cobras spotted a couple of boats on our side of the Euphrates, although they were empty. Cureton was drinking water next to me as the pilots described what they saw.

"Looks like we need to destroy these insurgent 'weapons of escape,'" I told Cureton, using technical terms that would help us get approval to destroy the boats. He knew precisely what I meant; the whole team felt the same. I was tired of seeing soldiers and marines get killed and wounded while we danced around the rules of engagement. Going to Lieutenant Colonel Huffman, I set my game plan in action. I would be honest.

"What do ya got, Captain Angell?" he asked, getting out of the back right seat of the gun truck.

Pointing into the air, I explained, "Sir, the Cobras have spotted two small boats on this side of the Euphrates. This is the same spot the patrol got hit the other day. I think those insurgents were originally planning on escaping across the river but changed their minds. They were probably nervous about getting caught in the river again and instead headed into the palm grove and eventually made their way back into the city."

Thinking, the colonel took a sip from his coffee mug. I turned to spit a bit of my tobacco out but noticed in horror that I was standing in some poor Iraqi soldier's blood. Before I could move, the colonel asked me, "So, you think we should destroy 'em?"

"Yes sir," I replied, stepping out of the blood and into the dirt. "As I see it, these small boats are used by the insurgents as weapons of escape." I'll admit that it was colorful language. I continued, "They use these boats as a means to flee after they try and kill us, and if they are gone, maybe they will be more reluctant to attack."

He smiled and agreed.

The Cobras, call sign Warrior One-Seven, seemed to perk up once I told them what I wanted. I'm sure they too were tired of playing softball with these flip-flop-wearing jihadists. The Cobras quickly dispatched and sank the small canoes with a few 20mm cannon gun runs and 2.75-inch rockets. In my view, it was a win-win, but not everyone agreed.

The team and I returned to Camp Hit shortly after to a welcome surprise: mail. It was nice to read the letters from Joni and decompress. We all headed to our team room and tried to tune out the war around us. It didn't last. A knock on our door revealed that I was wanted in the TOC. I turned to Anderson, who was engrossed in a letter from his family.

"Be ready just in case."

He knew what I meant. We could be called out at a moment's notice—another consequence of reactive war.

Down in the TOC, it appeared that 2-114 task force (TF) and I had ruffled some feathers. I'd known that the decision to destroy those empty canoes could be an issue. RCT-2, the regimental unit with tactical control over the Army battalion, wanted to know why we had diverted Warrior One-Seven from its mission of escorting the medivac bird. I hadn't even known they were for the medivac. The pilots sure didn't say anything.

Secondly, the Direct Air Support Center (DASC) wanted to know why we'd approved ordnance from the Cobras to destroy boats. Captain Morgigno, the 2-114 TF battle captain, was also doing the dance to explain to his chain of command why the battalion had destroyed the boats. We both got our asses chewed.

To be honest, it was kind of embarrassing. Here the Mississippi National Guard was aggressively trying to thwart the enemy's ability to attack American and Iraqi soldiers; then some midlevel career officer safe inside a huge airbase in Al Asad questioned our tactics. Captain Morgigno and I laughed about it. "We're kicking our own ass."

It didn't make any sense. About a week prior, we had been tasked with that terrain-denial mission targeting the empty banks of the Euphrates River. Now Captain Morgigno and I were tap-dancing because we'd destroyed a couple of canoes used by insurgents.

■ ■ ■

A few days later, on November 22, I was talking to the new Air Force combat controller assigned to Brent's ODA team. He was new, young, and very unfamiliar with how the Marine Corps conducts CAS, especially with gunships. It's all generally the same as dictated by the Joint CAS publication, but since the Special Forces combat controller was in battle space owned by the Marine Corps and would be receiving strike assets from the Marine Corps, he needed to learn a few things specific to the Corps. Brent asked me to help him out.

As I explained how to request air support in case his SF team is hit, Captain Morgigno interrupted us.

"You and your team need to head to COP-3. The IA by the bridge are under attack," he said, still holding the handset from the radio. Everyone in the TOC stared up at me. As usual, I dropped everything and ran. I had seen Sergeant Anderson in the internet center earlier, so that was my first stop. He was at a computer, instant messaging his young wife.

"Hey, Sergeant Anderson." He looked up expectantly. "We gotta go. There's a TIC at COP-3."

"Roger that, sir" was the reply. As he said goodbye to his wife, I took off in a shuffle to grab Dyer and Cureton. They had stayed up late playing poker with the soldiers the previous evening.

When I walked into the room, it was the same as when I'd left it two hours ago. Corporal Cureton and Sergeant Dyer were still asleep. A few nudges later, they were rubbing the sleep out of their eyes before jumping up and grabbing their gear. These marines knew what to do.

We had all our gear and weapons in the vehicle within seven minutes. We'd previously drilled this to get the time shorter and shorter. We could have been quicker if half the team hadn't been asleep when we started.

I "ground guided" the vehicle to the TOC and ran in for a quick update and to find out whose patrol we would be jumping in with. Coalition forces were required to have no less than three vehicles in a mounted patrol, and I had little ambition to drive through Hit in a lone gun truck. Back in September, the boys and I had been the rear security for a vehicle patrol flying through the back streets of the Tamim district when our vehicle stalled and died. When the dust cleared, we were by ourselves. It was an extremely uncomfortable feeling, watching Iraqis emerge from their homes to stare at us. Like wolves eyeing a lone calf, they drifted closer until we stepped out of the gun truck to assert ourselves. Eventually the patrol realized we were no longer behind them. We didn't want to repeat that here in Hit.

The TOC was crawling with marines. These weren't marines from EOD or CAG; these were majors, lieutenant colonels, master sergeants, captains, and others from the 3rd Battalion, 1st Marine Regiment (3/1) command element, listening to the drama unfold on the radio. They would be taking over for the Army when the Mississippi National Guard headed home. Ignoring them, I went straight to Captain Morgigno.

"Hey, man, COP-3 has been engaged from the ruins, the Sharky mosque, and from across the river. There is one Iraqi KIA. I'm getting air for you," he informed me. I felt the newly arrived marines scrutinizing me as I spoke, no doubt gawking at my three-week-old haircut.

"Roger that. I'll be waiting for my escort outside," I said.

As I moved back through the gauntlet of officers and senior enlisted on my way out, I looked a few in the eyes and nodded but said nothing; they said nothing in return. My team and I had a job to do, and I could not be bothered with pleasantries and customs. To their credit, they didn't stop me to ask questions. Of course, as I walked back outside, I ran into what must have been the battalion sergeant major. I did not look at him, but he stopped dead in his tracks, glaring at this young Marine captain. I walked briskly past him to my truck.

"We got a radio check yet with Copperhead One-Four?" I asked Corporal Cureton while the soldiers prepped their huge M1A1 tanks. These two monstrous Army main battle tanks would be our escort to COP-3.

"Yes, sir. We talked to them already," Cureton said. "You see all of these marines?"

Now they were everywhere.

Chuckling, I responded, "They're from 3/1 and will be taking Hit over in a couple weeks."

Up in the turret, Anderson was shaking his head. "Get ready for the games to begin."

I grabbed a magazine for my M4 from my chest rig.

"Negative," I replied. "Once the Army leaves, we should be headed back to the wonderful world of Ramadi." The tanks started churning up dirt and revving their engines. Cureton and I climbed into the gun truck and headed off to COP-3.

We arrived, moved through the barriers, and parked the truck outside the Iraqi Army OP overlooking the mosque and the bridge. The OP was little more than a few Iraqi soldiers with heavy weapons and a radio. From the information we'd received from Captain Morgigno, this was where the Iraqi soldier was killed. We were always more productive if we established ourselves in positions that were taking fire.

With our weapons and gear, the team and I made our way up the four flights of stairs to the roof of the Iraqi position. The moment we reached the top, I sensed the morale of the Iraqis had been decimated. The helmet and body armor of the slain soldier lay in a pool of blood. We moved to the southern corner of the building and started to set up, making communications checks with the TOC and orienting ourselves with our maps and the terrain around us. We crouched with the eight Iraqi soldiers behind the three-foot-high wall forming the edge of the roof. It provided concealment and limited cover.

"Look at these guys," Anderson said, shaking his head. The Iraqi soldiers' faces radiated fear. One of their fellow soldiers had been shot and killed right there, his blood still visible. Most of them stared into space; I couldn't tell who was in charge. They had no initiative and lacked any bias for action, a staple of Marine Corps doctrine. You have to have it if you want to win.

Sergeant Dyer contacted Dragon TOC.

"Sir, the TOC is reporting that we've got friendlies just outside of the mosque," he said while adjusting the radios. A quick peek over the wall revealed a couple of Army squads meandering outside the mosque below us. Dyer continued, "They're gonna raid the mosque."

It was quiet—too quiet. All of us were on edge.

Checking to make sure my PRC-148 was working, I asked Dyer to find out where the birds were.

"They're inbound and should be here any minute," he reported.

The earpiece to my radio awoke with the baritone voice of a Marine aviator: "Wild Eagle Two-Seven from Vendetta Four-Three on Salmon Two-One."

"Vendetta Four-Three, go ahead with standard CAS check-in," I replied, reading my watch. Following the check-in, I gave him a situation brief and had him establish in the overhead, watching for snipers on rooftops or large gatherings of personnel and people observing the area. Dyer had one of the handsets to his ear, listening to the TOC and keeping the rest of the team updated.

My main concern was friendly locations. Our position, the soldiers' position, and the various enemy locations were right on top of each other.

Sergeant Anderson and Corporal Cureton discussed potential enemy locations. Anderson pulled out his GRG map and reoriented himself by placing the map on the ground and lying down behind it. Corporal Cureton followed his lead. I noticed Anderson staring at the blood and body armor.

"Sir, they need to get rid of that damn gear," he said, crawling over to me. "Look at 'em. They keep just staring at it."

"Well, let's have 'em get rid of it, then."

Anderson directed an Iraqi soldier to take the blood-soaked body armor downstairs. It was another good call. The blood remained, attracting countless flies. The Iraqis were still motionless and showed no sign of initiative or aggression. The atmosphere started to affect me and my guys. Something had to be done to kick-start these Iraqis back into the war. Right now, the enemy held the initiative. This had to end.

My plan was simple: own the battle space and don't allow the insurgents to hold the initiative by pinning us down. Since we'd arrived ten minutes prior, there had been no enemy contact. Regardless, we had to push the fight.

I poked my head above the edge of the wall to study our battlefield, which wasn't more than streets, alleyways, windows, and buildings.

As soon as I could see over the wall, the sniper squeezed his trigger. He had been hiding in the shadows of a building, waiting for one of us to make a mistake. Although risky, I didn't consider my near miss an error. I had stood up to motivate the Iraqis. They were frozen by fear, unable to move. The blood of their fallen comrade was still shimmering in the daylight.

The loud and unmistakable crack of the 7.62mm round sent me diving to the ground. Over milliseconds, thoughts of death raced through my mind, and my wife's face popped up. I felt the overpressure of the bullet as it snapped past my right ear. My instinctive reaction was a loud expletive. "*FUCK.*" I instantly regretted that decision, but not as much as if I had been killed.

Anderson's eyes were about as wide as mine. He almost saw me die; I could see it on his face.

For some strange reason, this worked to our advantage. Before I could shake off the fear, Cureton popped up and started banging away with his SAW. The sound was deafening and disorienting since I was a mere foot from the muzzle of his blazing weapon. One of the Iraqi soldiers crawled over to our position and pointed out the sniper's location. I couldn't understand him, but his meaning became apparent when he let loose with his AK-47. He was about two feet away from me as I sat against the wall. The noise was painful. Empty shell casings and links fell from the belted ammo in a rhythmic song.

I turned towards Sergeant Dyer. He was enjoying his Copenhagen with his weapon oriented towards the fight, seeking a target.

"Fuckin tell Dragon TOC that we are receiving sporadic fire from the vicinity of building . . . 138 and we want permission to engage it with twenty-millimeter cannon fire from the Cobras," I yelled to him.

It took about five seconds for Dragon TOC to approve our request. This battalion had been in Iraq for just under a year. They were tired of taking casualties, and it showed.

With Cureton and Anderson, as well as some of the Iraqis, exchanging fire with the insurgents, it was difficult to pass information over the radio, but I needed to brief the AH-1 Cobras. I keyed the transmit button attached to my chest rig.

"Vendetta Four-Three from Wild Eagle Two-Seven."

He came up quickly. I heard his excitement. "Go for Vendetta."

"Be advised that we are currently receiving fire from building 138. They are firing at us from inside a window. We are looking at having you conduct a gun run . . . uh, a possible heading of north to south. How does that look to you?" I said before bringing my rifle up. It is always best to ask the pilots for their opinion. They know their weapons systems and aircraft. We were simply marines on the ground.

"Vendetta Four-Three copies, and I concur with the run-in heading of north to south" was his reply.

"We're going to mark the target with a smoke round. Stand by," I told him. Sergeant Anderson had already loaded a green-smoke round for his M203. *Thump!* The egg-sized projectile hit the side of the building and landed about fifteen meters to the north in a cemetery. As the green smoke released, I contacted the Cobras. "From the mark, south one-five meters. The building is lighter in color than the surrounding buildings and has a window in the center of it, facing north. That is your target; call tally."

"Vendetta Four-Three tallies the target" was his reply.

"Be advised that the nearest friendlies are in the mosque northwest three-five meters. We are going to have them take cover until you are done with your gun run. Just give me a wings-level call," I told him as my adrenaline soared.

"Vendetta Four-Three copies. Friendlies are northwest three-five meters, and you need a wings-level call. We are going to do a dry run first," replied the pilot. Conducting a dry run, meaning without firing, was a safety precaution to reduce chances of friendly fire and ensure that the attack geometry made sense.

Our position was still receiving fire, plaster from the stairwell wall behind us raining down with every burst from the enemy weapons. Sergeant Anderson noticed National Guard soldiers venturing out of the mosque to watch the gunships.

With enemy fire pelting over our heads, he got up and yelled to the soldiers, "You guys need to get back inside the building. There is an air strike inbound. You're going to have to get back inside!"

Anderson was forced to repeat himself a few times before they got the message and ran back in to take cover.

A section of F/A-18s came on-station, listening to the events unfold 15,000 feet below them. I briefed them on the situation. Like all Marine pilots, they wanted action but would have to wait their turn.

"Wild Eagle Two-Seven from Vendetta Four-Three, pushing," the Cobras reported. This meant they were on their attack run.

They banked left over the river. "Continue."

The lead aircraft started its short dive.

"Vendetta Four-Three is wings level," he reported.

He was oriented towards the enemy position.

"Vendetta Four-Three cleared hot for guns," I said, then warned the boys, "Here they come!"

We glanced over the small wall as we waited for the bird to unleash its 20mm cannon fire. The loud, penetrating sound echoed through the urban canyon as the pilot's ordnance slammed into the building, kicking up dust and shrapnel, piercing the window and silencing the enemy position. The pilot from the lead bird banked left. His wingman was next.

"Vendetta Four-Four, wings level," he reported.

"Hey, dash one is good. Hit lead's hits. Hit lead's hits," Anderson yelled, smacking the wall in excitement. The Cobras were right on target.

"Vendetta Four-Four cleared hot for guns. Hit lead's hits," I yelled over my radio handset.

The second bird bore down on the target. The AH-1 Cobra's

burst hit the house just to the west of the target building, but he adjusted before I could abort him or give corrections. Following the lead aircraft, the Cobra banked left.

We received no more fire from that building. The Cobras had silenced the insurgents for now. We'd recovered the initiative back. The Iraqi soldiers' attitude had visibly changed. Each one was now up against the wall, peering over with their AK-47s.

I jumped back on the radio to let the gunships know they had great effects on the target and directed them to establish themselves in the overhead as we tried to gain more situational awareness and allow the US soldiers in the mosque to finish clearing the building. Without my prompting him, Sergeant Dyer informed Dragon TOC that the Cobras were done with their gun run and the soldiers were cleared to venture out.

The team was working flawlessly, doing their jobs as expected. The Marine pilots, my team, the National Guard, and even the Iraqi soldiers were committed to taking the enemy out. Our exuberance was palpable. We felt like kings. During a lull in the fighting, Anderson and I were smiling. He laughed and told me he was going to reenlist. Like the rest of us, he was high on adrenaline and excitement.

Fifteen minutes after the Cobras silenced the insurgent position, they had to leave. Their fuel was low. The pilots wished us luck and told us to stay safe.

Out of all the various pilots I talked to over the radio during this deployment, I never met one of them. I didn't know their ranks or names, only their call signs. The Marine Corps had almost perfected the use of close air support, and we were proud to be a part of it.

The National Guard soldiers continued their sweep of the area. A couple of BFVs took up positions on the street as the dismounts moved about below us. For obvious reasons, there were no civilians nearby. The only sound now was the low rumble of the F-18s flying over the city and the distant melody of the Cobras' rotor blades as they flew west towards Al Asad Airbase.

Once the Cobras checked off-station, another section of gunships, Warrior One-Five, arrived to support us. We had worked with them before, and they knew the little city of Hit. I gave them an update and had them orbit overhead, looking for anything conspicuous while we waited to see what the enemy would do.

The Iraqis and my team continued to observe the battle space to our front while providing overwatch for the US soldiers on the street. Corporal Cureton and Sergeant Anderson were to my right, taking cover behind a small wall and using their ACOG scope and binoculars, patiently hunting the enemy. Sergeant Dyer had the radio handset to his ear, listening to the radio traffic from Dragon TOC. Occasionally, we'd get an update on friendly locations and other such information we needed.

I was a few feet away, towards the eastern side of the building, leaning against a wall and monitoring my radio as I talked to Cobras and jets. Using my ACOG, I searched for movement along the tree line on the far side of the river, the enemy's sanctuary. They loved to hide under the dense green foliage before melting back into the populace.

As I swept my ACOG scope across the tree line, I noticed activity beside a small, sand-colored building near the riverbank. This small outhouse-like shed held pumps that drew water from the river to the fields for irrigation. At first, what I was seeing did not register. Maybe it was some kids playing about or perhaps a farmer harvesting dates out of the trees. Then I focused in on them: about 400 meters away, two men wearing all black.

One was kneeling and leaning against a large palm tree. My heart raced as I leaned forward, trying to see what they were doing. Scanning their immediate area, I spotted an AK-47 leaning against the corner of the pump house, the buttstock sinking into the thick grass.

I yelled to my team, "Two insurgents to the southeast about four hundred meters, next to the pump house."

I was surprised. Usually, the most we saw of the insurgents was a brief movement in a window, a flash from an AK-47, or a quick dash between streets.

"Two males, weapons," I said, simultaneously taking my M4 off safe. I swiftly lined my ACOG scope on one of the two fighters. My finger squeezed the trigger, firing about four rounds of 5.56mm in rapid succession. The standing insurgent fell back out of my view and into the bushes. The man who had been kneeling by the tree vanished, melting back into the green landscape. I safed my weapon, not knowing if any of my rounds had met their target, although I was confident I'd smoked one of them.

"Where they at, sir?" Sergeant Anderson asked, moving to my position.

"Two MAMs with weapons. They were right next to that small building down there by the tree line," I said as I keyed the transmit button on my radio. My heart was still pounding.

I let the birds know what was going on. As I was on the radio, gunfire erupted from the tree line, coming at us from two to three different positions across the river. The insurgents' fire snapped over our heads. Cureton and Anderson returned fire, and some of the Iraqis rose and joined in.

I had to repeat myself several times as I talked to the aircraft. Sergeant Dyer informed Dragon TOC that we were getting hit. I crouched next to him as we both communicated on our various radios. One of the birds came back.

"Wild Eagle, we can tell you've got a lot going on down there."

My reply was "Affirm. I'm going to try and get clearance to destroy that small building with an LMAV. Stand by, Dealer."

Sergeant Dyer interrupted me. "Sir, they're dropping one-twenties."

About five seconds later, I heard the *krump-krump-krump* of three mortar rounds detonating in the palm grove across the river. The National Guard soldiers must have seen the insurgents as well and called in the mortars. Bringing indirect fire (IDF) to bear against the enemy while in contact is almost always a good tactic; however, with helos and jets flying around, I needed to deconflict the airspace.

I looked at Dyer. "Tell Dragon TOC to cease fire on the one-twenties and request a gun-target line." Knowing the location of the mortar position, Anderson got on the radio with the Cobras and F-18s and gave them the gun-target line—the imaginary line, in degrees, from the mortars to the target. This was a big deal in the world of fire support. Indirect fire and attacking aircraft must be deconflicted by either time, space, or both. Pilots do not like flying into a mix of artillery, mortars, or rockets. I don't blame them.

"Wild Eagle, Warrior One-Five can hit that building with rockets and guns while you wait for clearance."

"I'm aware of that, Warrior, but I need to get clearance for that as well. Just stand by," I replied.

The excitement in the pilots' voices was clear. That's the Marine Corps for you; everyone wanted a piece of the action.

The firing picked up in intensity as the Iraqi and American soldiers fired on the enemy positions in the palm grove. Anderson, who I'd thought was returning fire this whole time, told me he had a grid to the pump house. Dyer was talking to Dragon TOC over the radio, giving them a situation update and asking for clearance to engage with an LMAV. Anderson and I lay down next to each other to confirm our information and start coordination with the Hornets for an air strike. With so much gunfire, we had to yell. About ten feet away, Corporal Cureton was sending a steady stream of controlled bursts into the palm grove with his SAW. Somehow, we could still hear the AK-47 rounds as they cracked overhead.

It is hard to put into words how amazing this was. The adrenaline was flowing, and we could hardly hear one another, but everyone was calm and doing what needed to be done. Our team worked seamlessly. These marines were smart, disciplined, and extremely aggressive. It was situations like, with men like these, that made me want to forget all the nonsense and stay in the Marine Corps. This was what it was all about. This was why we joined the green machine.

"Sir, we're good to engage with the LMAV," Sergeant Dyer reported.

"Thanks, man." I keyed my radio and passed the F-18s the information needed for the air strike. Anderson moved back towards Cureton and continued to engage the insurgent positions.

The Iraqis still had not gotten back behind that big DShK 12.7mm Soviet-era machine gun positioned at the corner of the building behind a stack of sandbags. They were too intimidated since the last soldier behind it had been killed. Being the warrior that he is, Anderson grabbed an Iraqi and pointed towards the big gun. He got one of them behind the weapon to start suppressing the area. He did what their Iraqi commander would not or could not do: motivate these soldiers to fight.

As Sergeant Anderson pointed out enemy positions and directed the fire, this huge beast drowned out the AK-47s, M4s, and even Cureton's SAW as it spewed fire. Anderson and Cureton yelled encouragement—"*Na'am, na'am*," meaning "Yes, yes" in Arabic. The weapon quickly ran out of ammunition.

"Hey, he's red, he's red," yelled Cureton. Anderson started firing his M4 to cover the Iraqi soldier as he reloaded. Insurgent rounds slammed into the wall and sandbags. An Iraqi soldier in a firing position along the rooftop was shot in the shoulder. He simply fell to the ground, let go of his weapon, and grabbed his shoulder as he yelled out and ran downstairs. I shook my head and returned to the business at hand. I don't think anyone else even noticed at first.

Fifteen thousand feet above the city, the F-18s prepared for their strike by moving eight nautical miles to the south before turning for their attack run. I had the Cobras hold at a location where they were out of the way and safe.

Letting me know they were on their attack, the Hornets called out, "Dealer Six-Four, wings level."

The other F-18 was using her laser designator for Dealer Six-Four's LMAV.

Al Hit Bridge over the Euphrates River.

"Continue," I replied as I took my attention off the target and searched for the aircraft in the sky. Spotting him, I said: "Dealer Six-Four cleared hot."

Sergeant Anderson heard me and repeated it so everyone knew: "He's cleared hot."

"Dealer Six-Four, rifle" blared from my radio, telling me the missile was in the air.

"Rifle one away," I yelled to the team. I heard the thump as the missile's engine kicked on and started its short dive towards the target. Everyone's attention immediately went to the small building where the insurgents had been seeking cover. We saw the flash of the missile. It was a direct hit. The Iraqis yelled in excitement, as did the team; the small building disintegrated into brown debris and black smoke 400 meters away. The explosion was followed by a thunderous crack as the sound wave hit us.

"Dealer flight from Wild Eagle Two-Seven, be advised direct hit. Go ahead and establish yourself back in the overhead," I said with a grin. It was a clean hit. We had swiftly gained and maintained fire superiority over the insurgents. The Iraqi soldiers had snapped out of their traumatized reaction to seeing one of their brothers killed.

We all watched the smoke and dust drift downwind. It was a clear, brisk morning. Amazingly, despite all this madness, it was still a beautiful day.

The small-arms fire from across the river had stopped briefly, but we took cover again as the insurgents reengaged. *Damn, these guys are fuckin' tough*, I said to myself. Just because we thought they were on the run didn't mean they were.

The thick grove of date palms and brush, kept green by the life-giving Euphrates, provided excellent concealment. The insurgents were engaging from multiple positions, but we couldn't pinpoint any of them. They would shoot and then move to a new location. In retrospect, I should have had Sergeant Anderson call in artillery on the whole palm grove.

Summoned back for lethal work, the AH-1 Cobras were eager to get into the fight. I gave the birds a general talk-on to the target and had the Iraqis and US soldiers continue to suppress the enemy. As the Cobras were inbound for their run, Anderson fired a 40mm smoke round at the target. The round plunged into the cold Euphrates. Cureton laughed at Anderson. Even amid chaos and seriousness, marines will tease each other. It's who we are.

Anderson ignored the sarcasm and loaded another smoke round. This time, the projectile made it across the river, the egg-shaped projectile bounced before releasing the smoke. The Cobras came in at about a forty-five-degree angle. They peppered the palm grove with 20mm cannon fire and 2.75-inch rockets with good results. The insurgents were either killed or had scattered. Either way, we stopped getting shot at. Just like that, this short battle near the ancient city of Id was over.

The remainder of the day was quiet. I had the F-18s continue to conduct ISR of the area until they were bingo. They signed off as they headed back to Al Asad Airbase. Once they departed the area, the team and I linked up with the tanks and drove back to Camp

Hit. We were exhausted and hungry but in high spirits. Though we were proud, each man contemplated what could have happened and reflected on his own actions.

After parking the gun truck, we headed back to our team room. With my helmet in my right hand and weapon slung across my gear-laden chest rig, I noticed the boys were all smiles. Even the staunch professional, Dyer, revealed an uncharacteristic slight grin. *Job well done, boys.*

Today had been a success. I was proud of these three Marine NCOs. Dyer, Cureton, and Anderson had shown courage and initiative under fire. If that initial round from that sniper had been an inch closer, the day would have been drastically different, but it had been a calculated risk. In the end, it allowed us to take back the initiative and even motivated some of the Iraqis to fight.

Captain Morgigno informed me a few days later that intelligence indicated we had killed at least twelve insurgents. Even more important than that, though, we all returned to Camp Hit alive. Our time with these National Guard soldiers had been brief but filled with action. Lieutenant Colonel Huffman had allowed us to work as we saw fit because we brought results by being aggressive and smart. My marines were living up to the high standards of the Marine Corps because of our training and heritage.

■ ■ ■

As November ended, so did our time in the small but violent city of Al Hit, Iraq. For the next week, we conducted a few more operations with Lieutenant Colonel Huffman's battalion as the 13th MEU slowly took over. Besides a few artillery strikes across the Euphrates, these missions were calm and rather dull. Our team was asked to stay and support the MEU, but ANGLICO's headquarters in Al Asad had different plans for us.

I assumed we would be going back to Ramadi. From what I had

been hearing, those teams had their hands full. On December 1, we said goodbye to the National Guard soldiers of Mississippi. Huffman gave all of us a unit coin and thanked us. The whole team agreed: these soldiers were good people. With firm handshakes out of the way, we loaded up in our gun truck and jumped into a convoy headed to Al Asad. The boys and I figured we would get there and hop into a convoy headed to Ar Ramadi. We were wrong; I had a surprise waiting for me, and it wasn't good.

CHAPTER SEVEN:
PURGATORY IN AL ASAD

It didn't take me long to figure out something wasn't right when I got to 1st ANGLICO's headquarters in Al Asad. The XO, Major Stohs, was acting even more aloof than normal, and so were the various staff officers. I kept asking when the convoy the team and I would be taking back to Ramadi was leaving. No one could give me an answer.

The quicker I left this place, the better. Al Asad was Crazy Land with its painted rocks, normal business hours, and Sundays off. I wanted no part of it. My aggression was peaking. Fresh off the fight, I wanted more.

At around 1330, the XO called me into his office. He closed the door behind him.

"Captain Angell, the CO is going to talk to you about the blog you had." He paused.

Shock ran down my spine. I had a blog that detailed my experience in Iraq. It wasn't critical of the military; it simply described the general day-to-day nature of combat as a marine. It didn't even have my name or unit. I began writing it over a year before as a pro-military website to counter all the antiwar propaganda I was reading, believing it was important to share what was going on over here; plus, I loved to write. The Department of Defense (DOD) public affairs office had even contacted me through the blog, telling me how much they supported the site. But after arriving in Hit, I got an email from Major Grice ordering me to shut it down. Someone had seen it and brought it to the attention of the command. After that, I had not thought much about it.

The XO continued, "You won't be going back to Ramadi with your team. They will go back tonight, but you won't be going with them."

I felt as if my world had ended. I just stood there as he talked. There was nothing I could do, and I knew it.

"You will stay here and be part of the staff as the awards officer. It is unknown if you will return to your team," he explained with his hands clasped together.

It only got worse.

"Now we are going to go next door, and you will report to the CO. I highly suggest that you stay quiet and listen. Don't try and explain yourself or make excuses, and don't even mention free speech. Do you have any questions for me before we see the CO?"

"No sir," I replied emotionlessly. *Self-imposed chaos. Deal with it.*

We walked into the hallway, my proverbial tail between my legs. I stood outside the CO's door while the XO went in. In official Marine Corps tone, the XO called out, "Captain Angell, report to the commanding officer."

"Aye sir!"

Smartly, I stepped into the CO's office and centered myself six inches in front of his desk. I was now back in boot camp mode, something I had left over twelve years prior. Looking over his head, I focused on the cinder block wall behind him. Major Stohs closed the door.

"Captain Angell reporting as ordered, sir," I said, wishing I were somewhere else. I stood at attention, heels together and arms at my side. The CO's hands were on his waist, his eyes staring at me from his bald head. He said nothing for what seemed like an eternity but was probably only about ten seconds. Major Stohs stood next to the desk, quiet and stoic like always. The only sound in the room came from the hum of the air-conditioning unit on the wall and a ticking clock.

I would rather be blown up by an IED than be standing here right now, I thought. Getting killed would have at least been honorable.

As expected, the CO let me have it. He told me my actions were unbecoming of an officer in ANGLICO, how I might have violated operational security, how I let my marines down and violated his command philosophy of "quiet professional." Then he went on about how I was operating like a cowboy down in Hit, and how I was lucky he wasn't sending me back to the States and kicking me out of the unit. Heeding Major Stohs's suggestion, I stayed quiet and said not a word, unmoving, showing no emotion. Towards the end, he went into my punishment.

I was to receive a nonpunitive letter of caution (NPLOC), which would stay in my unit folder until the CO left once the deployment was over. Additionally, I was to stay in Al Asad for the month of December and work under Major Stohs as the "awards officer" while my team went to Ramadi without me. And finally, I was to write an essay on how, by having a military blog, I was wrong.

The CO knew that the silly little NPLOC or essay would be of no concern to me, but removing me from Wild Eagle Two-Seven and from combat operations was a sentence that felt just short of death. I would have preferred he kicked me in the stomach so I could get back to the boys. In the end, pushing aside my ego, I realized I was wrong. My actions, regardless of intent, violated the CO's command guidance. I was to accept his punishment, learn from it, and move on. There was no other choice.

A couple of hours later, after turning in my M4 and other serialized equipment at the armory and being assigned a "can" (small sleeping container with light, bed, and AC unit), I found Anderson and the rest of the team. They weren't scheduled to leave until the following evening, so they were staying in a four-man can for the night as well. Cureton opened the door. I asked them all to come outside. Putting my can of tobacco back in my pocket, I told them what was going on. It was humbling. I owned my mistake.

All three marines stood there with their arms crossed, shaking their heads.

"So, what's going to happen to us?" asked Dyer.

"Like I said, you're going to Ramadi tomorrow. Once you're there, you will be working with one of the air officers, like Captain Rard or Captain Elward, until I can get back down there."

Dyer spat out some tobacco and glanced over his shoulder at a marine walking by. He waited for the marine to pass before saying, "They don't realize how this affects us, just to prove a fuckin' point."

I reiterated that this was my fault, my responsibility, and not the command's. Anderson told me the sergeant major had been asking questions about me and how the team felt. Apparently, the command was very interested in the marines' opinion before deciding whether to remove me from the team. Whatever was said between Sergeant Anderson and Sergeant Major Morgan allowed me to stay with the team, minus a little time-out in December.

The following day, I shook hands with the marines and said goodbye before they headed off to Ramadi in another convoy. It would be a long month.

■ ■ ■

Every day in December was precisely the same. I woke up and made my way to the shower trailer. Then I headed off to the chow hall to eat breakfast. At around 0730, I'd go into the company office and sit at a computer, drink coffee, and chew tobacco. As the unofficial "awards officer," it was my job to gather the information from various teams and individual officers regarding awards they wanted to submit. Depending on the award write-up, I had to get witness statements and usually rewrite them so they fit with the official format. Once that was complete and the CO and XO signed off on them, I forwarded the awards to the MEF for approval or disapproval.

Sometimes I was required to go to the staff meetings, which were brutal. There was an internet café right outside the ANGLICO office, so at around 1000, I would take a break to call or email my wife. At 1200, I headed off to lunch, then returned to the administrative office to write awards and send off emails until 1800. After chow, I went back to the can to sleep. That was it. No firefights, no air strikes, no long patrols, no QRF.

Besides not wanting to be in Al Asad, I was apprehensive about being the "awards officer," based on my experience with the commanding officer. When I first reported into 1st ANGLICO, I was wearing my green service Alpha uniform. He noticed one of the ribbons I'd been awarded after the invasion and asked if I'd earned that award or if it was simply given to me.

Stunned, I replied, "I'd like to think I earned it, sir, but you can always ask Captain Sokol. He was the infantry company commander that had two KIAs and over twenty wounded during the invasion. He's the one that wrote and submitted the award."

The CO glared at me and changed the subject. If he was skeptical of combat awards, how would this affect our ability to properly recognize 1st ANGLICO marines and sailors?

This, with a few exceptions, was my life during December 2005. Of course, my wife was ecstatic; she was able to relax slightly as the fear of me being killed or wounded subsided greatly. She wanted to thank the CO. I also had the chance to email some of my fellow officers and apologize for my actions.

One of the first emails I sent out was to Major Grice. I apologized to him, as I was aware that my actions had caused friction between him and the CO. In usual fashion, the major said only, "It is what it is." In other words, "Deal with it, fucker, because there isn't anything you can do about it." He of course gave me some great advice. He highly recommended that I keep my head down, do my job, take my punishment, and before long I would be out of Al Asad and back in Ramadi. That is precisely what I did.

The sergeant major talked to me as well. A day or two after the

CO dropped the hammer, Sergeant Major Morgan pulled me into his office. One of the points he brought up was about the marines, his specialty. He had talked with Anderson and the team the day we arrived from Hit. In a fatherly tone, he told me that the marines really respected me. They didn't want to work with any other officer. He also told me that I'd get through this, even though I might feel like my world was crashing down.

"You'll be back with your team before too long," he said with a grin.

Al Asad felt like purgatory. The CO had me go to some lawyer with the judge advocate general (JAG) office on Al Asad for counseling. The lawyer was supposed to tell me what I did wrong as it pertained to the Uniform Code of Military Justice (UCMJ). But the JAG officer, a major, couldn't tell me what I did wrong. Nothing I wrote about violated operational security (OPSEC). He wasn't even sure why I was there. It didn't matter. I'd disregarded the commanding officer's guidance and trust; that was enough.

As the awards officer, I wanted to do the best I could. One thing I have learned in life that has done wonders for me is that when given a task I don't like, I should still give it 100 percent. I would lean into it and not complain. This wasn't always easy. To be honest, it was satisfying to support the command's efforts in recognizing the actions of individual men, but my thoughts were constantly with my marines down in Ramadi. I kept in touch with Anderson via email to see how the team was doing. They were as curious as I was to find out when I would return.

Not surprisingly, they were still in the fight. Insurgent attacks in Ramadi continued to increase. The boys were working with Captain Sean Elward, an F-18 pilot and FAC. Elward was a solid officer who brought an endless supply of CAS knowledge to the fight. The boys were taking care of this officer until I returned.

About halfway through December, Major Grice moved the teams. Captain Shane Murray's team, my team, and part of Supporting Arms Liaison Team (SALT) Delta based out of Camp

Ramadi went to Camp Corregidor in eastern Ramadi. Captain Mike Carroll's team and Staff Sergeant Orlando Ibanez's team moved to Camp Ramadi to support the Army there. Ramadi was dangerous, but eastern Ramadi was particularly hazardous. The threat there was IEDs and indirect fire, as well as complex attacks. Mike Carroll had been wounded early in the deployment when an IED destroyed his gun truck. He was lucky to be alive. Major Grice was attempting to spread the wealth of risk.

Towards the end of December, Sergeant Anderson started to send me reports about their operations in eastern Ramadi. He didn't go into detail for OPSEC reasons, but they were conducting missions with snipers and scouts. They would insert into houses in the dark of night and set up positions to observe and engage Iraqis who were emplacing IEDs or attacking coalition forces. It sounded like the counter-IED operations the team and I had conducted along Route Long Island. However, this was significantly more dangerous. During Operation Sand Eel, we were out in a rural area. Urban environments held considerably higher risks. The enemy could be next door or around the corner, hiding in the three-dimensional battle space. About a year prior, four US Marine snipers were overrun and killed conducting similar operations in the city. It was deadly business.

Just before midnight on January 2, 2006, I boarded a CH-46 helicopter in Al Asad and headed towards Camp Ramadi. My time in purgatory had ended. The bird I was on made several stops along the way, dropping off a soldier at some FOB and picking up a marine or soldier here and there. With all the stops, the flight took about three hours. I sat on my sliver of a seat against the fuselage with my M4 between my legs and tried to relax. Hydraulic fluid leaked from various hoses; it was futile trying to avoid the slow drips. The smell was oddly sweet.

For the first time in a month, I sighed in relief. This was rather counterintuitive when I thought about it. If anything, my anxiety should have increased as I neared Ramadi. But the more I thought about it, the clearer it became. In Al Asad, I had been worried about my men. I stressed about their safety day in and day out. Additionally, being with my team lowered my anxiety. They increased my combat effectiveness. Without them, I was only a Marine officer, about as useful as a steering wheel without a car. Our comradery and instincts, our ability to work together in this environment, drove me. This is what it's like to be a member of a real team. We supported and trusted each other. We watched each other's six.

To this day, I have no idea what their thoughts about me were. It doesn't matter. We didn't talk about a brotherhood—ever. For me, it was an unspoken bond. Knowing that three hard-charging Marine NCOs have your back in combat is almost indescribable. They would, and had, killed for me, and I had killed for them.

Men don't fight for their country, apple pie, or flags; they fight for each other. Words do not do it justice, but as William Shakespeare wrote in *Henry V*:

From this day to the ending of the world,
But we in it shall be remember'd;
We few, we happy few, we band of brothers;
For he to-day that sheds his blood with me
Shall be my brother

These men were my brothers, and I was going to stand and fight next to them. There was nowhere else on earth I would have rather been than with these men, fighting in Ramadi.

CHAPTER EIGHT:
BACK TO WORK

The CH-46s landed on Camp Ramadi in the early hours of January 3. Captain Elward was waiting on the small tarmac with a grin. I approached the F-18 pilot under a dark sky bursting with stars. The bird's rotors were still spinning, mixing the air with sand and grit that found its way into every possible crevice.

Loaded down with my gear, I lumbered forward, glad to put more distance between myself and Al Asad. Camp Ramadi hadn't changed since I left for Al Hit in late October. Large generators churned in the background. Eventually, your mind compartmentalizes the noise, and it becomes a simple hum. Lights illuminated the sprawling compound as bright as day, giving the feeling of being in a stadium at night.

I shook the tall, blond pilot's hand with a sheepish smile.

"Welcome back, Angell," he said, grabbing my rucksack. He had driven a small pickup from the ANGLICO CP to the tarmac. I didn't ask where it came from, but it felt odd to be sitting in a civilian vehicle. Embarrassingly, I flinched when two 155mm Paladin howitzers down the road fired. He laughed.

Elward was honest and straightforward. I had emailed him during my time in Al Asad to apologize for putting undue stress on the men due to my having a military blog. His reply was frank, telling me in no uncertain terms that I had screwed up. I readily agreed with his assessment. The conversation turned to the marines. As expected, he was impressed with all of the ANGLICO marines. He recounted one mission he'd gone on with the team in December.

It was a night-presence patrol. In the northern part of Ramadi, such missions usually didn't bring much contact with the insurgents. The team was with a platoon from one of the National Guard battalions and was inserted into the MC-3 area north of the river. Thinking ahead, Corporal Cureton had developed a few preplanned targets for mortars in the event they made contact.

As they patrolled near the river, searching for activity, F-18s flying overhead in support spotted two boats with armed men. Sergeant Anderson quickly notified the patrol leader. Being aggressive, the mix of soldiers and marines set up a hasty ambush and waited for the boats to round a bend in the river. Under a bright moon, the boats drifted into range. The ambush was initiated by an AT4—a disposable antitank rocket—fired at the insurgents. The rest of the patrol opened up on the boats.

Cureton, trying to get into a good firing position, wandered into the mud and fell. Though covered in greasy wet mud from the riverbank, he still managed to unleash the fury from his M249 SAW. Paddling for their lives, the insurgents tried to escape behind a small island as they were overwhelmed by 40mm grenades and small-arms fire. However, their effort was in vain. Seizing his chance, Cureton contacted the 120mm mortars on Camp Ramadi and called in a fire mission on the preplanned target.

With a big smile, Elward told me how aggressive and competent the men were. Truth be told, I was envious of the captain for being with the boys on that mission.

I didn't stay on Camp Ramadi long. The next morning, I jumped in a convoy headed to Camp Corregidor. The three-mile drive down Route Michigan was a reality check. The city was in ruins. Building after building comprised nothing but crumbled concrete and rebar. Stagnant pools of sewage and water collected along curbs and road intersections. The streets looked like Swiss cheese, marked with countless IED holes and craters. Weeds allowed to grow wild due to the lack of city services and maintenance stretched towards the sky. Smoke from burning trash and debris wafted through the air. Occasional pop shots snapped over our gun trucks as we made our way east.

I sat there and shook my head, resigned to the reality of this world. As a passenger, your fate is no longer in your own hands. I usually had to force these thoughts out by focusing on the mission and nothing else.

We sped down the road, swerving around obstacles. Civilians walking along what remained of a sidewalk picked up their pace. American outposts like the government center and OP Hotel sat in defiance of the enemy-controlled city. In the early winter of 2006, attacks against these strongpoints were a daily occurrence, and it showed. They bore the scars of relentless attacks, reminders of battles both recent and long past. The larger craters were the result of RPG attacks, while the small pits came from mortar shrapnel or small-arms fire. Huge chunks of concrete were missing down to the exposed and contorted rebar. But the marines and soldiers had stood their ground, repelling these assaults by fire and close combat.

The drive eastward was sobering yet good for me. I needed to get my head back in the game. There were two and a half months left of this deployment, and anything could happen.

As the convoy pulled into Camp Corregidor's north gate, I shifted in my seat to get a better view of my new home.

Camp Corregidor, about one square kilometer in size, was compact and located on the eastern edge of the city. Its proximity meant multiple attacks a day. There were no men running in PT gear, no soldiers playing volleyball. It was sparse and dirty. Old, demolished gun trucks—victims of IEDs—littered the area. All the soldiers and marines kept their helmets and body armor on. The reason why became apparent no more than five minutes inside the gate. As we were clearing our weapons, three mortar rounds detonated to the south, about 200 meters away. The previous day, enemy rockets had exploded right in front of the two-story command post, wounding three soldiers headed to the small chow hall.

I listened. After the all clear was given, we drove the short distance to my new home, a building called Full Metal Jacket.

Some of the marines came out to greet me. As expected, I was the target of amusing jabs and smart-ass remarks.

"How was Al Asad, sir?" They smirked. "How much fast food did you get?"

I laughed and shook their hands. "Too much," I replied.

"Well, you won't get that crap here," they retorted.

Captains Rard and Murray greeted me as well. Thankful to be with these men, I asked, "So, how is it here?"

Things got serious.

"Dangerous, dude. Fuckin' dangerous, but we're killin 'em—that's for sure."

"Can't wait to hear about it," I responded. With my pack over my shoulder, I grabbed my M4 and headed inside. Before I could enter the team room, Anderson, Cureton, and Dyer emerged. It was strangely awkward. For the past month, I'd thought of almost nothing else but this team. Now I didn't know what to say.

"Good to see you guys. I'm glad to be out of Al Asad," I humbly told them, setting my pack down on the dirt.

They each nodded. "Welcome to Camp Corregidor, sir," Anderson said as we shook hands. We headed into our team room. Anderson pointed towards a green army cot sitting on the dirt.

"That's yours, sir. I'm there, that's Dyer's cot, and that's Cureton's."

After throwing my rucksack on the cot, I removed my body armor and helmet. Anderson stood waiting to talk. The room was cold and damp, a 180 from when we arrived in Iraq at the end of August. I threw on a black fleece pullover, trying to warm up as Anderson went into the basic logistics of the base.

Bathrooms consisted of PVC pipes set into the ground called "piss tubes." The "shitters" were made from plywood with toilet seats screwed to a hole. Underneath the hole was a fifty-gallon drum cut in half and filled with diesel fuel. That was where the men did their business. Every few days, some of the marines pulled the drums out of the shitters to burn the diesel and excrement. There were no showers at all. A Corregidor "shower" meant using baby wipes to clean your body. You could occasionally use bottled water to clean off, but this would quickly reduce the amount of water we had to drink, which meant more logistical movements to and from Camp Ramadi, which meant an increase in IED attacks and more casualties.

The place was austere and rugged, worse even than Camp Hit. We were always armed. But the small chow hall, no bigger than a couple of household rooms, was surprisingly good. I wasn't in Al Asad anymore, and I loved it.

When Anderson paused, I interrupted to ask, "How's the team?"

He was always forthright with me; I trusted his opinion and advice. If something was screwed up, he would let me know.

"They're good," he said, shaking his head before continuing, "Sergeant Dyer is Sergeant Dyer—quiet, dependable, aloof, there when you need him like always."

"What about Cureton?" I inquired, crossing my arms to shake off the chill. It was starting to sprinkle outside.

Anderson chuckled before answering, "Cureton is doin' good. He'll act like a knucklehead occasionally, but he's quick to fix the problem once I point it out."

I knew precisely what Anderson was talking about, and it was clear not much had changed regarding Cureton's aggression. Cureton was a young, smart marine who had been unleashed in a world of violence, adrenaline, and raw power. At eighteen, he had seen and done more things than most grown men had in the United States. I liked that he was aggressive and had a bias for action; they all did. I respected and encouraged it. Occasionally, though, Anderson had to slow him down. He went on, "The missions are crazy—lots of contact."

"That's what I've heard," I replied.

"One thing that's nice"—Anderson paused and looked around with a smile—"is that when we're not on a mission, no one screws with you. No stupid games."

Stupid games meant doing busywork for what seemed like no reason. Here, the marines would conduct operations, prepare for ops, and get some downtime between missions, all while trying not to get killed. No one was painting rocks.

Captain Rard entered our team room, anxious to discuss operations.

"No problem," I replied, "just give me a few minutes to catch up with Anderson."

Rard left us to our conversation. Anderson explained that they had started to conduct operations with a sniper team and some scouts. The 1-506th designated it Task Force Dark Eagle. A team generally consisted of a four-man sniper team, about four Army scouts, and an ANGLICO team. These task-organized teams would insert into a house covertly in the dead of night and wait for the Army to conduct a patrol or sweep. When the insurgents came out to fight, the odd assortment of US soldiers, marines, and occasional Air Force TACPs would attack by fire and/or use precision-guided, air-delivered weapons to hit the insurgents.

There was significant lethal combat power in that twelve-to-fifteen-man team. I liked the idea. It was aggressive and didn't force the men to sit in a road-bound gun truck, waiting to get hit with an IED. For once, we were being proactive—forcing the insurgents to react to us.

We discussed a few more things. All in all, the marines liked it here. The only real concern was dying or getting wounded.

After talking with Sergeant Anderson, I went across the hall into the common area to see Captain Rard. Although austere, the space was impressive. There was a living room with a couch and some chairs, a TV with a marine's Xbox, and a table with a coffee maker and microwave. Behind the couch was a row of small rooms partitioned by two-by-fours and plywood walls. A whiteboard with upcoming missions hung next to the door. The floor was basically crushed rock and dirt, so a thin layer of moondust clung to everything. A radio connected to a speaker allowed us to monitor the TOC. There was even Wi-Fi. Rard had obtained a satellite dish from some Iraqi with the appropriate connections and service. The boys didn't have to go to the small internet café to use the internet. Most had laptops, so they could instant message and email their families back home whenever the opportunity arose.

Somehow—and I didn't inquire about this capability—service wasn't cut when the base went into a communications blackout after suffering a KIA. "River City" is the code name for this protocol. The intent is to ensure that the KIA notification to the family occurs through the proper channels and not some email from Iraq. Rard explained to me that the marines knew not to discuss operations or casualties over the system. These men were mature, even the few eighteen-year-olds. They knew what was right and what was wrong.

Full Metal Jacket housed a motley crew of enablers with unique skills and missions. There were marines from EOD and Civil Affairs Group, Navy Seabees, Air Force TACP teams, a couple of dog handlers, some sniper teams, the occasional SOF team, and of course our ANGLICO detachment. On the roof sat a few sandbagged bunkers to be used in the event Camp Corregidor was hit hard. The whole two-story building was ash gray, harsh, and lacked any redeemable aesthetic qualities. ANGLICO and a few other unit detachments were on the first floor. We were lucky. Mortars had put a hole between the roof and the second floor, wounding two soldiers.

January was part of the rainy season in Iraq. This year was particularly wet. The water created mudholes and shallow ponds. Everything around Full Metal Jacket was wet and cold. The temperature never dropped below freezing, but it was miserable enough to chill your bones. Bleak, cold, austere, and dangerous were four words that defined Camp Corregidor during the short winter.

Rard and Murray sat me down to talk about eastern Ramadi. As ANGLICO, we would be supporting the newly arrived US Army battalion, the 1-506th Infantry Regiment of the 101st Airborne Division. This battalion was made famous by the HBO series *Band of Brothers*. We would be supporting them and operating south of the Euphrates. The Al Mala'ab district lay just to the west of Camp Corregidor and south of Route Michigan. Most of the soldiers and marines called it the Mulab. South of there was the Albu Jabir district that bordered the east-to-west railroad tracks. To the north of Route Michigan and the Mulab was the Sina'a industrial district, simply referred to as the industrial district. To the northeast, the large Sufia district ran up against the Euphrates River. This area was primarily rural farms with small villages. It wasn't urban but was almost as dangerous as Ramadi proper. The 3rd Battalion, 7th Marines, was responsible for operations west of the 1-506th AO.

Rard and Murray got serious and talked about enemy contact. Almost every time a patrol left Camp Corregidor, it got attacked. Gun trucks were getting destroyed by IEDs and RPGs. Foot patrols, although more difficult for the insurgents to target, attracted complex attacks where insurgents would maneuver on the patrol after initiating the assault with an IED or RPGs. Many of these fighters on the east side of Ramadi actively tried to overrun American positions. If a patrol loitered too long in an area, insurgent mortars and rockets would rain down.

Insurgent snipers were creating havoc, filming their attacks and uploading them onto the internet. Suicide bombers attacked on an almost daily basis, targeting outreach efforts by American and Iraqi commanders. The dreaded suicide vehicle-borne IEDs (SVBIEDs) were becoming more deadly, targeting isolated outposts such as the government center and OP Hotel. American soldiers and marines were killed and wounded almost every day. This insurgency was growing under the leadership of the Jordanian jihadist Abu Musab al-Zarqawi, and we all knew it.

Rard went into the details of Task Force Dark Eagle. They developed the concept after conducting a mission with a National

Guard sniper team, Joker Four, led by a former marine. The 1-506th commanding officer, Lieutenant Colonel David Clark, and their operations officer, Major Dave Womack, signed off on the concept. It was aggressive and held significant risk but could potentially turn the tables on the insurgents. My curiosity piqued, I asked about the mission that had started the whole thing.

When the ANGLICO detachments switched out between Camp Ramadi and Camp Corregidor in December, the 2nd Battalion, 69th Armored (2-69), was preparing to rotate back to the United States. The newly arrived 1-506th was conducting their "relief in place" and taking over. Captain Rard was supposed to conduct an operation with one of 2-69's sniper teams. The sniper teams had been reluctant to work with the ANGLICO team so close to departing the AO, but Staff Sergeant Martinez—a sniper team leader and former marine who knew what ANGLICO did—volunteered to take the mission. The 2-69 readily agreed.

In late December 2005, the small mixed unit of soldiers and marines departed OP Hotel en route to a small two-story house in the Mulab. The eleven men forming the team left in the early-morning hours under cover of air support. They quietly inserted into a small house to establish an overwatch position while staying concealed. Platoons from one of the infantry companies were set to conduct a patrol in the direction of the occupied house later in the day. If enemy fighters started to harass and attack the soldiers pushing through the neighborhood, the snipers were to kill the insurgents. If the targets became big enough, ANGLICO would direct precision air strikes on key enemy positions; at least, that was the plan.

Entering the house, the men quickly secured and searched the family before separating the men from the women and children. A couple of scouts watched over them while Joker Four and the ANGLICO team cleared the top floor and roof. Once the house was cleared, they blew "loopholes" with small charges that allowed the snipers and marines to observe the area without silhouetting themselves.

As the sun rose above the buildings, Martinez noticed a young man digging a hole. He clearly wasn't planting a tree. He was nervous, looking around and shuffling away whenever a car drove nearby. This man was digging a shallow hole to hide an IED.

Martinez shot the insurgent and reported the incident to the team.

"I just dropped a man one hundred eighty-three meters to my twelve o'clock," he said, not taking his eyes off the target. He continued, "He accepted money from another man and started digging in the street. He's wearing a black man-dress and not moving."

On the rooftop, the men readied themselves. They heard women crying in the distance. Before long, one of the soldiers in the security element reported that a crowd of about forty people had formed around the body. The screams and wailing of the women had increased. The men prepared for what was coming. A bus pulled up, blocking the team's view. As more Iraqis gathered, the soldiers spotted more men with weapons, some even pointing in the direction of the task force.

Rard requested air support. A group of men was walking from house to house, knocking on doors, trying to locate the marines and soldiers. Joey Bennett, one of the snipers with Joker Four, shot a man pointing an AK-47 at their position. The tension rose. The low roar of American jets intensified over Ramadi.

More shots rang out as the marines and soldiers engaged armed Iraqi insurgents. Staff Sergeant Martinez saw several bodies in the street when he looked out the window next to Specialist Bennett's firing position. The Marine Harriers flying overhead were setting up to drop an LMAV on the attackers, but a glitch in their system called a "bent rod" meant they could not release the weapon. Frustrated, Rard brought the birds down in a show of force to ward off the gathering Iraqi fighters. Before long, the men were told the QRF was coming to get them for an exfil.

Anderson and the team, along with soldiers, were engaging insurgents to the north and south sides of the perimeter. As the Harriers dropped out of the sky, the Iraqis dispersed, not knowing whether a bomb was inbound. Staff Sergeant Martinez recalled how disciplined the marines' fire was, well aimed and deliberate. They were seizing the initiative and forcing the insurgents to react. Before long, the soldiers and marines were ordered to exfil the house as a monstrous BFV screamed down the road towards them, engaging insurgents popping out of alleys.

I sat listening to Captain Rard and Murray tell the story. They weren't boasting, merely sharing facts. The issue with the bent rod was disconcerting, but it occasionally happens; weapons malfunction. Shaking my head, I took a drink from a water bottle.

"All in all, I think the marines and I killed at least ten insurgents. That doesn't count the kills the snipers and scouts got," Rard reported with a sterile tone.

Later that day, Rard and Murray took me to the 1-506th TOC to show me around and introduce me to the commanding officer, Lieutenant Colonel Clark. He firmly shook my hand and welcomed me to the battalion when I met him on the second floor.

He was an impressive leader who appeared to have no ego. Open to ideas that would help rid this city of insurgent fighters so the civilians could get back to the business of rebuilding, he had nothing but positive things to say about his experience with ANGLICO. He expected nothing less from my team. The operations officer, Major Womack, shook my hand and welcomed me aboard. We all talked briefly. They were busy men, so we didn't take up much of their time.

A few nights later, on the fifth of January, I went on my first mission with Able Company, 1-506th—an operation called "Back to School." The team and I accompanied the patrol to an old schoolhouse north of Route Michigan along the western edge of the industrial district at around 2230. The objective was to find a weapons cache and try to roll up any suspected insurgents and deliver them to the battalion intelligence section for questioning. This was how they gained tactical intelligence. Unfortunately, the operation turned up neither hidden weapons nor insurgents. It was a quiet and uneventful movement through the dark neighborhoods of this restive town.

The men of the 1-506th operated like a hardened Marine infantry battalion. The officers and men sought out combat. I was honored to support them, but mostly I was thankful to have escaped Al Asad. Walking the cold, dark streets of this city was surreal. I was occasionally distracted by my awe at patrolling alongside the 1-506th, considering the unit's history and accomplishments during the Second World War. While soldiers like Dick Winters and Captain Spears had long since left this battalion, their legacy remained, and these men were proud of that. From what I could tell, they had been replaced by men of the same mold—heroic and tough.

After returning to Camp Corregidor, Anderson and Cureton went to sleep. Dyer stayed up to chat with his wife back in Texas. Still wired from the patrol, I grabbed my laptop and went into the common room to try to contact Joni. We chatted using Yahoo Messenger, and I even tried to use the small camera on my computer. The imagery was grainy and pixilated, but I didn't complain.

While I was in Al Asad, Joni had been relatively stress-free. Now our moods had switched. She hid her concern behind small talk about her day. After saying our goodbyes, I closed my computer. Looking around, I noticed Captain Rard had added another mission to the whiteboard. My next operation was another company cache search, this time with Bravo Company. Operation Away Game would take place on the morning of the eleventh of January, just south of the Mulab.

CHAPTER NINE:
OPERATION AWAY GAME

"**C**aptain Angell, it's that time." I stirred from my sleep as Sergeant Anderson returned to his cot.

Sitting up, I squinted around the cold, dark room, slightly confused. The dim light from a table lamp cast long shadows across the floor. Cureton and Dyer were awake and going about their routines. As I rubbed my eyes, my first thought was that I needed coffee. I looked down at my watch; it was 0515.

After shaking off the sleep, I swung my feet around, laced up my boots, grabbed my coffee mug, and walked next door to the team common area. I was strangely disoriented by the darkness. Gear and Xbox controllers cluttered the floor. The boys had been playing a few rounds of *Halo* the night before, trying to decompress and relax.

I poured a cup of stale coffee and went back to my cot. Sipping the bitter black gold, I focused on the mission's order. The rest of the team went through their usual pre-mission checks, inspecting magazines, lubing weapons, changing out radio batteries, eating what they could, and pouring water into their Camelbaks.

The mission was simple. Support Bravo Company, 1st of the 506th, call sign Outlaw, as they conducted a weapons-cache search south of the railroad station. ANGLICO was tasked with directing supporting aircraft. Once the enemy knew what we were up to, the question wasn't *if* we would get hit but when.

Cureton broke the silence. "What time are the birds supposed to show up, sir?"

"Around 0700, hopefully," I said. "The company commander wants the aircraft to check the route out before we step off."

"Well, let's hope they show up," Cureton quipped.

Tired and drowsy, everyone chuckled.

We jumped in our gun truck at around 0620 for the short ride to the south gate. Camp Corregidor has two entrances. The main entrance was on the infamous Route Michigan. The only other way to enter Camp Corregidor was through the south gate. We could have easily walked the 400 meters, but I figured we would be fighting the mud all day, so we drove and tried to stay dry.

This morning, with no breeze and low-hanging clouds, the smell of burning trash and sewage hung thicker and more pungent than usual. Mist floated through the cool morning air. The weather brought back memories of Southeast Texas in the winter: cold and damp.

As we neared the gate, I saw the sappers—combat engineers—and EOD teams waiting around. They collected in small groups, smoking, talking, checking and rechecking gear. Like us, they lived on Camp Corregidor, while Bravo Company worked out of OP Trotter to the east. Sergeant Anderson muscled the armored door open and got out to talk with the soldiers. The rest of the team and I hung out by the vehicle for a few more moments, trying to avoid the relentless wet mist. Finishing my coffee, I keyed the transmit button on my PRC-148 radio and contacted Captain Murray in the TOC.

"Wild Eagle Two-Eight from Wild Eagle Five-Seven on Cyan Three-One." For some reason, 1st ANGLICO command had changed my call sign from Two-Seven to Five-Seven before I returned to Ramadi. The reason for the change wasn't apparent.

"Go ahead, Five-Seven," Murray replied.

"Any word on Gunshot? Are they en route?" I asked.

"Negative, they will be a little late. They had some maintenance problems, but they should be Oscar Mike [on the move] shortly," Murray told me, to my dismay.

"Five-Seven copies," I replied.

Captain Shane Murray was another good officer. As a prior enlisted artilleryman, he was slightly older than the other captains. He was originally from Sealy, Texas, and earned his bachelor's degree from the University of Idaho, married his high school sweetheart, Patty, and had two young sons. During this deployment, I was married but had no kids. It wasn't until years later, when I had my daughter and sons, that I really appreciated the sacrifice those two had made. Being away from one's wife for seven months is tough, but being away from your children for seven months is entirely different.

Murray dealt with it as well as expected. He was never one to show much emotion or stress, especially around the marines. When the military bureaucracy reared its ugly head, he was quick to point out the stupidity of the green machine. He simply laughed at the clown show, knowing there was no way to fight the bureaucratic nonsense. His dry sense of humor was contagious. We would spend countless hours laughing at the ridiculousness of the whole situation during our time in eastern Ramadi. When it came to fighting, though, Murray was 100 percent business.

Captain Murray gave me the coordinates for the sniper team already in place outside the wire. Their mission was to cover our movement and provide overwatch as the sappers and EOD searched for weapons and ammunition supposedly buried under our objective. I noted the location on my GRG and shared it with the team. Avoiding blue-on-blue incident remained crucial.

A tall, dark-haired Army lieutenant approached us as we waited in the cold. Lieutenant Sheep was Bravo Company's fire support officer (FSO). We'd be with him for the patrol. He seemed bright and a little annoyed that he was doing more "information operations" than fire support. I hated informing him that the Cobras were late due to maintenance issues.

As the ground commander's fire support representative, Lieutenant Sheep would be our liaison with the company commander, who would be off leading his platoons. We couldn't authorize the release of air-delivered ordnance without the ground commander's approval; this approval would be relayed through Lieutenant Sheep.

With some free time, Anderson, Sheep, and I discussed the plan, double-checked the sniper position, and talked about the suicide bomber attack on local police recruits at the Ramadi glass factory. The attack had occurred about a week prior, killing a Marine dog handler, Sergeant Adam Leigh Cann; an Army officer, Lieutenant Colonel Michael E. McLaughlin; and a dozen Iraqis. It was another disheartening development. None of us said it, but we were barely holding on to this city.

About five minutes later, the Cobras arrived. Some of the soldiers joked that the pilots were warm and dry. I keyed my radio and asked for the standard check-in brief, gave them the location of the sniper team, and had them recon the route. The *thump-thump* of the attack aircraft flying overhead gave the patrol the reassuring sense that we weren't alone.

With the morning sun just above the horizon, we moved out. I was pumped to be on this patrol with the 1-506th and my marines. Yes, it was dangerous, but that was part of why I reveled in the experience. I loved being a marine in combat but despised the day-to-day monotony. The duality is difficult to explain to anyone who hasn't served in a war zone.

Soldiers and marines waited inside the gate until there was sufficient dispersion between themselves and the man in front of them before stepping off. The moment we departed the austere confines of the small base, our demeanor changed from tired and bored to alert and focused. We patrolled along a canal for about 500 meters before turning west, paralleling railroad tracks. Everyone was silent; most information was passed via hand-and-arm signals or in hushed tones through intersquad radios. As we moved towards Objective White, I maintained constant communications with the Cobras.

Gunshot Six-One notified me that they had seen a few men in a housing compound near the objective. Referred to as "the sheik's house," the compound consisted of three little houses encircled by a large wall. It was a dominating feature that overlooked our objective from the south. I reported the information to Lieutenant Sheep. He gave me a thumbs-up and reported the info to his CO.

We were at the very southern edge of Ramadi. To our north was the Mulab district, with houses stacked atop each other. The structures were shades of brown and gray, broken only by small alleyways and roads. Palm trees dotted the skyline, but other than that, the buildings all looked the same. To the south, except for the sheik's house, lay nothing but flat desert as far as the eye could see.

The team and I were positioned towards the middle of the patrol. Every few steps, I'd rotate around to keep aware of the marines and soldiers to both my front and rear. Our weapons were at chest level. My thumb rested on the selector switch so that I could quickly put the M4 into action. After years of training, the weapon was a part of me. Likewise, as an ANGLICO marine, using a radio and maintaining the ability to talk to aircraft while patrolling, update our position, and relay information to ground commanders was second nature to me. It sounds easier than it is, but we became experts at it. I loved it.

The company turned south as we closed on the objective, the platoons peeling off towards their areas of responsibility. I kept the Cobras updated on our status. They were flying low, cutting through the air in figure eights and circles, covering each other but trying not to fly over the city to the north. While the surface-to-air threat was not high, it was still there. In early November, Gunshot Six-Six had been shot down north of Ramadi by a surface-to-air missile, killing the two Marine pilots, Majors Jerry Bloomfield and Mike Martino.

These pilots flying in support of our January patrol were from the same squadron: Marine Light Attack Helicopter Squadron 369— the Gunfighters.

The patrol crossed the railroad tracks and headed south as Bravo Company's security element created a perimeter about the size of a football field. My team and I moved through the objective, avoiding detritus and brush as best we could. We took up positions along the southeast portion of the perimeter, facing the sheik's house. I stopped and took a knee near a dirt mound, focusing on the aircraft zigzagging in the sky above. Anderson was to my right, Dyer and Cureton to my left. We were surrounded by mud and garbage.

Anderson got my attention. "Hey, sir, let's move over here. It's a better position."

I agreed. The micro terrain he had identified gave us better fields of fire. We shifted about ten to fifteen meters to the west, and Jon Cureton grabbed his SAW and oriented it towards the entrance to the sheik's compound. Some of the soldiers near us adjusted their position, occupying our previous spot near the two-foot-high dirt pile, which stuck out like a pimple on a teenager's face. We wanted to create a perimeter around the engineers so they could search for hidden weapons and explosives.

Combat can be boring—until it's not.

As I peered over my shoulder towards the objective, a sergeant first class who had occupied our previous position was abruptly launched into the air by an explosion. The IED must have been buried deep in that mound because the explosion was forced up, not out and up as most surface IEDs tend to do. It looked like the soldier had been catapulted from a geyser; his body twisted and turned as he rose about fifteen feet into the air. His M4 rifle tumbled away. The elapsed time was milliseconds, but it seemed to happen in slow motion. As he hit the ground, time sped back up.

Calls of "IED . . . IED . . . medic" erupted from men nearby. I jumped up and ran to the dazed soldier lying on the ground as debris pelted us. Lieutenant Sheep and I arrived at the same time, examining the man for wounds. Amazingly, the gruff warrior wasn't bleeding, merely temporarily deaf and confused. Dirt and mud were packed into his right ear from the blast. Trying to overcome the ringing noise, the soldier yelled at the medics while they checked for more injuries, "I'm good. I'm good. Holy fuck."

I keyed my radio mic and updated the Cobras flying overhead while locking eyes with Anderson. We both shook our heads, thinking the same thing: we were just there.

Internally, I chastised myself. *Way to go, Angell. That could have been you, or worse, one of your marines.* The mound of dirt was conspicuous. I should have known better than to get anywhere near it. Over the last four months, the team and I had been in very close proximity to at least two dozen IEDs. Most had detonated harmlessly, while some had wounded and killed fellow Americans and Iraqis. The month I'd spent in Al Asad with 1st ANGLICO headquarters had dulled my edge. Anderson and the boys had been keeping sharp while I was taking Sundays off and watching movies and sitting in front of a computer. I only had myself to blame.

It was a command-detonated IED, which meant the insurgents had to be close.

I flinched at the sudden, sharp banging of Cureton's SAW. He had squeezed off a few bursts of 5.56mm at the entrance to the sheik's compound. Meanwhile, Anderson repositioned himself next to Cureton and a couple of soldiers. I keyed the transmit button on our intersquad radio.

"What's going on?" I asked.

"We got a peeker, sir. Probably the guy that detonated the IED," Anderson reported.

"Got it. Hold your position," I replied and heard the unmistakable *thump* from an M203. Anderson and a soldier had put a few 40mm HE rounds over the compound wall.

"He came back, this time with a weapon," reported Anderson

over the intersquad radio.

"Got it. Continue to hold your position. Outlaw Six doesn't want anyone gettin' drawn into an ambush," I explained.

I briefed the Cobras, asking them to look into the compound. They made a few orbits and reported an individual dragging a man's body away from the wall towards one of the houses. Again, I passed the information to Lieutenant Sheep so he could keep Outlaw Six informed. We should have immediately raided that compound, but it wasn't my call. That wasn't the company's mission.

The insurgents evidently didn't like us near the sheik's house or the cache site. By now, ordnance had been found and dug up. RPG warheads, C-4, mortars, and a few RPD machine guns were pulled from shallow pits. EOD and the sappers laid the deadly treasure out in neat rows for pictures and destruction. It felt good to see the operation find and remove weapons and ammunition, knowing everything here would have eventually been turned against us. Of course, it was a drop in the bucket.

Twenty minutes later, gunfire erupted from the north, near piles of rubble around the Ramadi train station. Everyone instinctively ducked and lowered their profile while searching for the shooter. The rounds snapped and zinged overhead. Lieutenant Sheep turned to me after a brief discussion on his radio.

"They're taking fire from the Mulab near the train station. Sounds like an RPK," he said with almost no emotion. The 1-506th had only been in Ramadi for a few weeks, but these soldiers were already hardened by the urban combat.

"Got it. I need to move to the north side of the perimeter," I replied before keying my intersquad radio. "Let's move; follow me."

The replies were short and to the point: "Moving."

We got up and shuffled north. EOD and the sappers lay in the prone and squatted in defilade to avoid the gunfire as we ran. The small-arms fire was sporadic, basically harassment, but could quickly become accurate and fatal.

There we were, running towards gunfire once again. Cureton was next to me with the M249 SAW; like me, he was smiling. As we moved towards the farthest edge of the security perimeter, I briefed the Cobras. When the gunfire increased, our speed picked up from a trot to a run.

We got to the northwest corner of the perimeter and took cover behind the elevated railroad tracks. The team and I talked with the company first sergeant and a few soldiers, trying to determine where the insurgents were hiding. I then rested on my knee while talking to the Cobras, trying to develop an attack plan. The automatic-weapons fire increased but remained inaccurate. Dyer and Cureton scanned for the fighters' locations as enemy combatants darted in and out of the alleyways, using the debris from the old train station as cover.

Close air support with helos isn't difficult, but it's important that everyone understands the attack geometry. The birds were holding · to the south. Anderson was going to shoot a 40mm green-smoke grenade from his M203 at the target. I would use that as the mark to talk the Cobras onto the enemy position. I knew precisely who the closest friendly units were: us.

The Cobras wanted to do a dry run. No problem. They came in without firing and circled back around. Anderson shot his smoke round about 100 meters away from our position. It landed in the rubble and unleashed green smoke that slowly wafted through the air. The presence of the birds hadn't scared off the insurgents. It amazed me how risk averse the insurgents were one day, only to become completely fanatical the next.

"From the mark, north one hundred meters."

The lead Cobra replied, "Copy, one hundred meters north of the mark; dash one tallies the target."

From my vantage point, the birds were pointed towards the enemy position.

"Cleared hot for guns," I said with a slight grin. The lead aircraft didn't hesitate and ripped the surrounding area apart with 20mm rounds. As the Cobra banked right, I gave the follow-on command, "Hit lead's hits; cleared hot."

The second aircraft sprayed the target again. We received no more fire from that position. However, we weren't sure if we had killed the fighters or simply scared them off. The company's CO didn't send a squad to look for bodies or a blood trail.

Once the objective had been cleared and the enemy weapons destroyed, we started our movement back to base, paralleling the railroad tracks east and passing the canal. We turned north towards Camp Corregidor. The team and I were with the forward element of the company. There was about a squad of Bravo Company soldiers, Lieutenant Sheep, me, Sergeants Anderson and Dyer, then Corporal Cureton. The rest of the company walked behind us in a staggered column. We were moving on a dirt trail about five meters to the east of the canal. Between us and the water were reeds standing about seven feet tall, obscuring the small buildings and road behind it.

With the south gate in sight, I relaxed slightly but remained alert. This was no time to celebrate. Still, I couldn't help feeling good. Everyone seemed relatively calm—at least, as relaxed as one can be in Ramadi. I was high on adrenaline and proud of the team. This operation allowed me to shake off the cobwebs and atrophy from my month in Al Asad. It's amazing how quickly the edge of a weapon is dulled. We still had about ten more weeks in Iraq. I had to stay sharp.

The ambush was triggered by two or three short bursts from an AK-47. The *clack-clack-clack* of the weapon halted our movement.

"Contact left," I shouted, dropping to the dirt, oriented towards the gunfire. The call was repeated up and down the column. The entire western side of the canal erupted in small-arms and automatic-weapons fire. The enemy was astonishingly accurate. I hear the rounds zipping by my head before impacting next to me, filling the air with mud and dirt. As I brought my M4 up to engage, enemy rounds slammed into the ground inches from my face. I fired about fifteen rounds from my M4 but couldn't see the enemy through the dense wall of reeds.

This scenario is considered a near ambush, but with the canal between us and the enemy, we couldn't simply assault through. Cureton's SAW was firing to my left as the FSO engaged with his M4 along with the rest of the column. Anderson and Dyer were also in the prone, firing away, all of us trying to overwhelm the insurgents with suppressive fire. It was deafening, confusing, and chaotic. I had tunnel vision.

While it had been mere seconds since the ambush began, I was surprised by my lack of situational awareness when I realized I still had a section of Cobras overhead. I rolled onto my back, keyed the handset, and yelled into the mic to let the Cobras know we were under attack. I could barely hear myself or the pilots. Knowing there were no friendly forces on the western side of the canal, I yelled at Lieutenant Sheep, "I wanna do a gun run along the canal with the Cobras." He gave me a thumbs-up in approval. I was amazed he could hear me.

I directed the Cobras to execute a gun run. Meanwhile, I went through the rest of my magazine to help relieve some of the pressure. The rhythmic cycle of my M4 was comforting. I inserted a fresh magazine and watched the birds come at us from the south. Twenty-millimeter rounds slammed into the reeds on the far side of the canal, creating geysers of water and mud with vegetation mixed in.

After the Cobras made their run, I glanced to my left and noticed that Sergeant Anderson had crawled into some defilade. He was firing his weapon and motioning to me. The enemy fire was still flying over my head, so I rolled three feet behind a small berm and looked back at Anderson. He told me Sergeant Dyer had been hit. Not knowing if I had heard him correctly, I asked again, then shook my head at the disheartening news.

The company needed to know about Dyer. I told Lieutenant Sheep to move back and yelled that we had a wounded needing medivac. Sergeant Anderson was lobbing 40mm grenades from his M203 across the canal. The low *thump* of the projectile as it left the weapon was soothing.

Cureton moved closer under fire to help our wounded marine. The enemy was pouring so much fire at us that he was forced to low-crawl to Dyer's position. I started to direct the Cobras in for another gun run, but Lieutenant Sheep shouted, "The sappers are moving into the reeds to the south."

I immediately aborted the attack. We needed to know where the soldiers were.

As I spoke with the helos, Cureton crawled to my position. Anderson informed us that Sergeant Dyer had only been grazed. Past Anderson, I saw Dyer firing his M4; he was a fuckin' warrior. The fire started to slow in intensity, and I noticed the company bounding towards the Corregidor gate. I notified the TOC that we needed a medical vehicle since there were now two WIA; one of the engineers had been hit by enemy fire.

Shortly after that, Dyer moved past Anderson's position behind me, and I had Cureton escort him to the gate. An ambulance would be there shortly. Anderson and I stayed in position and waited for the remainder of the company to move past us. The enemy fire had slackened but was still heavy.

I told Lieutenant Sheep that once all friendlies had passed our position, we would run more attacks on the western edge of the canal. The Cobras, Captain Rard in the TOC, and I speedily discussed the geometry and agreed on a southeast-to-northwest attack heading with rockets. Anderson found good defilade behind a small heap of mud. The rockets from the Cobras would be within thirty-five to fifty meters, well inside the danger-close range.

We set out an orange marking panel and took cover as I directed two more rocket runs. This effectively stopped the enemy fire. We stayed at the location until the remainder of the company moved past. Anderson, Sheep, and I were the last ones through the gate.

The company commander met me at the entrance and shook my hand.

"Good work, Captain Angell. Sergeant Dyer is going to be okay," he told me. I was impressed that he'd taken the time to learn Dyer's name. The guy had a few hundred men under his command at any given time. I was really beginning to like the 1-506.

"Good to go. Did they take him to medical?" I asked.

"They did," he said.

Anderson and I drove back to Full Metal Jacket. Our adrenaline was high. Once it peaks, it's tough to come down from. We talked about the morning's events. Dyer had been struck by a 7.62mm round that hit his skin and traveled up his arm but failed to hit bone or muscle. He was lucky. A quarter inch to the left or right, and Dyer could have been in serious trouble. The randomness of combat has perplexed warfighters for centuries.

I was relieved that his wounds weren't life threatening. Dyer is a good man and an outstanding ANGLICO marine. He always brought calm and professionalism to the team, and his absence would have been catastrophic.

My friends and family outside of the Marine Corps have never really asked me about combat or what I did in Iraq besides generalities. It's not that I'm unwilling to talk about my experiences, but it's not easy discussing the subject without feeling guilty—though I'm not even sure the uncomfortable feeling is guilt. On some unconscious level, it might be apprehension.

Those who have not experienced combat will have considerable difficulty understanding the experience of trying to kill other human beings who are trying to kill you or your fellow marines. Hearing someone talk about getting shot at and almost blown up isn't easy to process. For some, it can be hard to deal with on a psychological level. For others, it's not an issue at all; it was just business.

What allows us to overcome the fear is repetitive and nonstop training. Couple this with the knowledge that your brothers are relying on you, and you them, and it's clear how marines and soldiers function in the chaos of combat. Instead of thinking about dying, your training kicks in and focuses all your attention on eliminating the threat and supporting the man next to you. You must be in the present. Every thought and move must be fixated on the job at hand.

Major Grice was at Full Metal Jacket when we returned from the mission. He had arrived earlier to see the marines and conduct an inventory of our serialized equipment. As usual, he was straightforward and fatherly when he greeted the marines and officers. He had been in the TOC when we were ambushed outside the south gate. Sitting next to Captain Rard, the major listened intently as the action unfolded.

Shaking hands, he asked how the team and I were doing.

"We're doing good, sir. Dyer was wounded, but it wasn't bad, thankfully," I told him.

He replied with a smile. "I just saw him. He'll be fine."

Major Grice's words had a deep impact on all of us, and they meant a great deal to me.

This operation was important. It got me back in the game and allowed me to bust off the rust from my month in Al Asad. The warriors of the 1-506th proved outstanding. They were tough and intelligent, not easily distracted, and not risk averse. These men had identified the hidden weapons by exploiting intelligence gained through previous operations. They were living up to the proud lineage of their battalion.

■ ■ ■

A few days later, I participated in my first Task Force Dark Eagle operation. It was void of significant contact but allowed me to meet and work with some of the scouts from the 1-506th and Joker Four, the National Guard sniper team. On that night, we departed Camp Corregidor at around 0100 and pushed through the industrial district covered by air support from a section of F-18s before arriving at our target house.

As intel had reported, the house was abandoned. For whatever reason, construction was never completed. The scouts quickly cleared the three-story house while my team and a few soldiers provided security for the entrance and bottom floor. Once cleared, the curious assortment of soldiers, national guardsmen, marines, and a lone sailor went about preparing the position for what could become a tough fight.

Priority of work went to establishing and maintaining communications with the 1-506th TOC and supporting aircraft. A few scouts stayed downstairs to provide security. The rest of us took turns banging holes into the rooftop walls to create loopholes before the sun rose. No one wanted to stick their heads above the four-foot-tall wall and silhouette themselves. The snipers draped blankets, ponchos, or mosquito netting behind the loopholes to reduce the shadows. A few of the holes were almost impossible to break through until Sergeant Anderson took a turn with the sledgehammer. He was one of the few able to power through the stubborn brick and plaster.

When the sun finally rose above the horizon, the streets were quiet. From what we could see, Iraqis weren't moving about. We figured that we had been compromised or an attack was imminent. We weren't too concerned since one of Task Force Dark Eagle's tasks was to establish a small foothold in an insurgent-dominated area and have the insurgents react to our presence. We would sit and hold a defensible position. As the insurgents attempted to maneuver on us, we planned to repel their advance with precision sniper fire and close air support.

About an hour after the sun rose, someone heard movement next door. A scout peeked over the side of the wall and spotted an Iraqi woman and boy who kept staring up at the roof. We had been compromised, but we weren't sure what this meant. The aircraft reported that Iraqis were standing in the street about 300 meters to our south and were turning cars away from access to our direct front. Staff Sergeant Martinez, the Joker Four team leader, grabbed a few soldiers to hit the house next door. They came back a few minutes later, telling us that the civilians had heard us breaking through the brick earlier in the morning. One neighbor talked to another neighbor and warned everyone. We were officially compromised.

Staff Sergeant Martinez contacted 1-506th TOC to report our situation. The call came back that we were ordered to exfil the position, since we'd be compromised, and link up with a platoon of gun trucks. The small twelve-man task force would have to exfil during broad daylight and move to a rendezvous point. This was a risky situation.

The most dangerous part of the Task Force Dark Eagle ops was the exfil. In an exfil, the enemy knows there are only a few points of departure. They can sit and wait for you to emerge from the protection of barriers or overlapping fields of fire. In a perfect world, an armored column of gun trucks and M1A1 tanks would pull up to your position. We didn't have that luxury now.

Martinez attempted to persuade 1-506th to send the exfil vehicles to our position, but he was wasting his breath. For unknown reasons, we were required to link up down the road through the abandoned industrial area. There was no use arguing about it.

Everyone grabbed their gear and packed it tightly. We didn't want to worry about gear and equipment falling out of packs as we aggressively departed the area in expectation of getting hit.

The only card we had was close air support. High above the city of Ramadi, two Marine Corps Harriers would be watching our movement, covering our exfil. Captain Rard and I worked out a quick plan. Considering that I'd be moving with intensity, trying to focus on the three-dimensional world of the city, Rard would talk to the aircraft. Occasionally, though, I'd report our progress and location to the Harriers. I used an earpiece to listen to the radio. If the birds saw something, I would relay it to our small team of Americans, and if the circumstances dictated, I'd be in position to direct an air strike.

Outside the house, we stacked up against the interior of the perimeter wall next to the large, blue metal gate. It was a bright, sunny day; the January weather was cool and pleasant. Anderson told the team to ensure their grenades and spare magazines were easy to reach.

Staff Sergeant Martinez reminded the team, "Cover each other's movements."

I glanced over at Doc Vissing, the lone sailor on this operation. Vissing was an old-school ANGLICO doc who sported the gold jump wings. He was a great corpsman—very experienced, yet with a jolly side that made you like him. When I met Doc Vissing's gaze, he smiled—and then promptly threw up. It broke the tension.

Anderson was quick to react. "Doc, you okay, man? What's wrong?"

"I'm okay, Sergeant Anderson. I feel better now," the doc replied, looking slightly embarrassed.

Everyone smiled before getting serious. Martinez opened the gate. Each man exited in a direct and focused manner. As one man stepped out into the neighborhood and oriented his weapon to the left, the next man focused his weapon to the right. I keyed my radio to inform the Harriers and Captain Rard that we were Oscar Mike. One of the scouts was on point in front of Martinez, who knew the direction to the rendezvous point. When we came to an intersection, we would bound across and turn to cover the man behind us.

I was amazed at how smoothly the process went as we fed off each other's movements and cues. These basic tactics allowed soldiers, sailors, and marines to move together through the streets of Ramadi with maximum security.

Finally, we reached an alley comprising abandoned storage units void of civilian activity.

"They aren't fuckin' here," announced Staff Sergeant Martinez, frustrated. I informed Rard that we were at our linkup point but our ride wasn't here. In theory, Rard could inform the TOC personnel that soldiers and marines were in the industrial district waiting for their extraction.

Everyone instinctively took up positions to support one another while we waited. Before long, a platoon of gun trucks turned the corner and sped towards our location. Minutes later we were back in our dreary home, Full Metal Jacket.

The mission, while unsuccessful, proved to me that this unique task force could work together for a common cause. Each team's capabilities complemented the others' in finding and destroying the enemy. While our numbers were small, the potential was huge.

CHAPTER TEN:
TASK FORCE DARK EAGLE

For the rest of the month, we got into a routine. Most of our Task Force Dark Eagle missions started in the early morning and lasted anywhere from seven to twenty hours, depending on the situation. The team and I would conduct an overnight operation followed by a couple days of rest, an overnight operation, a couple days of rest, and repeat. The occasional daytime patrols or QRF would be thrown in. In between missions, we prepared for upcoming operations. Occasionally, I threw in some limited training, usually on communications, our critical vulnerability.

As the team's communications chief, Sergeant Chad Dyer was the subject-matter expert. I had him teach and reteach me the intricacies of using the PRC-148. ANGLICO had some great laminated cheat sheets, but I tried to learn the details of the system by memory. My fear was that we'd lose communications while fighting in the streets. I didn't want to rely on Dyer to fix it all the time.

He was an excellent instructor, patient and extremely smart. His Texas accent reminded me of home.

Dyer was instrumental to our team's success. Technically, he was senior to Anderson with regards to time in the Marine Corps and could have been the team chief, but ANGLICO T/O (table of organization) stated that the senior 0861 scout observer would be the team chief. Both Anderson and Dyer were more than capable of performing the required tasks of the billet. I feared possible animosity about the situation, but Dyer never showed it, and I don't think he cared. Out of sheer luck, 1st ANGLICO had blessed me with three outstanding NCOs who consistently outperformed my expectations. They were gritty, clever, and proven assets in combat.

Our downtime consisted of rest and scrolling through the internet. Corporal David Donnelly, Captain Murry's team chief, was the one who had brought the Xbox. The marines fought off boredom by battling aliens with the space marine character Master Chief. It was a great way for them to decompress.

A stocky young man with a bushy mustache, Corporal Donnelly was esteemed and liked by the men and had a dry sense of humor that drew the ire of senior enlisted leaders. He also knew what to do and when to do it while out on the streets of Ramadi. At the end of the deployment, his vehicle was hit hard by an IED, disabling the gun truck and all communications. Captain Murray was wounded badly. Donnelly and their other two marines, Lance Corporals Cain and Hamilton, saved his life and led the team out of a perilous situation on Route Michigan in the dead of night.

Eastern Ramadi was always full of danger. The marines were at a high risk of being wounded even within the perimeter of Camp Corregidor. The indirect-fire threat was constant. The marines never complained about the requirement to wear their helmets and body armor when outside of a building, knowing the reality of their situation.

One day in January, I was discussing an upcoming operation in the 1-506 TOC when insurgents to the north launched two 120mm mortars at the base. We heard the explosions, followed by reports of injuries. Word soon arrived that one of the wounded was with ANGLICO.

Doc Vissing had wanted to get to the chow hall before it closed. The first round exploded to his east, between two buildings. The following 120mm exploded near the front gate, wounding Doc: a piece of shrapnel hit his leg. Luckily, the wound was not serious enough to require evac out of the country. After a short visit to the aid station, he returned with minor lacerations. Everyone welcomed him back with the usual smart-ass comments. He took it like a champ. Deep down, we were all simply grateful his injuries weren't serious.

■ ■ ■

I respected Harry Martinez from the moment I met him. I had only been at Camp Corregidor a few days when the dark-haired, olive-skinned staff sergeant came by the ANGLICO room at Full Metal Jacket. Martinez's stature of five feet eight inches hid the fact that he was an absolute warrior who dealt death to those unlucky enough to meet the crosshairs of his sniper rifle.

A former marine, he had seen combat during the Gulf War. Now he was older and a team leader for Joker Four, part of the 3rd Battalion, 103rd Armor Regiment, 28th Infantry Division. In his civilian life, Martinez was a cop for the Cambridge, Massachusetts, Police Department. He was mature, aggressive, and lacked the ego and attitude that usually comes with someone of his experience. He was easy to get along with and had one thing on his mind: killing insurgents.

Introducing insurgents to the black hole of death requires a team. Staff Sergeant Martinez and three young soldiers made up Joker Four. There was Specialist Jarrod York, Martinez's spotter; Specialist Joseph Bennett, lovingly called "Joey B."; and Specialist Rick Taylor, the youngest. These four men put the nail in the coffin of any remaining bias I had against the Army or National Guard. They had been operating in Ramadi since the brigade arrived in the summer of 2005, about seven months prior. They had extensive experience and a long list of confirmed kills earned while attached to the sniper section of the 2nd Battalion, 69th Infantry Regiment called Shadow Team. By the time I arrived at Camp Corregidor, the 2-69 had rotated back to the States, replaced by the legendary 1-506th.

Our first mission with Task Force Dark Eagle had been relatively uneventful, but our second mission, Operation Sky Train, provided proof of concept for bringing together snipers, scouts, and ANGLICO. At around 0800 on the seventeenth of January, the boys and I linked up with Martinez's team and four other soldiers from the scout platoon of the 103rd Armored Regiment. The scouts from the 1-506th had been replaced by the 103rd for this operation due to internal US Army politics, which I cared nothing about.

It was a sunny, cool morning as we awaited the gun trucks from Delta Company for our insertion. During the mission brief the previous day, I'd had a chance to meet all the men scheduled for the operation. Anderson, Dyer, and Cureton had worked with them before, and I had discussed Joker Four with Anderson. His opinion held significant weight with me, so I was pleased he held them in high regard.

The 1-506 scouts and snipers were eager to accomplish the mission and take calculated risks and had a bias for action. Of course, as with all alpha males, there was some ego and standoffishness between the soldiers and our ANGLICO team. We simply hadn't worked with them enough to build a solid relationship.

They were as curious about our tactical capabilities as we were about theirs. This was amplified by the fact that we were working in small teams on relatively unconventional operations. For the marines and I, this dance was familiar. ANGLICO doesn't own ground or have "areas of operations." We are enablers who support the US Army, SOF units, and our allies through the weight of US Navy and Marine Corps fire support, usually by integrating ourselves into the supported unit—the "liaison" part of our mandate.

Waiting outside the battalion headquarters building, the twelve-man team was geared up and ready to go. We milled about, conducting pre-mission checks, smoking cigarettes, and making nervous jokes. Everyone was loaded down with ample gear, ammunition, grenades, and various weapons, such as light anti-tank weapon (LAW) rockets and shoulder-launched multipurpose assault weapons (SMAW-Ds).

I would have never admitted it, but I was anxious. There are plenty of unknowns when dealing with new units. This concern is heightened when the enemy becomes a factor, which was always the case in Ramadi. But in true Marine Corps fashion, we didn't have a choice. We had to improvise, adapt, and overcome. We would deal with the uncertainty and build a solid relationship with these men through mutual respect, communication, and partnership.

After a one-month time-out, I was behind the curve. Captains Rard and Murray, as well as the rest of the ANGLICO detachment, had already built a good relationship with the command of 1-506th. My concern was the soldiers on the ground. We needed to have confidence in each other so there would be little to no hesitation during a firefight. This takes time.

The mission was simple. The dozen men of Task Force Dark Eagle would be driven into the Mulab and take over a house on the corner of Easy Street and Farouk, just south of the Ramadi soccer stadium. The scouts would secure the occupants of the home and provide security. ANGLICO and the snipers of Joker Four would move to the roof, establish a strongpoint, and wait. Wait for what? Wait for the insurgents who were no doubt seething that we dared be so bold as to come out of hiding. We needed them to react to us.

This wouldn't be too difficult. The battalion had pushed out a heavy presence of M1A1 tanks and gun trucks in the Mulab. This always infuriated the insurgents. They would be drawn to the tanks like moths to light.

The gun trucks from Delta Company pulled up along the road to the west of the 1-506th HQ building. A blanket of silence and brief apprehension swept over us as we prepared to load up. Martinez came up to Anderson.

"ANGLICO is in those two trucks," he said, pointing out the vehicles. Cureton glanced at me before shuffling to the back left door of the gun truck. To my left, Anderson and Dyer opened the doors to the vehicle behind mine and climbed in. I took a moment to gaze around at the motley crew of US Marines, National Guard, and regular Army soldiers. It was always exciting to watch eager young men prepare for battle. I relished the time.

Pulling out of Camp Corregidor, the vehicles made a left and headed west down Route Michigan and then quickly made another left south into the Mulab. I leaned forward to look out the small, armored window, keeping an eye on the slums of this restive and dangerous neighborhood. Local Iraqis going about their business stopped and glared at us.

At the time, we were losing the war. The Iraqis didn't trust us. We were unable to provide them with security from the brutal insurgents, one of the primary missions of counterinsurgency operations. The fight had fallen into a state of attrition, with victory defined by the number of bodies. Meanwhile, the "hearts and minds" mission was a catch-22: it required Americans to be on the streets, but this drove the elusive insurgents out of hiding. Task Force Dark Eagle was developed to take advantage of this.

Once in the Mulab, the gun trucks made a right and headed west down Farouk towards the target house. I rapidly conducted another check of my equipment, ensuring I hadn't left anything behind. My final step was a "brass check." I pulled my charging handle back on my M4 ever so slightly so I could see the brass of the 5.56mm cartridge. The last thing I wanted was to squeeze the trigger and hear nothing but a *click*—the dreaded sound of a firing pin finding an empty chamber. I obsessively performed this check throughout missions. Cureton kept checking his SAW. Reaching over to my left, I got his attention.

"You good to go?" I yelled over the noisy truck. Behind his issued Oakley sunglasses, Cureton gave me a smirk and a thumbs-up.

Just as I faced forward, an explosion erupted to my right—a small IED hastily placed along the curb. The young, hardened soldier driving the gun truck simply kept going. Reports on the radio were cold and rehearsed. All vehicles came back "green," meaning there were no injuries, and everyone was operational.

"IED. Keep pushing." About 200 meters down the road, the gun trucks slowed. The time was 0830. The sun was out, and so were the Iraqis. There was no sneaking into houses under the cover of darkness during this mission. We were going overt.

As the vehicle slowed, we opened our doors. The moment I stepped out of the gun truck, my M4 was covering the target house. We maneuvered towards the large metal gate forming part of the house's perimeter courtyard. I checked behind me to get accountability of Anderson and Dyer. They were rushing towards the gate with their weapons ready, as were Joker Four and the scouts. Unsure of what was going on, many civilians scurried to their homes or nearby alleyways; others stared, while many simply ignored our presence.

Lucky for us, the metal gate wasn't locked. Martinez kicked it open, allowing the scouts to clear the courtyard while Joker Four ran to the front door and banged on the metal frame. My team and I took up the rear, providing security. I kept glancing over my shoulder, trying to see what was taking so long.

A middle-aged woman cautiously opened the door, speaking in Arabic. Joker Four rushed in, followed by the scouts and my team. They started clearing the downstairs as one soldier watched the woman and her two children. We followed Joker Four up the concrete stairs, blood pumping. Joker Four, Dyer, and Anderson headed right down the second-floor hall while Cureton and I went left to clear rooms. The sounds of "Clear!" echoed through the house. We burst into the last room and found nothing but pillows and blankets and a large wardrobe dresser. Cureton grabbed the wardrobe's handles and made eye contact. I gave a nod. He yanked the door. It was empty. I yelled out, "Clear."

Thinking back to our pre-deployment training, close-quarters battle (CQB) was a sensitive subject, although I wasn't sure why. Some SNCOs and officers thought FCT teams didn't need to focus on CQB because it wasn't our job to clear rooms or houses. This was antiquated thinking, in my view. FCTs need to be able to get into position to terminally control aircraft and direct artillery, mortars, and, if available, naval gunfire. We were put in numerous situations that required us to help clear and secure rooms and buildings, especially when working with Task Force Dark Eagle. ANGLICO teams couldn't be a liability to supported units. We had to be an asset.

Luckily, experienced 1st ANGLICO leadership knew this and insisted on CQB training, although probably not enough. We would be fighting on the urban battlefield; some of these leaders saw to it that we were ready.

With the house cleared, the scouts maintained security downstairs. Joker Four and my boys made our way to the third-floor rooftop courtyard. Breaking through a rusty, warped metal door, we crouched to stay below the wall. The sky was clear with a hint of warmth as the sun rose. The house was perfectly positioned to provide us with observation west down Farouk Street and north on Easy Street. We held the high ground. Staff Sergeant Martinez and Anderson talked about fields of fire while Joey B. and Specialist York went back into the house to grab furniture to set up their shooting positions. Taylor and Cureton used a sledgehammer to break through the brick wall to form loopholes. Meanwhile, Dyer and I checked our communications with 1-506th TOC and Captain Rard on the air support net.

Below our position, at the intersection of Easy Street and Farouk, an M1A1 tank pulled up. The scream and whine of the sixty-ton beast could easily be mistaken for a jet. We felt the vibration and weight of this colossal instrument of war as it angled into position. While its presence was comforting, it was a deterrent to the insurgents, which we didn't want. However, this operation wasn't a typical Task Force Dark Eagle operation—if there was such a thing—considering that we inserted during daylight under the overt cover of heavy armor.

It was interesting watching these snipers deploy their urban field craft. They wore no ghillie suits, as those would have done no good in this environment. Instead, Staff Sergeant Martinez had his team bring tables, dressers, and chairs to the rooftop. There, the readily available household items were used to provide a steady platform for observation and shots while scanning the streets for insurgent activity. Placed behind loopholes, the snipers could sit back and wait. Anderson, Dyer, and Cureton created their own loopholes, enabling them to observe west down Farouk Street. I sat in a white plastic chair behind the team and listened to radio chatter while we waited for contact. The men talked among themselves, pointing out details and activity that warranted more scrutiny.

After about an hour, civilians started going about their daily routines, ignoring the presence of the M1A1 tank and the gun trucks driving around to the north. Men smoked cigarettes on the sidewalks. Women covered from head to toe in dark, substantial garments walked about. Small cars came and went, although never coming close to our position or the M1A1. Children played and kicked soccer balls down alleys and sidewalks; hesitantly, some waved.

These people were living their lives as best they could. But within the rather innocuous behavior were signs of nefarious action. The snipers of Joker Four were experts at seeing the trees through the forest. They studied the movement of certain individuals who caught their attention, and suspicious activity was relayed between themselves and my team. It became apparent we were being watched.

"Two hundred and forty meters to the west on the south side of the street is a large pile of dirt next to a white car," Joey B. announced at one point, sitting behind his bolt-action sniper rifle.

The team replied, "Got it."

He continued, "Okay, to the left of that pile of dirt is a white sign with some Arabic writing about five feet above the ground."

"Don't see it. Wait . . . got it."

"Watch the doorway to the left of that sign. A man in a white man-dress will slowly peek out, looking in this direction."

Everyone stared in that direction, waiting to see if someone would appear. About two long minutes later, the body and head of a man in a white robe eased out of a doorway, staring east towards our position. Martinez directed his team to continue to observe; something was happening.

My guys kept watch as well. Back and away from the wall, I searched the area with my ACOG under the shade of a low awning. One of my guys noticed the man looking across the street at another man, who was on a cell phone. Martinez noticed as well. They were communicating. Martinez informed the TOC of the situation and got approval for a warning shot.

Warning shots were not something we trained for in the States. In fact, there was a saying in the Marine Corps about warning shots before the intricacies of fighting insurgents caused a change: marines don't give warning shots. However, it had become a tool in the ever-evolving "escalation of force." The general rule was that troops must use a graduated escalation of force in ambiguous situations before resorting to deadly force. If time and situation permitted, verbal warning, the use of flares, and warning shots, as examples, were acceptable to deal with situations that weren't so clear cut.

This was one of those cases. In Ramadi, the insurgents wore no uniforms; their camouflage was the populace. You couldn't tell them apart from the locals until they decided to engage you. From experience, they knew our rules of engagement, so insurgents would hide behind women and children, hide weapons in mosques, and occasionally fight from them, knowing that such sensitive sites were off limits without specific approval. We Americans fought with rules and limitations; the insurgents did whatever they wanted.

The warning shot slammed into the plaster above the man's head. He vanished, as did the man across the street. Civilians scattered briefly but returned minutes later, hardened by the reality of life in Ramadi amid a war.

These people lived a life that was almost unfathomable. The Iraqis who could leave had already left for Syria or beyond. Iraqis who stayed in Ramadi had no choice but to live caught between the fanatical violence of the insurgents and foreign fighters and the behemoth

American occupation. If they sided with the Americans, insurgents would cut their heads off and film it, accusing them of being traitors and apostates. If they sided with the insurgency, they risked a speedy death by American firepower. These people were in a no-win situation, and they knew it.

I tried not to dwell on this. Whenever a marine or soldier was killed by an IED that had been planted in front of civilians who ignored the danger, my concern about their plight dwindled like a flame without oxygen.

After the warning shot, things got boring. The men fought the monotony by studying civilians and vehicles. We examined the area for possible IEDs and glassed the windows of shops and homes for snipers but found only shadows. As the boredom pushed my attention from one mundane issue to the next, I noticed Joey B. and Martinez using a strange device to peer over the wall without silhouetting themselves. It was a handheld periscope about the size of a police baton.

The use of periscopes for soldiers and marines is nothing new. In World War I, soldiers used periscopes to see from the trenches without fear of being shot. These simple devices saved lives. Marines still had to expose themselves to engage the enemy, but for instances where they were merely scanning or trying to increase situational awareness, periscopes were extremely valuable. Many Americans lost their lives looking over walls and around corners in Ramadi and other Iraqi cities. In fact, in the summer of 2006, a young marine from 5th ANGLICO, Corporal Christopher D. Leon, was shot and killed while on a rooftop overlooking the street. It's a hard lesson. At the end of the deployment, I and other ANGLICO marines recommended that the company purchase periscopes for the men, especially those returning to fight in the various cities.

The familiar *clack-clack-clack* from an AK-47 came from the south along Easy Street. Everyone shifted forward, ducking slightly out of instinct. From the sound, we could tell we weren't the target.

We adjusted our views through the loopholes, and Martinez and Joey B. used their periscope to investigate what was happening. The incident could be a ruse to make us expose ourselves to insurgent weapons. Alternatively, they could be attempting to distract us or the M1A1 on the street.

This was our mindset in Ramadi. The enemy was as smart and cunning as we were. In Al Hit, insurgents had distracted the soldiers with small-arms fire while another group brought in a mortar tube. To underestimate these fighters would be foolish.

One of the soldiers reported the small-arms fire to the TOC. Word came back that the rounds had harmlessly hit the tank. Around the same time, a section of Cobras arrived overhead to support us. *Clack-clack-clack. Clack-clack-clack.* Another few bursts erupted from the south. None of us could identify the source, but the tank was once again the target. They despised our armor. This American beast sitting on their streets infuriated them more than our presence did. Everyone in the position stayed calm as we sought out the shooters.

The double boom from an RPG increased our apprehension. Stepping from behind a corner to our south, an insurgent had fired, hitting a wall next to our position and missing the tank. These rather simple weapons can damage and destroy even the most advanced tanks; the M1A1 is no different. Before we knew what had happened, the tank fired at the insurgent position. Dust and dirt kicked up all around us from the overpressure and blast.

"The tank just fired at those motherfuckers," yelled Anderson.

"I'm requesting a fuckin' gun run from these Cobras," I announced. About a mile away in the TOC, Captain Rard approved the attack.

Knowing that the birds didn't like flying over the city if they didn't have to, I brought them in from the south along Easy Street. It was a sketchy attack angle, with the birds coming towards our position firing. In training, this would not have been approved, but in combat, tolerance for risk changes. After relaying my six-line CAS information to the Cobras, Gunshot One-Two quickly set up.

Knowing I needed to observe the area, I stood to see over the roof's wall; I had no choice.

My PRC-148 earpiece crackled: "Gunshot One-Two in-heading three-five-zero."

Satisfied with their position and heading, I gave the required call: "Gunshot One-Two cleared hot for guns."

The lead Cobra dove towards his target like a mechanical monster and unleashed the 20mm cannons along the western portion of Easy Street. I watched nervously as the HE rounds showered two alleyway intersections and about 200 meters of Easy Street. Insurgents trying to escape the firestorm were cut down or scurried off to lick their wounds.

The sounds of the rounds impacting the concrete and building facade were alarming. Some ricocheted off the pavement and whizzed over our heads. It was sketchy and dangerous, so I aborted the attack. I was relieved no one was injured and satisfied the exercise had given us a little breathing room against the insurgents maneuvering on our position.

"Gunshot One-Two from Wild Eagle Five-Seven, be advised the reason for the abort was your rounds were getting too close. Good effects, though. Establish yourself to the south," I reported.

The pilot agreed with the call. He had thought our proximity to the target in relation to the aircraft's movement was risky, but in Ramadi, if you didn't respond with violence of action, these insurgents would make you pay in blood. They respected one thing: death.

After the Cobras flew south over the desert, we heard the screaming and wailing of a woman. Everyone stared at each other in quiet curiosity but didn't verbalize our concern. We were all thinking the same thing. The noise came and went over the next five minutes; I tried to ignore it. The hope was that an insurgent had been killed and someone who knew him was crying out in anguish. We didn't want to hurt civilians.

After the tank shot its main gun, piercing an unknown number of homes, and the Cobra gun run, the streets cleared out for a while. The snipers and my marines continued scrutinizing the area down Farouk and north on Easy Street. Technically, the 3rd Battalion, 7th Marines, owned the ground west of Easy Street, but the 1-506th had requested the boundaries be pushed west, temporarily giving us more terrain and reducing the possibility of fratricide.

To our front, the streets were mostly empty. The once-teeming traffic circle was quiet and void of movement. Trash skipped and tumbled in the wind. Small dust devils swirled about, creating a sand-colored haze. It looked like a scene from a movie. Beyond that and to the north along Easy Street, the rectangular and boxed homes sat atop each other, broken by narrow alleyways and the occasional date palm covered in beige sand and dirt. Each of us sat quietly, occasionally murmuring observations.

We started to notice a curious phenomenon. All around us, Iraqis had thrown colored rugs over their rooftop walls. As we studied this change in scenery, we noticed these rugs weren't positioned facing the other directions. They all faced us. Viewed individually, these seemed the result of daily chores as women went about cleaning their homes. When we'd first arrived earlier in the day, there were none, but now they were everywhere. We suspected that the insurgents were marking our position for others to see. It was ingenious and simple, proving once again that these fighters running around in Adidas tracksuits and flip-flops weren't as dumb as others had claimed.

Once again, an AK-47 fired. This time it was to our northwest, along Easy Street. The rounds were inaccurate and high. Specialist York moved to the north wall, careful not to let his head rise above the four-foot barrier, and searched the area with his periscope. I remained in the shadows, using my ACOG. The insurgents were no doubt trying to find a weak spot not covered by observation from the M1A1 or us. We couldn't see them but knew they were out there, stalking us like wolves in the mountains.

Martinez contacted the TOC and reported the small-arms fire. From what we could tell, the insurgents were positioned in an alley leading to Easy Street. They would pop out from behind the corner, spray a few bursts from their AK-47, and retreat to relative safety. More bursts came from the north. Martinez directed his team to keep watch of their sectors, fearing that the fighters were trying to draw our attention away from Farouk Street or Easy Street to the south.

Clack-clack-clack. Now more AK-47s were firing. We heard the snap of the rounds as they screamed over our heads. The insurgents grew more accurate as their comfort level increased. Another section of Cobras arrived to support us, compliments of Captain Rard in the TOC.

As I was briefing the Cobras on the situation, one of my marines spotted the insurgents using a white sedan as cover—driving it slowly out of the alley while two insurgents hid behind the vehicle and sprayed our position, then retreating back behind a house. I'm not sure why the M1A1 didn't light up the vehicle, but it was a perfect target. The tank's loss was our gain. I quickly got approval for a Hellfire missile.

As I gave the Cobras the attack details, some of the soldiers and marines stood and started engaging with their weapons. The outgoing gunfire added to the stress, but I made sure the Cobras had the information they needed. The AGM 114 Hellfire slammed into the sedan, exploding and killing three insurgents. The hulk of metal lay burning in the alley, black smoke rising into the sky above the city.

Not long after the air strike, we were ordered to exfil the house and link up with gun trucks for the short ride back to Camp Corregidor, but not before another brief firefight erupted. An insurgent had made his way to the rooftop about two houses to our south. Without warning, we were briefly suppressed by surprisingly accurate AK-47 fire. One of the scouts came to the roof and swiftly silenced the insurgent with a LAW rocket.

∎ ∎ ∎

I was drawn to this war. By itself, that statement might seem grotesque and unholy, but it is the truth, which I neither celebrate nor hide. As a Marine officer, and as a young infantry rifleman before I received my commission, enemy contact was this mysterious event our lives revolved around. We talked about it, trained for it, and dreamed of it, never quite sure if we would live up to the high standards of our Marine forefathers. Before earning one myself, those who had received the coveted Combat Action Ribbon (CAR) were almost mysterious.

All marines have a fascination with combat prior to seeing it. They want to know how they would hold up. Will they crumble under fear and stress, or will they thrive in the chaos of battle? No one truly knows—until they do.

At this point in our deployment, as the dawn of our departure approached, one thing that I knew for sure was that Sergeant Michael Anderson, Sergeant Chad Dyer, Corporal Jon Cureton, and the rest of the 1st ANGLICO detachment at Camp Corregidor had lived up the high standards of the Marine Corps. It was humbling to work next to these men.

■ ■ ■

The scout and sniper teams of the 1st Battalion, 506th Airborne, were rough, smart, and highly trained, thriving in the combat environment. They treated us well, but I would be lying if I said we blended in with them seamlessly. There was always a distance between the teams, an invisible barrier that cast a slight shadow. I chalked this up to the usual interservice or interunit rivalry ANGLICO teams are accustomed to. As enablers, this is how it goes. We don't have to like it or even acknowledge it. Unless it becomes a problem that interferes with the ability to accomplish the mission or the safety of marines, it is simply something that has to be dealt with.

From what I could tell, the slight standoffishness hadn't caused any issues, and I was more than proud to work beside these warriors, regardless of their funny berets. There was no question that these men would fight for us, as we would have and did fight for them. Regardless, the shadow was always in the background. This was never more present than with the scout platoon leader, First Lieutenant Jones.

A former Special Forces enlisted man, First Lieutenant Jones was experienced and brought a certain quiet, methodical leadership. I'm not sure how his platoon viewed him, nor was I too concerned, because it didn't matter to me or my team. Outside of operations, we never really talked. Our short professional relationship focused on nothing but the mission.

Like a good officer, First Lieutenant Jones supported the task force's operations to the best of his ability. However, he seemed uneasy about going on missions with ANGLICO teams. More to the point, I believe he wasn't sure how to act on operations with Marine captains such as myself, Rard, or Murray. Staff Sergeant Martinez and First Lieutenant Jones appeared to occasionally butt heads, but I figured this was natural when an experienced NCO and an experienced former Special Forces operator turned lieutenant were forced to work together. At any rate, Jones wasn't some boot second lieutenant; he'd cut his teeth as an SF soldier. That was more than enough for me.

ANGLICO was a rather odd animal when it came to dealing with various tactical leaders while on missions in Ramadi. As an example, the team would be attached to a patrol led by a lieutenant. The lieutenant would technically be in command of the patrol, meaning as a captain, I would take tactical direction from the younger officer. This was anything but conventional. Some officers struggled to put their egos aside.

On one operation, three separate Task Force Dark Eagle teams were out in the Mulab. We had covertly inserted into three locations that mutually supported one another. When the battalion commander for the 1-506th gave the mission brief, ANGLICO was designated as the "main effort." The mission centered around an ANGLICO team being in place to identify the target and direct supporting aircraft ·

to destroy the threat. However, the house we took over had a large six-foot wall lining the roof. I wouldn't be able to see the engagement area as required, so my team had to break loopholes into the wall.

First Lieutenant Jones was worried, and rightfully so, that we might be compromised. I understood his concern, but the battalion commander needed us to see the engagement area. This caused friction between Jones and me, but in the end, we made the loopholes.

Situations like this didn't help reduce the invisible barrier between Jones and ANGLICO. Just more proof that ANGLICO is peculiar. To excel within the odd, unconventional nature of this unit, marines must check their egos at the door and find ways to solve problems. So that's what we did.

CHAPTER ELEVEN:
ANOTHER DAY IN RAMADI

Sergeant Anderson and I studied the white mission board in the team common room. For the next couple of days, we weren't on any planned ops. Captain Murray had a mission, but my team had some downtime before suiting back up and heading into the city.

"Looks like we have a few days off," I said, smiling with my hands in my pockets, a faux pas by Marine standards.

"Yes sir," replied Anderson with a smirk. "I'm not complaining."

I chuckled. "Neither am I. Let's try and remain productive, though."

Ahead of the game as usual, Anderson informed me that he'd make sure the guys attended to weapons and gear maintenance if they hadn't already.

Trying to maintain our "vampire" schedule, no one was going to force the marines to wake up at 0530 as if we were back on Camp Pendleton. Our next operation, so far unnamed, was the usual late-night insertion followed by a long day slugging it out with insurgents or fighting boredom. I looked forward to a little rest. There was even the remote possibility of a Corregidor shower: baby wipes.

It was around 1000. I'd already drank a few cups of coffee and was bored. I sat on my cot and opened my laptop, trying to relax. With the knowledge of the world in my hands, I decided to waste my time reading news stories written by someone thousands of miles away. I was a glutton for punishment. As usual, I gravitated towards articles about the Iraq War. None of the reporting was good. More Americans killed, more American civilians upset, sectarian violence ripping the country apart. Ramadi was all over the news.

Frustrated, I closed my laptop and sighed. It was tough not to question the war and the whole situation.

Ramadi was saturated with insurgent activity. The scuttlebutt was that there were plans to conduct a Fallujah-like takedown of this stark, gray blot of buildings and rubble some called a city. No one believed it. Politics wouldn't allow such a thing, and most of us, jaded and sullen, didn't believe the DOD had the balls to pull it off. On a tactical level, we knew it could be done with the right number of soldiers and marines, but the politicians didn't have the nerve to try, especially with 2006 being an election year with control of Congress at stake. We were stuck fighting a war of attrition. Like the Marine lieutenant says in the movie *Full Metal Jacket*, "It's one big shit sandwich, and we're all goin' to have to take a bite out of it."

Putting my laptop back on my green cot, I stood and stretched. Cureton and some other marines were headed outside to burn shit, a required duty every couple of days when the situation warranted it. Trying to feel useful, I followed them outside.

I was hit by a wall of cold, damp air. Others were often bewildered at the extreme temperature differences between the parched, dry heat of the long Iraqi summer and the short, cold, damp winters. Being from Southeast Texas, I was relatively accustomed to such changes. I've always done well in the heat and humidity; however, the cold in Iraq, although not freezing, pulled the heat from my body. I retreated back inside to get my black fleece and a coyote-tan beanie. I could see my breath as I walked back out to help the marines do a duty no one wanted to do.

Outside, Corporal Cureton and Lance Corporals Cain and Hamilton were pulling the fifty-gallon drums from the makeshift shitters. Looking more like a boy's fort than a bathroom, the shitters were made of plywood and very austere. The drums of filth were heavy and cumbersome. The marines joked with each other as they tried not to slosh the contents. I approached them with a grin.

"You get any on you?" I asked rhetorically.

"I think Cain got a little in his mouth, sir," Cureton laughed, lugging a large jug of diesel fuel.

Cain responded without diverting his attention. "Bullshit."

As he adjusted his gloves, Hamilton asked if I came to watch or help.

"I'm here to help, although you might have to give me a class on this," I answered, staring regretfully into the contents of the refurbished drums.

"Oh, Hamilton and Cain are experts. They can help you out, sir," Cureton quipped.

Lance Corporal Cain was a muscular blond radio operator on Captain Murray's team. A football player from Florida, he had an edge of street to him and loved being behind the M2 .50 cal. He was quick to talk trash with the other marines. Like the rest of the crew, he was hilarious and more than happy to mix it up with the flip-flop-wearing guerrillas in the Mulab.

Lance Corporal Hamilton, with dark hair and thick eyebrows, was another radio operator on Murray's team. From Mount Washington, Kentucky, Hamilton was another Southern boy who played football in high school before joining the Marine Corps a few years after 9/11. He was quick to give advice on radios and comm. Smart and wearing a constant grin, Hamilton also had a serious side and was well liked.

For the next half hour, I helped the marines pour diesel fuel into the drums, light the concoction, and stir the disgusting mixture of urine, feces, and diesel. Underneath large date palms and the threat of mortar fire, the marines poked fun at each other and complained about their current duty. Their conversation ebbed and flowed, switching between girls, one of their mothers, football, the Marine Corps, Ramadi, and then back to girls. For the most part, they left me out of it besides the occasional question. I wore a smirk broken only by a chuckle here and there.

It was foul work but required nonetheless. The smell didn't bother us; if we had thrown some Styrofoam into the mix, we could have bottled it up and given it the name Essence de Ramadi. In the back of my mind, I knew this was all fleeting—experiences that become memories, fading with time. We would all look back on these days with a mix of pride, aggravation, and maybe a little regret and fascination. The camaraderie and brotherhood would be replaced with a gaping hole once we were civilians.

With the work done, the marines and I headed back into Full Metal Jacket. The cloud-covered sky succumbed to drizzle and light rain. I carefully placed one boot in front of the other, trying not to slip in the mud. The once fine, powdery dirt had become a slimy mess, attaching itself to everything just like its dry predecessor.

The team common room was packed with marines and soldiers. Even the Air Force was present, represented by Airman Paul Williams. Williams was a former marine who had gotten out and signed up for the Air National Guard. A member of the 118th ASOS supporting the 2-28 Brigade, he was on a TACP team led by Technical Sergeant Patrick Scoggins. Williams was accustomed to our aggressiveness and brash humor. When the marines harassed him, he gave it right back. Everyone liked him. He visited us regularly and played video games with the men, joking and laughing, trying to forget the realities outside.

I sat in a cheap folding chair as the digital combat unfolded on the TV. Corporal Donnelly and Sergeant Dyer were competing in a first-person combat game. Each man tried to outflank and kill their opponent for bragging rights and a little entertainment. A couple of Staff Sergeant Martinez's boys were waiting their turn while talking trash and laughing with the marines. Before long, Captain Rard came into the room. His usual smile was missing; I knew it wasn't good.

"Hey, you and your team need to grab your gear and link up with a couple vehicles from the 506," Rard told me before letting the door shut. All conversation stopped. Donnelly paused the game. Standing, I asked what was going on.

"A patrol from Bravo Company got hit with a coordinated attack to the east on Route Michigan. You'll be taking your gun truck, so hurry up. Major Womack will be waiting for you with the QRF," replied Rard.

Cureton, Anderson, and Dyer jumped up and flew out the door. I followed them into our team room. As per our team's SOP, our gear was ready to go. However, this mission required our gun truck, while we had been doing nothing but dismounted ops for the past three weeks. The vehicle was filled with fuel, but Dyer had to ensure the radios were updated with the current communications crypto. This is a quick process unless the radios won't take the crypto fill for whatever reason. Professionally, I don't like people having to wait on me, so my stress level increased as we focused on prepping the vehicle.

It took us about ten minutes to get everything ready to move. I would have preferred keeping it under five. Irritated with myself, I put a pinch of tobacco in my lip before attempting to wipe the condensation off my Oakley sunglasses.

Driving through the mud, we swiftly arrived at the front gate. Anderson jumped out to ask the QRF for the patrol frequency. He returned dripping wet.

"Two sixty-three," he said urgently. Dyer punched the frequency into the vehicle radio located in front of the dashboard and slammed down the gas pedal. The gun truck bounced and rolled through large, water-filled ruts and out onto Route Michigan. Cureton absorbed the drizzle and rain up in the turret as it started to dwindle.

Elements of Bravo Company 1-506th had been on a vehicle patrol about five miles to the east. As they were moving west on Route Michigan, an IED exploded. Soon after, the patrol began receiving heavy small-arms fire and RPGs. Soldiers reported that insurgents in a large, elaborate home were attacking while other insurgents tried to maneuver between houses and in ditches. A couple soldiers were wounded, so the battalion sent the QRF.

Route Michigan always increased our apprehension. As we drove east, we were on edge, waiting for an explosion to rock our world. The congested urban environment gave way to lush green farms and small villages. Ornate homes with huge columns dotted the countryside. It would have been pretty if it hadn't been Iraq.

Watching the gun truck's wiper blades work back and forth, I realized we had never been this far east. The only imagery I had of the area was a 1:50,000-scale map. My GRGs didn't cover this part of Al Anbar Province. Since August, we had been using nothing but imagery and rarely, if ever, used the 1:50,000 maps. It wasn't a big deal considering that most of my training was with maps of this size. I simply didn't like surprises.

The vehicle's radio beeped with the tone of frequency hopping before the transmission came through. Captain Rard informed me that he had requested air support. It was quickly approved, so a section of AH-1 Cobras was en route.

"Captain Rard is pushing us some Cobras," I announced to the team over the whine of the engine.

"Check, sir" was the response.

On the radio, I asked for a situation update on the attack against Bravo Company. What was the estimated enemy strength and location? Where were the friendlies located? Any suspected IEDs? The QRF didn't know. They were having problems communicating with the soldiers.

Frustrated, I tracked our position on the map with my GPS. The last report we'd received conveyed that the insurgents had set up a support-by-fire position in a house north of Route Michigan. If that was still the case, I'd have the Cobras hold to the south while we linked up with the soldiers. While the surface-to-air threat was minimal, it was still a worry, and as the JTAC, I had to consider the threat against supporting aircraft.

In the distance, down Route Michigan, we saw multiple gun trucks spread along the road. Turret gunners appeared to be suppressing a white two-story house with four pillars facing southeast. As we approached, I heard the unmistakable signature of multiple M2s banging away.

Soldiers were out of their vehicles, using the armored doors as cover. Most had weapons pointed up towards the house, while other soldiers were shooting into a tree line at another group of enemy fighters.

Dyer stopped the gun truck about twenty-five meters from the QRF vehicle we were following. I jumped out to talk with Major Womack behind his vehicle, taking advantage of the cover.

"What do we got, sir?" I said, shaking his hand. The tall Army officer greeted me with a smile, informing me that Bravo was still in contact with the enemy in multiple locations. Around that same time, the earpiece attached to my PRC-148 radio crackled with a transmission. From the southwest, two Cobras were approaching. I gave them a brief situation report and requested they hold south.

Motioning to Major Womack, I informed him that a section of Cobras was available. I explained that considering the proximity of his soldiers, I could have the Cobras hit the house with a Hellfire missile. Our conversation was interrupted by a burst of machine-gun fire that snapped over our heads. Instinctively, we ducked and looked behind us for the impacts before returning our focus to the target house. A gun truck across the road opened fire in reply.

I reiterated that Major Womack's dismounts by the ditch were considered danger close. "If you approve it, I'll need your initials."

The tall VMI graduate didn't hesitate: "No problem, Captain Angell. Let's use the Hellfire. My initials are Delta Whiskey."

"Check, sir," I said with a grin. Kneeling behind the major's gun truck, I briefed the Cobras. The process took less than two minutes.

"Gunshot Five-One from Wild Eagle Five-Seven, my position is on Route Michigan, marked by VS-17 panels. Your target is northwest three hundred meters; insurgent-occupied house is marked by machine-gun tracer fire. I need you to come over my right shoulder in a southeast-to-northwest heading, using a Hellfire. Be advised this is danger close; initials are Delta Whiskey."

The pilot repeated key portions of the six-line to ensure there was no confusion.

"You need a talk-on?" I asked.

The bird replied calmly. "Negative. We tally the target."

To ensure he was aiming at the right building, I asked how many columns the house had. He came back with the correct number: four.

Turning towards Major Womack, I asked that he have his soldiers continue shooting at the house to mark the target for the birds. More enemy fire wracked the gun trucks to our front. Fifty-caliber and 7.62mm rounds chewed up the building. It was glorious.

"Lasing," crackled from my earpiece as the Cobras used their laser designator for the Hellfire missile.

I mashed the transmit button on my body armor: "Continue."

Machine guns from Bravo Company's gun trucks continued to mark the target.

"Wings level, in-heading three-oh-five," stated the pilot.

Satisfied, I approved the attack: "Gunshot, cleared hot." Then I yelled to those around me, "He's cleared hot. Here they come!"

I turned as the Cobra bore down on the target. These are truly magnificent weapons of war, sleek and deadly, their rotor blades giving off that telltale sound as they muscle through the sky. My left hand rested over the transmit button attached to my chest rig in case I needed to abort the attack.

We waited for the missile to be released. Finally, after what seemed like an eternity but was probably only a few seconds, the hundred-pound missile streaked through the sky, swiftly gaining speed.

"Missile away. Stand by," I yelled at no one in particular.

Everyone watched the missile sail through a second-story window and detonate, shooting out white-hot shrapnel.

"And Gunshot from Wild Eagle Five-Seven, be advised good hit, good hit. Continue to push south towards your holding area. Target's quiet; unknown EKIA," I advised the pilot.

I continued to track the Cobra as it banked right west and then south to a holding area. In the event some motivated insurgent with an SA-7 decided to attempt a takedown, I was prepared to announce,

"Missile in the air, missile in the air." Thankfully, I didn't have to. We received no more fire from the target house. The insurgents, dead or running away, were no longer an immediate threat.

We waited around for another half hour as Bravo Company sent a platoon to search the house. Finding hundreds of spent cartridges and multiple blood trails, we were satisfied that either the machine-gun fire or the Hellfire missile had wounded and killed multiple insurgents. The fact that the bodies were gone wasn't surprising. The insurgents almost always removed their dead if they could. While that was frustrating, we understood it.

The drive west was quick and eventless. The rain had stopped, but the streets were wet, and the sky hung low, threatening more of it. Anderson and I discussed the need to ensure the gun truck was always ready, though it wasn't as if we were unprepared. The vehicle had been full of fuel, with the two PRC-117s locked in their station. All we had to do was load the crypto fill, grab our gear, and put the machine gun in the turret. We would never leave the M240 in the gun truck unsecured. Packed away in the vehicle was extra ammo, water, radio batteries for dismounted ops, a couple of AT4s, smoke grenades, VS-17 panels, and the blowout medical bag; basically, everything we would need was in the gun truck. The one thing we needed to keep on top of was new crypto fill. This was an easy fix.

We arrived back at Camp Corregidor a few hours after we left. Once we cleared our weapons inside the gate, we headed to Full Metal Jacket. The standing water had accumulated, but still I preferred the cool, wet weather to the oven-like temperatures of late spring, summer, and fall. The heat was an almost insurmountable obstacle that we dealt with most of the year. But at the end of January, the temperature was relatively pleasant.

As we approached Full Metal Jacket, Dyer stopped so I could get out. I walked in front of the vehicle to ensure we weren't running over anything we shouldn't be; this was a required safety practice near buildings and personnel. Dyer turned the gun truck around and slowly backed in. Mud clung to the tires. Finally in place, everyone else got out and started removing their gear.

A loud *whoosh* came out of nowhere, instantly followed by an enormous crack and explosion. I felt it in my teeth and chest.

"Incoming," yelled one of the marines. Dyer, Anderson, and Cureton raced towards the entrance to Full Metal Jacket. Like an idiot, I knelt between the gun truck and building, thinking I had cover. Another round screamed in and exploded somewhere behind the building. *Boom.*

"Captain Angell, come on," yelled Anderson. He was at the entrance to the building, motioning for me to follow him. I turned towards him and slipped. A third round slammed into the roof of Full Metal Jacket. The sound was painful. Finally gaining traction, I ran through the thick mud towards the entrance. The fourth and final round exploded nearby in the palm grove covering the east side of Camp Corregidor.

In the team common room, everyone was standing, waiting for more impacts and trying to account for all the marines and Doc Vissing. Taking indirect fire was always stressful. It appeared random, and our only protection was our ability to seek cover and hope the rounds would detonate somewhere else. Hope wasn't a particularly effective strategy.

A couple miles west, at Camp Ramadi, the AN/TPQ-48 counterbattery radar system registered a POO north of the Euphrates River. They sent the ten-digit grid to the 2-28 BCT TOC for assessment. The grid was assessed for possible response via counterbattery fire. If approved, the fire-support representatives would send the 155mm Paladin battery or 120mm mortar platoon the grid to fire on.

There would be no response today, though. The insurgents' proximity to a two-story house violated the collateral damage estimate (CDE) instituted by someone in Baghdad. No one wanted to risk destroying a civilian's house—at least, no one in Baghdad.

Back at Full Metal Jacket, we waited for the "all clear" from the

1-506th TOC. Everyone was talking about the IDF, thankful that none of us had been injured in those few seconds of violence and mayhem.

Before long, the excitement was over, replaced by the tediousness to which we were accustomed. A few of us headed up to the roof to inspect the damage. Not 100 percent sure we wouldn't get hit again, Captain Rard, Corporal Cureton, myself, Lance Corporal Cain, and a few others emerged cautiously. About ten feet away from the top of the stairs, twisted rebar and jagged concrete encircled a hole about four feet in diameter. Through the hole, we saw the top bunk of a bed used by some of the CAG marines. Someone downstairs was lucky they hadn't slept in. When I woke that morning, I'd anticipated a mundane day. I was wrong. It was just another day in Ramadi.

CHAPTER TWELVE:
OPERATION BLUE FALCON

At 0100 on January 30, we stepped out of the main gate of Camp Corregidor and headed west on foot towards OP Hotel. The sky was awash with stars; a thin sliver of the moon glowed above the horizon. Varying shades of green shimmered through the monocular NVGs hanging over my right eye from my helmet. Sixteen separate beams darted out from the small patrol, one emanating from each man's AN/PEQ-2 Infrared Target Pointer/Illuminator/Aiming Light device. The light show was only visible through our NVGs.

Route Michigan was quiet. The only sounds came from barking dogs in the distance and the crunch of rocks and concrete under our boots. There was no nearby movement or activity. Sleeping in their homes, Iraqi civilians were nowhere to be seen. But we knew from experience that somewhere within the darkness and catacombs of Ramadi, insurgents were waiting.

It took the patrol about twenty minutes to get to OP Hotel. We weaved through multiple layers of barbed wire and concrete barriers, then passed several fighting positions manned by soldiers defending the beleaguered outpost. These men greeted us with the occasional nod, while others simply ignored us. We climbed a few flights of stairs to an empty room.

OP Hotel had taken countless attacks and multiple SBVIEDs, and it showed. Inside, the building was dark, cold, and musty. The only lights came from red-lensed flashlights as soldiers and marines completed various tasks. The windows had long been replaced by layers of sandbags. The interior reminded me of medieval prison cells I'd read about in books. Our hardened group of young Americans—a mixture of ethnicities and backgrounds, some marines, some soldiers—settled against the concrete walls to wait, trying to get comfortable with their individual combat loads.

We were to depart OP Hotel for our target house deep in the Mulab at 0200. First Lieutenant Jones went into the small TOC located behind a curtained door. I followed to check for intelligence updates.

Operation Blue Falcon was originally named Operation Kinetic Fury, but the 1-506th requested that Captain Rard change the name. The 2nd Marine Division, who oversaw all combat operations in Al Anbar Province, had made statements that the 1-506th was possibly being too aggressive in a time when the division was trying to gain more support from the civilian populace. I suspected the new name was a passive-aggressive swipe. "Blue Falcon" reflected a common phrase used to describe marines who backstabbed their buddies— Buddy Fuckers, or Bravo Foxtrots for short. The 1-506th approved the new name.

A platoon from Charlie Company, call-sign Gunfighter, comprised the main effort. They were to insert into a house on the north side of the Ramadi soccer stadium and lay low. Our element, which consisted of my team, Joker Four, four scouts, and First Lieutenant Jones, would enter a home and go firm on the east side of the soccer stadium. Once compromised, we hoped the insurgents would believe our element was only a small team. When the enemy came out to fight, Gunfighter would destroy them with fire and maneuver while Task Force Dark Eagle came in with precision sniper fire or air-delivered ordnance.

Waiting to step off towards the Mulab, everyone checked and rechecked their gear. Dyer was having difficulty contacting Captain Rard back at the 1-506th TOC. He wasn't too concerned, knowing that the thick concrete walls would hamper our communications until we left the safe confines of OP Hotel. Glancing over at Corporal Cureton, I had to laugh at the sight. He had an AT4 strapped to his pack, and as an M249 gunner, he also had over 700 rounds of linked 5.56mm, eight hand grenades, a couple bottles of water, and other miscellaneous combat gear. Anderson had told Cureton he could take the AT4 as long as he could hump it. Our experience so far proved that the more weapons and ammunition we had, the better. Walking around the Mulab with just over a dozen men required that we be prepared for whatever the enemy threw at us. All of us were similarly loaded down—not because someone required it but because we wanted to have all the tools we might need.

"We leave in five minutes," Staff Sergeant Martinez said after emerging from behind the curtain. It was almost 0200. Gunfighter had departed Camp Corregidor's south gate and were en route to their target. Anderson grabbed Cureton's hand to help him up. Snagging the mouthpiece from my Camelbak, I took a long pull of cold water while attempting to clean my ballistics glasses.

At 0200, the patrol was outside OP Hotel and crossing Route Michigan, heading south into literal darkness. The deeper we pushed into the Mulab, the less the electricity seemed to work. Only a few lights emanated from homes. We bounded across the streets, covering each other as we moved through the dark in a choreographed dance. The continual barking of dogs was the only sound except for the occasional burst of distant gunfire. We scanned for possible threats along the roads cutting through the neighborhood. The usual smells of Ramadi followed us deeper into the back alleys. After about forty-five minutes, we made it to our target.

Even with NVGs on, the darkness and looming shadows played games with the mind. Night vision equipment allowed us to penetrate the lack of light to some degree—through a window, we could see if someone was standing just beyond the glass—but we couldn't see as if we'd turned on the light. They gave us an edge, but they weren't perfect. Where the lights were working, our NVGs would get washed out from time to time. It wasn't unusual to flip the small black NVG cylinder attached to my helmet up and down constantly as we walked through light and back into the shadows.

Everyone took up positions along the road next to the target house. Staff Sergeant Martinez and a few scouts jumped the courtyard wall. The owners had secured the large metal gate with a huge lock. Unable to break it, we were forced to climb over the barrier. Resembling turtles with our gear and packs, and about as graceful, we scaled the wall, helping each other over one by one. Once inside the courtyard, my team was tasked with providing rear security while the scouts unsuccessfully attempted to pick the lock to the front door. Frustrated, they started knocking. I chuckled at the frustration.

Sergeant Anderson and I had a long-standing joke that "it's never sexy." The movies like to show marines or soldiers on patrol making no mistakes, gliding towards their target in a violent yet graceful manner. Hollywood never shows soldiers or marines slipping in mud, fumbling with a door, or dropping a magazine. The reality is, for the most part, we were a bunch of young men trying to solve some very dangerous problems on the modern battlefield. Mistakes happened; people tripped and fell. We used whatever worked: we improvised, adapted, and overcame.

Through a window, I spotted the small glow of a candle finally approach the door. Staff Sergeant Martinez told the Iraqi man to hurry up. Once the door was open, Martinez gave the man the traditional "*Salam alaykum*" greeting and went into the house. The man was short and thick with a balding head and bushy mustache. I was surprised to find him smiling. As per our usual SOP, the scouts held the family in one room. I tried to ignore them.

After the house was cleared, the snipers and my team went to the roof. Cautious, we looked over the rooftop wall. It was imperative that our observation and potential fields of fire were good. Divided by a small road, the house was located along the eastern corner of the soccer stadium. Local fans would have been able to sit and watch a game from the roof. We had clear fields of fire down an east-to-west-running road to our south and southeast. To the west and southwest was a road, the stadium compound, and fields of dirt. Behind the stadium and its green concrete bleachers rose an enormous water tower.

As the team and I looked around, one of the scouts, Staff Sergeant Geise, prepared small detonation charges. These would be used to blow our loopholes. Lieutenant Jones and some of the scouts provided security in the house, keeping guard over the occupants. We wouldn't blow the loopholes until 0530 when the mosques blared the call to prayer over their loudspeakers in the minarets. The intent was to provide cover for the explosion and reduce our chances of getting compromised; that's how accustomed to explosions the inhabitants of Ramadi had become. Sometimes this strategy worked, and sometimes it didn't.

With an hour left before the charges were blown, Joey B. and Specialist Taylor went into the house to try to get an hour of sleep before the long day. Anderson and the boys followed them.

Staying on the roof for a little while longer, Staff Sergeant Martinez and I discussed the mission. While our position was not perfect, we were satisfied with it. Shortly after, I made my way down the concrete stairs to the first-floor roof and into the warm, dark house. It smelled of foreign spices I couldn't picture. Finding a spot against the wall, I sat and rested my eyes.

Movement woke me up. It was 0515. Wishing I had a cup of coffee, I stood and stretched. My team and Joker Four were digging in their packs and preparing to move back outside once Staff Sergeant Geise blew the loopholes. Awake and ready, we waited downstairs. Sergeant Anderson and I talked briefly about what time the first section of aircraft was due to arrive. We had a couple of hours but were anxious to get in position.

At around 0535, the morning call to prayer echoed throughout the Mulab. As the muezzin recited the adhan into a microphone, five small charges detonated. Staff Sergeant Geise went to confirm that all charges had blown. He returned quickly with a thumbs-up.

One by one, the men of Joker Four and my team headed back up the stairs and onto the roof. Faint streaks of light stretched from the eastern horizon. The air was cold and still. The long melody from the adhan rose and fell like the tides as we stretched mosquito netting in front of our loopholes and tied blankets overhead to create shade and more shadows. Dyer, Cureton, Joey B., and Taylor grabbed several blankets and sofa cushions from the house for warmth and comfort. The cold concrete sucked the warmth from our bodies, so we sat on the blankets. The only words we could make out from the call to prayer were "Allahu Akbar": God is great.

With the position set up, we sat back and observed the neighborhood coming to life. The locals drifted down the streets to the Haji Mosque. Men walked in groups while the women followed closely behind. The occasional car drove past to points unknown. As the sun climbed above the horizon, the activity increased. I tried to ignore the cold enveloping my legs. Thoughts of my wife popped into my mind. It was about 1830 in Southern California. She was probably home or at her parents' house. I missed her warm smile.

About an hour later, around 0830, Staff Sergeant Martinez, Corporal Cureton, and Sergeant Anderson noticed movement across the street, on the other side of the fence between our position and the soccer stadium. There was activity in what was once an auto repair shop. Two men kept peeking over the wall at our loopholes. Everyone grew still. Quietly, Staff Sergeant Geise contacted the scouts below to let them know something was going on. Everyone gradually moved into a position to engage. This was a dangerous situation. If we were compromised, we would deal with what unfolded, but if these were insurgents, we could be in trouble. One well-placed hand grenade thrown over the wall could take out everyone on the roof.

The men on the other side of the wall were talking in Arabic. Despite the tension, we dealt with the situation calmly, by waiting. A few minutes later, the men must have left. We couldn't hear them, and we'd stopped seeing them. Everyone remained on edge, unsure if these were curious civilians or enemy fighters.

The reality was that someone had left to report our presence.

I was reading my GRG map when a short burst from an AK-47 erupted from the auto repair shop. The gunfire went far above our heads. From our loopholes, we couldn't see the insurgent, but we knew he was trying to draw us out. My instincts were to stand and start suppressing the area, but I knew that wasn't the best decision. Showing discipline, we stayed hidden.

Corporal Cureton and Joey B. readied fragmentation grenades, removing the safety clips and pulling the pins but keeping a tight grasp, ensuring the "spoons" stayed in place. Martinez counted down. I saw no grin on Cureton's face, just 100 percent focus as he prepared to throw the small explosive. On the count of three, they stood and lobbed the grenades across the small road and over the wall. About four seconds later, they exploded. Dark-gray smoke wafted above the wall. There were no screams of pain and no more gunfire. The insurgent had either been killed, run off wounded, or had already left, leaving the grenades to explode harmlessly.

"We've been compromised," Anderson said, peering through the loophole and beyond.

"That didn't take long," chuckled Cureton.

"No, it didn't. Just get ready," I said, looking at my watch. The birds wouldn't be arriving for a while. Staff Sergeant Martinez and his team were gathering their gear, ensuring water and magazines lay within arm's reach. The brief exchange was reported back to the TOC.

At this point, we awaited the attack we knew was coming. The streets were now void of civilian activity. Each man had a sector of fire and observation. Staff Sergeant Geise and Sergeant Dyer were covering the east. Cureton and I kept an eye out for movement to the south. Sergeant Anderson and Martinez's sniper team were covering west across the soccer stadium. The scouts, located inside the house, covered the north, providing local security and still watching over the Iraqi family.

Maintaining this intense focus was mentally draining. It always amazed me how quickly monotony became the enemy. Adrenaline is a drug. The more it rushes through the body, the faster it subsides. I equated boredom to adrenaline withdrawals.

A few hours after Cureton and Joey B. had lobbed their grenades into the repair shop, we started to get probed. Sporadic gunfire came in from the south and southwest. The insurgents were trying to figure out if other Americans were in the area. The platoon from Gunfighter had been compromised as well. We'd known this was going to happen; it was part of the plan. Sneak in, set up, get compromised, and fight. That was the mission. Now we had the insurgents reacting to us.

From what we could tell, there were at least four groups of enemy fighters. Consisting of three- and four-man teams, the insurgents would pop out from behind the corners of buildings or down dusty allies and unleash long bursts from AK-47s, RPDs, and RPK machine guns. They would rapidly displace to a new location. Shoot and move, shoot and move. When they stayed in a location too long was when mistakes occurred.

The Gunfighter platoon to our west maintained contact, the roar of gunfire increasing and waning. For the most part, we held our fire, waiting for the insurgents to make a mistake.

"They fuckin' know we're here," Staff Sergeant Martinez announced.

"No shit," Joey B. said, sitting behind his sniper rifle.

"No, that old man, the owner of the house, told us that they've known we're here," answered Martinez.

It was a warning. We'd been compromised since we got here. It didn't change anything. A burst of fire hit the other side of the wall Cureton and I were next to. Bits of plaster pelted us. We hunched lower.

"They must be right down the street. I can't see anything from here," Corporal Cureton yelled, frustrated. He had his M249 SAW against his shoulder as he peered through the loophole behind mosquito netting.

I glanced to my right. Anderson, Martinez, Joey B., and Taylor hadn't even noticed the impact. They were focused on something near the soccer stadium. Staff Sergeant Geise and Sergeant Dyer continued scanning for movement to the east. They were disciplined.

"We're takin' fire from the southeast. They're fuckin' right on top of us," I yelled, ensuring that everyone knew the situation. Multiple bursts of enemy fire hit the rooftop wall again. This time, it came from the south and southwest. Using the defilade provided by the three-dimensional world of the city, a small team of insurgents had closed on our position.

Fearing the insurgents' proximity, Cureton and I counted to three, rose over the wall, and engaged. Two Iraqis darted back behind a street corner about fifty meters away as Cureton poured 5.56mm rounds down the road. I couldn't tell if they'd been hit.

We continued to get attacked. Cureton wanted to fire the AT4, targeting the road beyond the street corner where the fighters were seeking cover.

"Negative," I replied as I put a new magazine in my M4. We needed to save the AT4 for a better target. This fight was only beginning, and we had to be smart with our ammunition. Staff Sergeant Martinez was thinking the same thing; he told his team to watch their ammo usage.

I keyed the transmit button on my plate carrier. We needed air support. "Wild Eagle Two-One from Five-Seven, be advised, we are troops in contact. What's the status on the Harriers?"

The battle was unfolding in earnest. Using their targeting POD, fixed-wing aircraft could help us locate groups of insurgents. Besides, while I loved being a rifleman, I was out here to control air strikes in support of 1-506th. From what we could see from our location, the enemy was gathering in small groups on the far side of the soccer stadium. The Gunfighter platoon was still being engaged as well.

"They'll be checking on-station soon," replied Captain Rard over the radio.

Targeting the south side of the stadium, Anderson and Cureton requested mortar fire but were denied. The machine-gun fire from our east had stopped, but the fire from the soccer stadium had increased. Using the bleachers from the stadium as cover, groups of insurgents maneuvered closer to us and the Gunfighter platoon.

About five minutes later, a section of two Marine Harriers, call sign Duster Three-Four, arrived. I immediately briefed the pilots on the situation. Meanwhile, Cureton and Anderson worked together to get 40mm HE rounds from Anderson's M203 onto the insurgents.

"I'll observe through the loophole so we don't have to expose ourselves," Cureton told Anderson.

"Tell me when you're ready," Anderson ordered.

"I'm ready," replied Cureton, squinting through his loophole. Anderson fired, popped open the chamber and let the empty canister fall to the floor, and quickly loaded another one.

The chatter around us was constant. Rard approved a gun run from the Harriers, but I had to talk them onto the target. As this was going on, the mix of soldiers and marines were focused on suppressing the insurgents.

"Ready on three. One, two, three," Martinez counted. On three, we all stood and engaged, planting a wall of lead near the insurgents.

"I see their shots."

"They're in the press box."

"They're in the fuckin' press box."

"They're fuckin' right there."

Our adrenaline was spiking, and everyone was yelling over each other. The crack and snaps of enemy 7.62mm surrounded us.

"I fuckin' hit 'em," yelled Martinez.

I was caught up in the moment. The meaning of my whole existence at this point resided in putting ordnance on insurgents.

I yelled over the gunfire, "I'm bringing those fuckin' birds in."

I was forced to yell into the mouthpiece of my PRC-148 so the pilots could hear me.

Cureton was trying to fire the AT4, but it wasn't firing. These systems are known for misfires. They have to be recocked and fired again, but it's nerve-racking not knowing what the misfire will cause.

"Man, I think I almost got hit. I felt that bullet. It went right by my fuckin' face," Anderson muttered, shaking his head while loading a new magazine. He was lucky; he almost got killed on his birthday.

Joey B. had noticed as well. "Yeah, I heard that shit. That thing was fuckin' close."

You can feel the air pressure change for a split second when a bullet comes within six inches of you. That was way too close.

Everyone verified their ammunition count. Martinez was down two magazines but had about six left. We all readied ourselves for the insurgent response. About 250 meters away, we saw movement but couldn't tell if we'd killed any other insurgents.

Behind his sniper rifle, Martinez had had enough: "I'm gonna take this shot."

Anderson continued putting 40mm HE rounds near the bleacher doorways at the soccer stadium while Cureton directed his fire: "Bring those rounds to the left." "That round was close." "Come to the left with those shots."

"Hey, on the count of three, we're gonna suppress while Joey B. shoots the LAW."

Staff Sergeant Martinez counted, "One, two . . . three."

Again, everyone stood and engaged, aiming for the covered portion of the soccer stadium known as the press box. Joey B rose and fired the LAW after ensuring the backblast area was clear. The sound was oppressive.

The LAW round went long. "It went over. It went over," yelled Joey B.

I maintained communication with the Harriers to ensure they knew what the target was.

"Watch your mags. Watch your rate of fire," ordered Martinez.

Satisfied that the Harriers knew the target, I gave them my abbreviated nine-line for a gun run. This transmission was interrupted by the exchange of gunfire. I was forced to repeat myself at least three times.

"Okay, they're coming in from the northeast to the southwest over our right shoulder," I yelled to the men as I traced the path with my right hand. As the Harriers were setting up for the attack, 1-506th contacted Anderson to report that they could use mortars now. The battalion could tell we were in a big fight and were thankfully trying to give us all the tools we needed.

"Negative. We got these birds inbound," I replied.

"Duster Three-Four is wings level, in-heading two-oh-five," reported the lead aircraft. I needed to see the jet to ensure he was pointed in the right direction, and Harriers are notoriously difficult to see in the sky. I had everyone looking to the northeast.

"Anyone see 'em?" I asked, straining to see the bird. The sun's bright reflection off the jet's wings caught my eye. "There it is. Fucking right there." I pointed. "Duster Three-Four, cleared hot."

The beautiful jet descended from the heavens. A loud, long *bbuuuurrrpptttt* echoed over the city from the GAU-12's 25mm rounds. The jet ascended back into the sky, disappearing from sight. Dirt and rocks were kicked up about 300 meters away. They were off target.

Knowing that the second aircraft was inbound, I gave a correction: "Duster Three-Five from Wild Eagle Five-Seven: from lead's hits, south one hundred."

The second pilot responded, "Duster Three-Five copies. South one hundred. And Duster is wings level, in-heading two hundred."

"Duster Three-Five is cleared hot," I replied.

This time the aircraft hit their target. The bleachers were showered in 25mm rounds. The men cheered and hollered as the second Harrier vanished into the blue sky to circle the city at about 15,000 feet.

Everyone resumed watching for enemy movement through their loopholes. The incoming fire had stopped, but we weren't sure for how long.

"Wild Eagle Five-Seven from Wild Eagle Two-One, be advised that 3/7 is reporting insurgents running away from your area into their zone," reported Rard. The unit boundaries had been switched again for this operation, providing breathing room between the 3rd Battalion, 7th Marines, to the west. The mission was working as the battalion had planned. Our presence had brought out the insurgents. Now we were hitting them with air power.

With a lull in the fighting, we all double-checked our ammunition again. Most of us had blown through two or three magazines. Anderson only had a couple of 40mm M203 rounds left. Joey B. had fired the LAW, but we had an AT4 rocket remaining. Things were quiet for the next half hour.

Scanning the area, we once again noticed that Iraqis had placed rugs and blankets on their rooftop walls, facing our direction. Not long after noticing this, the Haji Mosque speakers erupted in angry speech. This was no normal call to prayer. Battalion contacted us to let us know that the mosque was calling for insurgents to come out and battle the infidels in a jihad.

Waiting for the inevitable attack, we all just sat back. Another section of Harriers had arrived about twenty minutes after Duster Three-Four flew back to refuel. Anderson had them use their targeting POD to search for insurgents gathering near our location. So far, they hadn't found much of anything. The insurgents were waiting for us to make a mistake.

Specialist Taylor noticed movement again near the press box about an hour later. Staff Sergeant Martinez got behind his sniper rifle, fired a round, ejected the empty shell casing from the bolt-action rifle, and fired again.

"I think I fuckin hit 'em," he said, peering through his scope. "He's not moving anymore."

Our spirits were high. Every one of us was entirely focused on finding and destroying the insurgents. Sporadic jokes and laughter intermingled with military jargon. We fell quiet when the Gunfighter platoon started shooting from their position to our west.

"What the fuck are they shooting at?" asked Martinez. Staff Sergeant Geise was in radio contact with the platoon.

"They've got enemy activity near the stadium again," replied the scout. Captain Rard contacted me. They'd heard about the insurgents and gave me permission to control an LMAV.

Upon hearing that, Anderson handed me the radio handset. Having hit the stadium press box with a gun run a couple hours earlier, I was quick to provide the Harriers with the abbreviated nine-line. By now it was late afternoon. The sun dropped towards the horizon as I talked with the birds. The rest of the team tried to determine what the various shadows in the press box were.

"And Duster is ramping" came the call from the Harriers over the radio's speaker box.

"The Harriers are getting ready. Stand by," I informed the men on the roof. Martinez and Joey B. were still inspecting the press box.

"I think it's a shadow," replied Joey B., looking through his periscope.

"That ain't no fuckin' shadow," replied one of my marines. "That's a man in the prone with a rifle." The afternoon sun was creating strange images.

"Duster Three-Four, spot and wings level," declared the pilots. His wingman was lasing the target. They awaited my approval now. Staring at the target, I gave it.

"Duster Three-Four, cleared hot."

We silently observed the attack. Sergeant Anderson and I discussed the aircraft's heading as the bird announced, "Rifling," meaning release of the LMAV.

Staff Sergeant Geise reported down to Lieutenant Jones, "Twenty seconds to impact."

About ten seconds later, the boom of the LMAV's propulsion

system echoed throughout the city. With the sun in our eyes, we watched the missile make a direct hit into the press box of the stadium, blowing the roof off with a high-order detonation. The clear blue sky was obscured by dark smoke.

Once the smoke cleared, we realized the Gunfighter platoon had been right. The odd-shaped shadows had been a sniper. Hiding among the bleachers and small overhangs of the stadium, he must have been trying to get into a position to shoot. His efforts were wasted; now he lay motionless.

After hitting the stadium with the LMAV, we had no more contact with the insurgents. We sat on that rooftop for another four hours, waiting for another attack that wouldn't come. Our morale was high. We had gone toe to toe with the enemy on our terms, and it had worked once again. But we knew we had also been lucky.

A few days later, Staff Sergeant Martinez and his team came by Full Metal Jacket to show us video from the operation. One of his men had placed a small recorder on the rooftop wall. As we were engaging the enemy near the stadium, the grainy imagery showed two men carrying a dead insurgent down the road away from our position. The grenades thrown by Corporal Cureton and Joey B. had killed one of the fighters who attacked us earlier in the day. We hadn't noticed the movement as we focused on engaging the insurgents around the stadium. This was a mistake that could have cost us dearly. We weren't sure why the scouts in the house hadn't seen or reported this. The fog and confusion of war could lead to dead marines and soldiers.

While we had come out on top during this mission, this remained a war of attrition. We measured success, at least in our area, by how many insurgents we killed. I even had a tally of how many air strikes the boys and I had controlled. While I'm sure the big brains at the 2-28 BCT, 2nd Marine Division, and MEF had a plan to win, those of us walking the streets of this city had nothing but killing insurgents on our minds.

It wouldn't be until after we left Iraq that the US Army and Marine Corps would start setting up more outposts in these dangerous neighborhoods. These small outposts would eventually provide an increase in security for the civilians, leading to the Al Anbar Awakening.

CHAPTER THIRTEEN:
MAROON TRACKSUIT

The Mulab was a festering boil of insurgency. Intelligence reports had indicated that the notorious terrorist al-Zarqawi had made the Mulab his home after fleeing from Fallujah in 2004. Scores upon scores of his henchmen followed, setting up a base from which to wage war against the American infidels and their Iraqi apostates.

Almost every single time we stepped foot or drove a gun truck into this area, we got hit. These terrorists didn't like when we entered their domain. At no time was this clearer than when we penetrated the neighborhood during daylight hours.

About half a week after Operation Blue Falcon, Charlie Company requested ANGLICO support for a daylight patrol. They wanted to do a push through the area with gun trucks. Never one to turn down an operation with machine guns and close air support, we happily accepted the invitation.

The days in early February were all the same. The nights and mornings were cool, while the temperature increased slightly as the sun rose. Iraqi men went about their daily routine of smoking cigarettes and drinking chai as we drove slowly by, simply staring at us with blank expressions. They wore contempt for our presence like bright-red paint. The children, usually full of smiles in other parts of Iraq, frowned at us with disdain. The women ignored us.

We were one of seven gun trucks patrolling through the

neighborhood north of the soccer stadium. Second- and third-floor windows had a clear view down onto our gun trucks, which was dangerous because our vehicles were vulnerable from the top of the turret. Sergeant Anderson was manning the M240G machine gun while Dyer drove. Corporal Cureton sat in the back seat next to Captain Murray. Murray wanted to come along, knowing we'd see some action. This was the culture of the Marine Corps; marines sought the fight.

The patrol moved through a couple streets and stopped while the platoon leader tried unsuccessfully to chat with locals. This was called "engagement," an effort to help the Iraqis so we could gain their support of the coalition forces. I was never involved with such endeavors except to provide support if attacked. This day was no different.

After creeping along one of the backstreets, the patrol stopped. Sergeant Dyer oriented the gun truck into a position to cover a street to the east as half the patrol made a right, moving west.

"All elements, we are stopping here for now while we talk to these older men next to the shops," reported the young blond lieutenant.

"Here we go. This is where we get hit," Captain Murray said, gazing through his side window.

One of the marines replied, "You're right about that."

Rolling around in the gun trucks always made me anxious. Ramadi was a minefield.

We noticed a few soldiers getting out of their vehicles for security.

"Let's get out with these guys, Cureton," I said, double-checking that I had a round in the chamber of my M4.

Outside the vehicle, we focused our attention above us, towards the roofs and windows. Captain Murray had gotten out as well. Wanting to keep an eye down the road, I moved towards the street corner ahead of us. Cureton was directly behind me, with Murray a few feet behind him. I popped my head around the corner barely enough to see down the road. As soon as I did, AK-47 fire ripped into the concrete and plaster of the building just above my head.

I immediately jumped back.

"Fuck, they were right there, two corners down," I said, startled. An insurgent in a white man-dress and flip-flops had fired at me from his hip. It wasn't well-aimed fire, but we were only thirty meters away.

As soon as I had jumped back, Corporal Cureton took my place and put a steady stream of 5.56mm down the road with his SAW. Another short burst hit the corner as Cureton pulled back. A few feet next to me, Dyer edged up in our gun truck so Sergeant Anderson could cover the road. Using multiple quick bursts from the machine gun, Anderson briefly silenced the insurgents. These three marines never ceased to amaze me with their smart, aggressive action. They weren't waiting for me to give orders or directions. They knew precisely what needed to get done and did it.

A sergeant first class and specialist ran over to us.

"What's going on?"

"We're taking fire down that alleyway," I said before drinking from my Camelbak. "We need to move on these motherfuckers."

Somewhere a couple streets over, insurgents were probably trying to get into a better position to engage us. They were maneuvering; we needed to move and move quick.

The two soldiers stood next to the gun truck.

"What do you want to do, sir?" asked the sergeant first class, who towered over me. I asked how long we were going to be here. I was told it could be twenty minutes.

The house across the street had three stories, was located on the corner, and appeared to have good observation. I wanted high ground.

"Let's take that house right there," I said, pointing.

"No problem," replied the Currahee soldier. "Let's fuckin' do it."

After throwing a yellow-smoke grenade to conceal our movement, Cureton, Murray, and I followed the two soldiers across the street and into the house. Anderson and other gunners in their turrets were suppressing the streets.

The large soldier kicked in the door on the first attempt. I was glad he didn't try knocking. The specialist was the number one man into the house as all five of us quickly cleared the rooms. "Violence of action" is the term used to describe the unrestricted use of speed, strength, surprise, and aggression to achieve total dominance over your enemy. In this case, we weren't going to sit and let the insurgents take pop shots at us. We needed to dominate the zone until the patrol leader wanted to depart. Additionally, the house would provide me with better observation in the event I needed to direct air strikes. At the very least, this would allow us a little breathing room. The hard-charging sergeant first class would be our link to the patrol's command element.

The roof wasn't very big, only about ten by twelve feet. The wall was a mere four feet high with decorative grates.

"Stay low. The wall isn't very tall," advised the specialist as we got into place. Everyone knew the dangers of looking over these walls.

We peered through the decorative grates, searching for enemy fighters. Dyer had reported our position to the rest of the patrol to prevent friendly fire. I keyed the handset to my PRC-148 and gave Captain Rard a situation report. He had already requested air. The two soldiers with us were busy talking with the platoon leader on the street via their radios. Not long after getting into position, bursts of AK-47 fire hit one of the metal grates.

It was effective fire. The 7.62mm rounds snapped between Cureton and I, while others slammed into the grate and wall. Everyone hit the floor. We started laughing—a typical combat response. We couldn't wallow in fear; we had to deal with the situation.

Using their usual tactics, the insurgents engaged and then displaced. Everyone got back up but stayed low, looking back down on the streets, alleys, doorways, and windows.

We were unable to get a fix on the enemy positions, so I had the Harriers conduct a show of force. The bird descended to about a thousand feet and rolled into an inverted position before ascending back to his holding altitude of about 15,000 feet. We didn't receive any more fire from the street.

Five minutes later, we were back in the gun trucks, pushing through the neighborhood. The rest of the afternoon was quiet. In Ramadi, combat action was quick and violent.

■ ■ ■

About a week later, we were hunting insurgents once again. This time, it was a larger operation centered around Task Force Dark Eagle.

Operation Camel Spider was designed to draw out the enemy and destroy them with precision rifle fire and air-delivered ordnance. There were three elements. Two platoons inserted into two different houses near Easy Street and Farook. We were part of a twelve-man team located on Easy Street to the north. At around 0100, we inserted into the house. One of the platoons had made their way to their objective on foot as well. The third element was inserted by Task Force Dagger.

Task Force Dagger was the IED clearance team that supported operations in Ramadi. These soldiers' sole job was to find IEDs and disable them. They were on the road every night, clearing streets and highways of the deadly IED. Route clearance was a job performed by sappers and EOD. They rode in specialized mine-resistant ambush protected (MRAP) vehicles with V-shaped frames that deflected mine and IED blasts. In contrast, the typical armored gun truck had an extremely vulnerable flat bottom. An explosion under a gun truck usually ruptured the cab, wounding the occupants or worse. When an IED detonated under a Buffalo or other MRAP vehicle, the blast was typically deflected out and away, thus protecting the soldiers inside, at least in theory.

The men of Task Force Dagger got hit by IEDs every single night as they tried to clear the roads. They drove slowly, searching and scrutinizing. An ANGLICO team went out with them on most of their missions, led by Navy lieutenant John Van Meter, US Naval Academy class of 2002, and Staff Sergeant Travis Williams. They operated solely at night and rode in a vulnerable gun truck alongside the MRAP vehicles.

Van Meter was technically a naval gunfire liaison officer (NGLO) assigned to 1st ANGLICO. However, there would be no naval gunfire shot anywhere near Ramadi. Before departing the United States, Van Meter went to TACP school to become a JTAC. Now he was in Iraq, fighting IEDs and boredom at three miles an hour, waiting to get blown up. It was a grind for him and his men, but they endured.

In the early part of the deployment, before I left for Al Hit, I would ask John how many IEDs Task Force Dagger had hit the night before. The numbers were always staggering. Without the soldiers, marines, and sailors conducting these missions, significantly more Americans and Iraqi civilians would have been killed.

Due to the nature of Task Force Dagger's mission, they were occasionally used to insert soldiers and marines into the various neighborhoods. One of the platoons with 1-506th inserted via Task Force Dagger during Operation Camel Spider. My team and I, along with the scouts and sniper team, simply patrolled in from OP Hotel.

ANGLICO was the main effort. We were to get into position and deliver precision air strikes when the muj came out. As per our usual SOP, we secured the target house and headed up to the roof at around 0100. Staff Sergeant Martinez and his team were located to our south with one of the infantry platoons. Captain Rard was actually out in-sector with the company commander, located in another house. All our positions supported one another with observation and fire.

The day started out very quiet for my team. Surprisingly, our position hadn't been compromised. Lack of everyday activity was often our first clue something had gone wrong; however, on this day in early February 2006, civilians were everywhere. From our loopholes we watched as children journeyed to and from the few schools still open. Men walked the streets. Even women covered in head to toe were out and about.

The other elements weren't as lucky. Over the radio, the two other positions to our south reported they'd been compromised and were getting probed. Iraqi cars and trucks turned around as the word got out that the Americans were in the area. Rard's position had received sporadic fire, and he'd hit a small building with a Hellfire missile via a section of SuberCobras, killing two insurgents. As morning became afternoon, word came that the exfil was starting. We were slightly annoyed; we wanted to stay and fight the insurgents, but the CO for Charlie Company had made the call.

Corporal Cureton and I were behind a loophole providing a view of Easy Street, parts of the soccer stadium, and a section of dilapidated houses across the road. Sergeants Dyer and Anderson surveyed the action from their loophole, as did two snipers from the 1-506, Sergeants Hernandez and Tommarello. Hernandez's loophole overlooked the same area.

As the soldiers and marines started their exfil down the street, Sergeant Hernandez spotted possible insurgents: two men trying to hide behind a building at the entrance to an alley. They kept peering around the corner at the teams getting into Bradley Fighting Vehicles. To make the situation more interesting, one of these Iraqis was talking on a cell phone. This certainly wasn't a discussion about the weather; these men were reporting the activity to someone on the other end of the phone. They were getting excited. What they didn't know was that multiple heavily armed Americans awaited them behind mosquito netting on a rooftop about 150 meters away.

Lying in the prone, I shifted to my right to get a better understanding. A large, dusty date palm blocked my view, but through my ACOG, I could focus through the gaps between the leaves. It all became clear to me the moment I shifted to the right. There they were, two Iraqi men in their midtwenties, one with a maroon tracksuit, the other a teal jacket. Their eyes were wide but determined. Not once had they looked in our direction.

"I've got 'em. There are two MAMs in tracksuits," I announced to Sergeant Hernandez without moving my gaze. "These guys are defiantly muj. They've got a cell phone and keep watching the exfil, reporting the activity to someone on the other end."

No one else had a clear line of sight. I studied their movements. Neither of these men had shaven in days. The MAM in the teal tracksuit was angled towards me, his head to his left, away from our position. His partner had his back to us. They were only visible from the waist up behind a car. The man in the maroon jacket held an RPG in his right hand, the weapon dangling awkwardly.

One hundred percent of my focus was on these two insurgents. The crosshairs of my ACOG in the center of the man's back, I drew in a breath and used my right thumb to switch my M4's selector switch to fire. As I exhaled, I put pressure on the trigger. The loud, sharp clap of my rifle was followed by my loophole filling with the dust kicked up by the shot. The insurgent wearing the maroon tracksuit fell forward, and the other man moved to the left, out of view.

I had engaged insurgents and enemy positions before with my rifle, directed my team's fire, and used artillery, mortars, and air support to eliminate the threat posed by the enemy. As the man through the ACOG fell, I felt as I usually did: nothing. There was no overwhelming, life-altering emotional experience as Hollywood tries to portray. This was warfare, and no matter how the politicians and generals—far removed from the dangerous streets of Ramadi—downplayed the situation, we were fighting for our lives, trying to accomplish our mission and get home to our families.

As soon as I'd squeezed the trigger, Corporal Cureton woke up, startled, and grabbed his M249 SAW. "Sir, I'm up. What's going on?"

Still looking through my ACOG, I replied, "Nothing. We just capped an insurgent across the street."

"You get him, sir?" Anderson asked, sitting up with his weapon in his lap.

"I think so. One of 'em fell forward when I shot," I replied calmly despite my pounding heart.

"Shit. You might have got both of those fuckers, Captain Angell," announced Sergeant Hernandez. "Those guys were muj for sure."

I sat up on my knees and moved over so Cureton could get behind the loophole. After checking to make sure my weapon was safe, I grabbed a water bottle and took a drink. Fifteen minutes later, we were ordered to prepare for our departure. The time was around 1500. We'd been in position for just over twelve hours. After grabbing our gear, we headed downstairs to await the vehicles.

All twelve of us lingered by the front door. Sporadic fire rang out down the street as the large six-wheeled vehicle located between two BFVs pulled up in front of the house. Sergeant Tommarello threw a yellow-smoke grenade into the street.

"Go, go, go, go," he ordered the men rushing out of the house. The four scouts ran first, followed by the sniper team. I made sure Anderson, Cureton, and Dyer went before me; I was one of the last men out of the house. When I glanced back, a young kid waved. It surprised me.

Into the street, my combat load weighed heavily on my back as I ran through the yellow smoke. The sun was bright and warm. The *clack-clack-clack* of AK-47 fire ripped through the street. I tried to ignore it as I grabbed Sergeant Dyer's hand, climbing into the back of the truck. Everyone lay down in the bed of the vehicle as we sped off towards Camp Corregidor.

CHAPTER FOURTEEN:
THE LAST DAY OF OPERATIONS

By the end of February 2006, our time in Ramadi and in this country was ending. I had previously forced that knowledge to the back of my mind in order to survive and operate with a clear head. Thinking about leaving Iraq was a luxury. The reality of going home was one I wasn't certain I'd ever see. None of us really talked about it, but being a marine in combat, especially in Ramadi, meant there was no guarantee we were going home alive. But there we were, discussing our last day of conducting combat operations.

We were all silently ecstatic and dealing with it in our own ways. No one wanted to jinx matters by talking about going home—a.k.a. retrograde, going in an alternate or opposite direction, a cold and callous word to describe our return to the US.

The 1-506th was set to conduct a large operation in the rural Sufia district to the northeast of Ramadi, on the south side of the Euphrates River. ANGLICO was needed to both support Task Force Dark Eagle and accompany a mounted patrol with Charlie Company and some Iraqi special forces. Rard let me choose.

Since I'd gotten to Camp Corregidor back in early January, the team and I had been working almost exclusively with the snipers and scouts as part of the task force. These missions were eminently preferable to rolling around in gun trucks and getting hit with IEDs. However, the task force operations could be draining and demanding.

Joker Four was an outstanding team, and I gravitated towards them. These ops had been quite successful, with minimal casualties, but they weren't easy on us. I knew it and they knew it. So when given the choice for our last operation, I volunteered for the mounted patrol. Captain Murray and his team would support Task Force Dark Eagle. However, my team and I would be required to also support a "soft knock" raid on a house in the Mulab later that evening with a platoon from Bravo Company.

I gathered the team to give them the warning order.

"It's a mounted op," I said. "Since we haven't used the gun truck in a while, we will need to ensure it's fully prepped."

The men looked relieved. Sergeant Dyer, usually as stoic as an oak tree, smirked. They were all nodding as I went into the details.

"You and I will attend the operations order tomorrow at Charlie Company's CP," I said, pointing at Anderson. "I'll let you know what time when I find out." I had one last comment they needed to know: "Also, we have to do another mission later that night."

Anderson seemed apprehensive about the raid. "What's the deal with that?"

"It's a quick soft-knock raid in the Mulab with a platoon from Bravo," I said, tucking my little notebook back in my pocket. "We will be doing a left seat/right seat for the turnover with the Air Force TACPs and their OIC, some major, so I have to go, and we need a turret gunner. Any volunteers?"

"I'll go, sir," replied Cureton with a matter-of-fact expression. He didn't hesitate. While it wasn't surprising, it caught me off guard. I smiled.

"All right, man. Sounds good."

Later that night, I went to the top of Full Metal Jacket to make a phone call with the detachment's satphone. Like everything else in the country, the staircase to the roof was dirty, half-finished, and dangerous. The rebar poking out at varying angles gave the structure a medieval aspect.

I sat on the roof with the thick, heavy phone in my hand. I wanted to hear my wife's voice. We hadn't talked much due to my operational schedule. If we had shared regular calls, any interruption in regularity would have made her anxious, so I kept the phone calls to an absolute minimum. Now I punched in her number and waited for the line to connect—no answer. I left a brief message, told her I loved her, and hung up. I didn't want to tell her I'd be home soon, although she knew the deployment schedule.

I called my parents instead. My father wasn't home, so I talked with my mother. About two minutes into our conversation, I heard the distant *thump-thump-thump* of mortars. I paused, unsure if the rounds were outgoing or incoming. About thirty seconds later, I realized these were incoming. They impacted about 200 meters away: *kurump-kurump-kurump*. I tried to conceal the sound with my hand over the phone, but it didn't work.

"What was that?" she asked.

"I've gotta go," I replied and hung up. I cursed myself for making that call.

■ ■ ■

A few days later, on our last official day of operations, we found ourselves sitting in our gun truck, driving through the lush green landscape to the east of Ramadi. We were in a patrol with eight other vehicles from Bravo Company and a few trucks of Iraqi SF. The sun had just risen; the air was cool but getting warmer. We would push into an area, dismount, and patrol. The soldiers would clear a few houses, looking for insurgent activity, and then we would mount back up and do it again as we moved through the zone.

Captain Murray and his team, along with some snipers and scouts from the 1-506th, were in a house in the area to interdict any fighters trying to harass our movement. So far it had been quiet except for a few bursts of gunfire. Captain Rard was in the 1-506th

TOC, working with aircraft support.

As we patrolled, I marveled at the beauty that hid the reality of this land. Date palms hung over the green pastures and wheat fields. Kids were out playing soccer while farmers tended their crops. Women glanced at us from windows before retreating out of sight.

About two hours into the mission, we got a call over the radio that changed our momentum. Some of the Iraqi SF soldiers had received actionable intelligence, so we hurried towards the target house. Anderson, Cureton, and Dyer were quiet and focused. The expressions on their faces, their mannerisms, reminded me of my first patrol with Gunnery Sergeant German and his team almost seven months ago. My marines now looked like his team did—tired, exhausted, yet determined.

Over the radio, the Bravo Company CO briefed us on the raid as we traversed the narrow roads. Americans were to secure the perimeter while the Iraqi special forces raided the house. Everyone was to stay in their vehicles.

With the rest of the gun trucks, we encircled the house in preparation. Dyer oriented the gun truck north on a north–south running road. Another gun truck sat to our left and slightly in front of our position, facing the same direction. I radioed Captain Rard our location. He tasked a section of F-18s to conduct ISR around our position; they found nothing.

Our friend boredom returned as we waited. We had been on the objective for about twenty minutes when I had to get out of the gun truck.

"I'm getting out to take piss," I told the team. "I'll be right back."

"Roger that. Be careful. The muj know we're here now," replied Anderson from the turret. He was right. Insurgents usually attacked within fifteen minutes of us arriving on any objective. You could almost set your watch to it. By our calculations, they were already late, but I had to piss regardless.

I got out and scurried to the back of the gun truck, using the vehicle as cover. The hair on the back of my neck stood on end as I relieved myself. None of us wanted to get killed days before we left. Standing behind the gun truck, I noticed myself swaying and moving around out of fear of being shot. An automatic response had kicked in. This frustrated me. While I was focusing internally, I wasn't focusing externally. I wasn't giving the situation the attention it deserved. This is how you get killed.

Before climbing into the gun truck, I spotted an embedded journalist strolling around and taking pictures. I yelled over to the oblivious man.

"Dude, you might not want to walk around here," I said, shaking my head. "We are bound to get hit soon, so try and get some cover."

He told me he was okay but thanked me for my concern. I got back in the gun truck, annoyed that this reporter wasn't taking the risk to his life seriously.

Cureton asked what the reporter said. He laughed when I told him.

"Well, it's his ass if he gets shot," he said, smiling. We all laughed at the craziness. The reporter continued taking pictures in the middle of the road. As expected, the marines made various comments.

"Does this guy know where he's at?" Anderson asked. "He's gonna get killed."

What upset us was the knowledge that if he got hit, one of us or one of the soldiers from the 1-506th would have to risk his life to help the reporter. This was something civilians couldn't understand. If they wanted to risk their lives trying to get a Pulitzer Prize photo, we would have to risk our lives.

The crack of the rifle interrupted our conversation. The reporter got hit, spun about at the impact, and dropped to the ground next to the gun truck to our left, writhing in pain and screaming that he'd been shot. He was between the target house and the vehicle; this meant the sniper was either to our front or behind us.

"Here we go. Anyone see anything?" asked Dyer in the driver seat.

I yelled up to Anderson, "You see anything?"

"Negative, but I think the sniper is in front of us," he replied. We'd had a front-row seat to the attack but couldn't identify the sniper's position before he shot again, hitting the reporter in the leg. I immediately requested air support from Captain Rard, who pushed the F-18s to me. A soldier jumped out of the adjacent gun truck and started to provide first aid, despite the risk to his life. The sniper fired again, this time hitting the soldier.

"Shit. Stay low, Anderson. Don't give him a target," I yelled up to the turret. Needing concealment, one of the soldiers threw a yellow-smoke grenade. The sniper fired again. We heard the screams from the reporter and the soldier. They needed cover.

"Fuckin' move up, Dyer. Block the road," I ordered.

The gun truck's engine whined as Dyer slammed the gas pedal down. He moved us about thirty meters down the road, blocking the casualties from the sniper's line of sight. All of us strained to find the shooter. There were a couple of houses mixed in with thick vegetation; he could be anywhere. All of us were on edge. The radio erupted with reports of the attack. None of the other gun trucks could identify the sniper's location either.

I had a pair of binoculars up to my face as I peered through the windshield. We scanned the area but found nothing. This wasn't some muj spraying pop shots. This man was calculated and disciplined.

Out of what seemed like nowhere, a large orange dump truck sped around the corner about 300 meters to our front. The driver accelerated towards us, the roar from the engine increasing. In milliseconds, we had to make a decision—Anderson had to make a decision.

"Dump truck! He's not slowing," I yelled up to Anderson.

"Oh shit," said Dyer to himself.

Up in the turret, Anderson leaned into the M240G and fired a barrage of 7.62mm into the windshield. The glass exploded as rounds penetrated the cab, spraying shards in all directions. The driver slammed on the brakes, and Anderson sent another burst into the vehicle. This time the dump truck stopped, 100 meters from our position. The man in the passenger side jumped out and ran off, disappearing behind a home. The driver slumped over the steering wheel.

My pulse was racing. I looked to find my hands shaking. Embarrassed, I shook them until they stopped.

"Good job, Anderson," I yelled, unable to take my eyes off the dump truck.

We all cursed under our breath. We couldn't know the driver's intention, but SVBIEDs via orange dump trucks were notorious killers in this city. Insurgents had used them during multiple complex attacks. Our gun truck was the only thing between the SVBIED and the perimeter, so there had been no time for escalation of force. Anderson had to make a life-or-death decision in a matter of seconds, and he made the right one. We couldn't simply wave the driver down, and we sure as hell were not going to abandon our position. Marines don't retreat.

The F-18s overhead searched for more threats and spotted none.

"We're Oscar Mike back towards Ramadi to drop off the wounded at the aid station," the Bravo Company CO ordered over the radio. "Start moving."

Dyer hit the gas and turned the vehicle around as Anderson traversed the turret to maintain cover down the road. We sped off towards Route Michigan to the south, cursing the reporter's actions and the elusive insurgent.

A few days later, someone sent us a link of an insurgent video. The enemy had filmed the attack. The grainy video showed the scene from the insurgents' perspective. The reporter was taking pictures as propaganda music played. The video showed him and the soldier getting shot while screams of "Allahu Akbar" sounded in the background. Fearing they'd been compromised, the insurgents cut the video off when our gun truck moved into a blocking position. The boys and I were furious. The enemy had been directly to our front, but we hadn't seen them.

From the nature of the video, intelligence believed that the shooter was Juba, a notorious sniper who had killed dozens of Americans and filmed the attacks since the previous summer. He was a cult hero in the shadowy world of insurgents and terrorists.

After returning to the US, I read the reporter's article about the incident. It was the usual journalistic fluff but well written. The author wrote one thing that really irritated me. He claimed that he was a neutral figure in this war. He wasn't on our side nor the insurgents'. This was of course nonsense. If he were truly neutral, he wouldn't have ridden with our patrol, enjoying the security the soldiers provided. Furthermore, if he'd been caught by the insurgents, they would have cut his head off with no questions asked. Jihadist fighters wouldn't have risked their lives to provide him aid. An American soldier was almost killed helping this man.

After dropping off the casualties, we made a quick stop at the fuel farm to top off the gun trucks. No one said much. Each of us dealt with the situation in our own way, as we always had. I couldn't help thinking about how nervous I had been as I stood next to the gun truck before the attack. My body or mind must have sensed something wasn't right. What if that had been me, or worse, what if it was Anderson or Dyer who got hit, in the turret, so close to going home? No one ever really believes they will get hit, but every time we saw our brothers fall, we couldn't help but think, *What if?*

After the vehicles had refueled, we made our way back into the Sufia district. There were reports of a firefight between insurgents on the north side of the river and one of Charlie Company's platoons on the south side. The CO wanted to get my team into position in the event air support was required. As we headed through the back roads, we listened to the radio traffic. RPGs and machine-gun fire had been exchanged near the banks of this ancient river. I informed Captain Rard that we were en route. In response, he sent a section of F-18s to support.

When we rolled up to the platoon's position, their gun trucks were spread out on Route Nova, a narrow road that paralleled the Euphrates. Some of the soldiers were out of their vehicles, taking up positions overlooking the river. I needed to get to the closest friendly unit that was engaged, so I contacted the CO to ask where that was.

A platoon leader and some soldiers had cleared a house on the banks of the river. Dyer stopped the gun truck in the hasty perimeter.

"Let's go, Cureton," I said, grabbing my assault pack and weapon. Anderson, manning the M240G, stayed in the vehicle with Dyer.

Pushing the armored door open, I got the attention of a soldier standing near another gun truck.

"Where's your platoon commander?" I asked.

"He's in the house over there," the soldier replied with a smile. "You gonna drop some bombs, sir?"

"We're going to try," I said, shuffling towards the house. Cureton was directly behind me with his SAW at the ready.

As we ran towards the large home, Cureton gestured to the smoke across the river. Between the date palms swaying in the warm breeze, an old white Chevy Suburban sat smoking. Black clouds rose above the vehicle and drifted west.

Sporadic fire from both sides of the river reverberated off the walls of the house, momentarily confusing me. The earpiece in my right ear squawked with activity; Captain Rard and the F-18 pilots discussed setting up an attack on the vehicle but were waiting until I was in position to control the strike. My heart rate increased. As Cureton and I ran up those steps, I smiled at the situation. I strangely loved combat but hated it at the same time; the duality and contradiction were both confusing and real.

My inner dialogue corrected me. Killing your fellow man wasn't supposed to be exciting, but I didn't care about the morality of it at this point. These insurgents had actively been trying to kill my fellow marines and soldiers. We'd seen torture rooms where insurgents murdered civilians. We'd seen Americans maimed and killed. When we managed to stop our enemies with overwhelming firepower, I liked it. It was a drug that could never be purchased on the streets of America.

Cureton and I climbed to the patio roof of the house. Oddly, it was void of furnishings. The occupants had long since left, abandoning it as the insurgency raged. The walls, ceilings, and floors were all white, causing a mental distortion. The house looked bigger and more formal than was typical.

On the roof, six soldiers stared across the water. The platoon leader, a large Hispanic lieutenant, gave me a quick situation report. His platoon had been pushing through the area when they started taking fire from the other side of the river. Insurgents had rolled up in the Chevy Suburban before jumping out and engaging the soldiers. Some of the enemy fighters were now pinned down behind the vehicle.

I contacted Captain Rard on my PRC-148 radio and let him know I was in position, able to observe the target. The low rumble of the F-18s overhead raised my blood pressure even more. Taking a knee next to the platoon commander, I had him contact his CO and request permission to hit the target. It was quickly approved.

Flipping through my CAS notepad, I double-checked that the information Rard had sent was correct. His data wasn't a concern— as a Harrier pilot, Rard knew his business when it came to close air support—but I wanted to make sure I was fully aware of the details. Behind me, the soldiers gleefully told each other, "ANGLICO is gonna bring in some gun runs."

The pilots reported they were inbound towards the target.

I keyed the radio: "Continue."

The birds would be coming in low. Everyone watched for the F-18 as it dropped altitude. Sporadic fire from the far side of the river continued. The soldiers returned fire, trying to keep the insurgents pinned down. I took off my sunglasses and strained to see the aircraft.

"In-heading two-eight-zero," reported the pilot.

Cureton picked up the bird's position. "There he is. There he is." He motioned towards the northeast. Seeing that the aircraft was pointed towards the target, I gave the required call.

"Cleared hot for guns."

The massive F-18 became bigger and bigger, appearing like an angel of death. The pilot let loose a long burst of 20mm cannon fire, belching flames and smoke. By now the F-18 was pointed back towards the sky, but it kept descending. Vapors from condensation engulfed the bottom of the aircraft as it appeared to struggle to gain altitude. Everyone flinched from the deafening shriek of the engines.

"Pull up, pull up, pull up," I screamed into my radio, fearing the pilot was fixated on the target. The noise was so loud and piercing that I worried my request had gone unheard. The aircraft's engines finally outmuscled the downward force, and the bird pulled back towards the blue sky from whence it came.

I was nauseous at the thought of the aircraft slamming into the earth in front of us. I shook off the disorienting noise and looked back towards the northeast, searching for the other F-18.

"Dash two is in-heading two-eight-two," came the report from the pilot. This time I saw the second bird before Cureton.

I keyed my radio: "Dash two, cleared hot."

The sun was high in the sky as I struggled against the glare. All of us on that roof watched as the second F-18 came down at a noticeably higher altitude than its predecessor and delivered a deadly burst. The rounds impacted along the length of the Chevy Suburban, pelting it and the pinned-down insurgents with the hate and discontent of American firepower. The target erupted in more black smoke.

The small-arms fire had ceased from across the river. I glared at the out-of-place Suburban as it sat in the field behind date palms, an environment that appeared oblivious to the war around it. Pockmarked and in flames, the Suburban seemed more like it belonged in Ramadi than before. The insurgents were either dead or had escaped. No one was going to risk a patrol to conduct a battle damage assessment (BDA). The 1-506th estimated that half a dozen insurgents had been killed, but no one knew for sure.

For about fifteen minutes, we stayed in our position, watching. Cureton and I joked with the soldiers for a bit, the kind of dark and twisted quips only men in such situations can make. As the river flowed south on this sunny day, boredom returned, but we were soon ordered to load back up and continue the push.

Making my way to our gun truck, I gazed around with disdain and contempt for this whole city and its rural suburbs. I was tired and jaded. I saw changes in myself that I didn't like but felt helpless to correct.

Under my breath, I muttered, "Fuck off."

The remainder of the day was relatively uneventful. We patrolled through the area, dismounting, searching a few homes, getting back into the vehicles, and doing it again. We returned to Camp Corregidor around 1600.

Back at Full Metal Jacket, the various teams started returning. Captain Murray and his boys had a fairly quiet mission. They had exchanged fire with insurgents, but their position was otherwise calm. This amazed me; we had been seriously engaged almost every time we went out with Joker Four and the scouts. I was still on edge, though. Cureton and I had to go on the soft-knock with a platoon from the 1-506th and the new Air Force OIC.

At around 1900, after the sun had set, Cureton and I grabbed our gear and went to the 1-506th command post to link up with the Air Force major, the driver, and the platoon. As usual, we shook hands with the other marines before we left. This was standard, but we noticed throughout the deployment that when we told each other good luck and shook hands, the handshakes lasted a bit longer. We would look each other in the eyes and make a smart-ass comment, but we never knew if this was the last time we would see each other alive.

"Don't fuck it up, dude," we'd say. In the backs of our minds, we were really saying, "Good luck, brother. Semper fidelis."

At the CP, the Air Force major introduced himself. Standing at about five feet, ten inches, with dark hair and a thin mustache, he had an edge of arrogance to him. He'd previously been a pilot with the US Army's elite 160th Special Operations Aviation Regiment known as the Nightstalkers. For whatever reason, he transitioned to the Air National Guard as a member of one of their Tactical Air Control Party

(TACP) units and had been ordered to Iraq. At the time, I simply didn't want to know much more about him. He seemed in over his head, but I'm sure I did seven months ago as well.

We discussed the mission, and I told him how we conducted these operations. He didn't seem to like that we had a gun truck. He felt that it was the Army's responsibility to provide protection for them. This was the exact opposite of how the Marine Corps viewed such things. In my view, the more machine guns, the better.

The patrol leader, a young, stocky, blond first lieutenant from Bravo Company, approached me to discuss the raid. He wore a big smile that hid the weight of his responsibility. We laughed at a few things, briefly talked about the earlier mission, and got down to business. A small house with a suspected insurgent in the Mulab was our target. We wouldn't be kicking in any doors today. We were to take gun trucks to the Mulab, dismount, and hit the house.

Reading from a tan notebook, the young officer provided a basic order of march: "Captain Angell, your vehicle will be third, just behind mine."

Flipping the page, he continued, "Once we get to our dismount position, we will head west towards the house." He paused and held up a picture of the target, showing it to the platoon and the assorted enablers such as myself and the K-9 team: "This is who we are after."

I chuckled; the insurgent resembled every other fighter I'd seen in this city: dark-olive complexion, facial hair with about a week's worth of growth, and wearing an Adidas tracksuit that made him look more like a wannabe mafia gangster from New Jersey than an urban guerrilla. We all listened intently as the lieutenant discussed the raid. I sucked on the water tube from my Camelbak, trying to quench my thirst. Cureton stood next to me. I tried to suppress the thought that this was our last mission, but it was a losing battle.

Before long, the mission brief was over. The Air Force major asked me a few questions about the briefing as we headed to the gun truck. I answered his query before jumping into the back left seat. Cureton was up in the turret behind the machine gun. The major sat in the vehicle commander's seat, and Airman Williams sat behind the wheel. It felt like I was going through the motions, apathetic and void of the aggression the mission deserved. I'd felt this way before, towards the end of my first deployment when we were closing in on Baghdad. I told myself to focus on the task. American lives depended on it.

As the vehicles moved out of Camp Corregidor's main gate, I took a deep breath and forced myself into the present, ignoring the distractions bubbling up in my mind.

Focus, Angell, I said to myself.

After exiting the small combat outpost, we drove west on Route Michigan before turning south into the Mulab. I set my monocular NVGs down over my right eye as darkness engulfed us. The gun truck squeaked and bounced past potholes and blast craters. Cureton moved the turret around to maintain his sector of fire along the narrow roads, sitting low so as not to give a motivated insurgent a target.

Before long, the gun trucks stopped. There were no civilians on the road. The major and I dismounted, and the soldiers formed up on the other side of the road. Nodding at the platoon commander, I brought my M4 up, scanning the street for possible threats as we moved briskly towards the target house. All the buildings looked the same. We had to count the courtyard doors to ensure we had the right place.

We simply opened the large gate to the courtyard and walked in. There were no flash-bangs or grenades, no rush of adrenaline. The soldiers cleared the house quickly and efficiently with an edge of softness. The women and children were moved to a bedroom with blankets and mats. The only man there was old and feeble; he wasn't our target. As the interpreter and platoon commander talked with the Iraqi, I moved outside into the courtyard to maintain communications with Cureton over our team radio. Our target wasn't there. After about twenty minutes, we prepared to leave.

The platoon shuffled to the gun trucks that had set up a blocking position down the road to the east. I noticed shadows in the windows above us. They could have been insurgents or curious civilians, but with no PID, we merely kept our weapons trained on the threat, passing the information down the column with hand-and-arm signals. Through my NVGs, I watched the infrared laser pointers from our PEQ-4s dance around.

When we neared the gun trucks, Cureton jokingly asked what had taken so long. The comment held a hint of concern. He didn't like sitting on the street in the Mulab. The longer we stayed on an objective, the more the risk of an attack increased. Darkness typically gave us an advantage, but on this day, the city's power was still on. This negated our NVGs and made us nervous.

Back in the gun truck, I exhaled in relief, drank some water, and stared through the small, armored glass window at the alleyways and small buildings, shaking my head at this city. The major was talking with Airman Williams as we started back towards Camp Corregidor. My neck and back ached from the weight of my gear and helmet, and I was thirsty and tired—tired of this whole deployment, ready to go home. The annoying squeaks and jolts of the gun truck returned as we drove through the streets.

A huge explosion erupted from underneath the lieutenant's vehicle twenty-five meters in front of us. The detonation caused a split second of unconsciousness as the shock wave slammed into our chests. No one in our vehicle said a word for about two seconds.

"God damn it," I said to myself while squinting through my armored glass window, waiting for insurgent gunfire. Leaning forward, I told the major to contact the TOC at Camp Corregidor to request air support before I opened the door to get out. The quiet street betrayed the reality of what had happened. I ran towards the lieutenant's vehicle, resigned to another IED going off. With each step, I expected a flash and then darkness. Fear engulfed my being, but my training and dedication forced me to move forward.

With my right hand, I opened the back left door, surprised when it opened easily. Inside the vehicle was something I still see. A soldier was screaming in agony, his face white and contorted. I looked down at his left leg, and it was gone to just above the knee. There was a mangled hole in the vehicle floorboard where a large piece of shrapnel had burst through and torn his leg off. I saw the concrete below.

All I could muster was "Fuck."

Then "You're gonna be okay, buddy. We're gonna get you taken care of," I told the soldier, providing meaningless comfort. I grabbed my tourniquet from my gear and slipped it over what remained of his leg. He cried out, not acknowledging my comment or actions. He couldn't hear me; his ears had ruptured from the overpressure of the explosion.

The other three soldiers were in obvious pain as well, but I was unsure of their condition, still focused on this young man's wound. The exposed flesh and bone were covered in dirt and bits of concrete, and a dark layer of soot from the blast covered the soldier's skin. Bright-red blood had spattered the inside of the vehicle; the smell of iron and cordite filled my nostrils.

By now, other soldiers had arrived to help. A medic pushed me aside to get to the wounded. I stepped back so he could treat the soldier with his experienced hands, then lowered to one knee behind the medic, facing away from the vehicle to provide security. A familiar feeling rushed over me. I felt hollow and empty.

The lead gun truck backed up towards the disabled vehicle. It would have to be towed back to base. The soldiers were quick at recovery, their experience gained through countless IED attacks. Standing, I noticed that I was dizzy but shook it off. I ran back to my gun truck, thankful I had not fallen.

Before getting in, I looked up at Cureton. Always the consummate professional, he was searching the area for threats. I slammed the armored door shut behind me. No one said a word for what felt like minutes.

"How are they, sir?" Cureton called down from the turret.

Staring off through the window, I replied, "He lost his leg—fuckin' cut right off."

"Fuck" was his reply. It was always the same reply.

The disabled gun truck limped to base on the slow ride back to Camp Corregidor. Radio communications were short. Once we pulled into camp, our gun truck drove to Full Metal Jacket. I helped Cureton take the M240G machine gun off the turret mount and wipe it down. The major and Airman Williams, the former marine, had been forced to face the reality of their deployment.

Neither Cureton nor I said much of anything. We'd seen and experienced these things before, but it was different this time. We were so close to going home. That could have been us—mangled and bleeding, crying out in pain and fear. I walked with my weapon and assault pack to the stairs inside the entrance to Full Metal Jacket. Not wanting to talk with the other marines, I sat on the concrete stairs and moved my feet through the powdery dirt. My helmet and NVGs felt heavy, so I removed them, placing the gear next to my weapon.

Cureton briefly disappeared into the team room before reappearing with a pack of cigarettes. He handed me one, lit his, and gave me the lighter. I leaned back on the stairs and closed my eyes, inhaling the smooth tobacco to calm down.

When Cureton had finished his smoke, he left me alone in the dark, cool, musty air of Full Metal Jacket. Every time I breathed in, I smelled this city. The pungent odor of burning trash and filth singed my nose. Tears welled up and rolled down my cheeks. I thought of that young soldier's face as he screamed in pain. He didn't want to look at his leg because he knew it was gone.

I felt guilty that I was unharmed. The lead vehicle had rolled past the IED. The lieutenant's gun truck could have driven past the IED with a minor alteration to their course. Our vehicle could have been the one hit. We were lucky, they were not, and I felt guilty about it.

Fearing one of the marines would see me with tears, I quickly wiped my face, took a deep breath, and stood up. It was 2236. Grabbing my gear and weapon, I went into my team's room and went to sleep, thinking of the young soldier whose life had changed forever.

Our last day of operations during this deployment had ended, and I wanted to get as far away from it as I could, physically and mentally.

But to this day, Ramadi remains with me.

■ ■ ■

A few days later, the 1st ANGLICO detachment departed Camp Corregidor for Camp Ramadi to link up with the rest of Major Grice's platoon and start our journey back to the United States. At around 1900 on March 2, 2006, we loaded into gun trucks packed with our gear and equipment and rolled out of Camp Corregidor in the darkness. We were anxious to leave this desolate and violent part of Iraq.

Staff Sergeant Martinez and his team, the scouts, and various members of the command element from the 1-506th, to include the CO, came to say goodbye. They shook our hands and teased us about being crayon-eating marines. We laughed at the lighthearted ribbing. After getting back in the gun trucks, we drove west down Route Michigan.

Just past OP Hotel, a large IED exploded behind our vehicle and in front of Captain Murray's gun truck.

It was later estimated that the IED consisted of two 155mm artillery shells. The explosion hit both gun trucks and penetrated Captain Murray's vehicle, wounding him. One of the escort vehicles helped us get the captain to the battalion aid station at Camp Corregidor before he was evacuated to Germany and eventually the United States. The rest of us would have to wait to leave eastern Ramadi the next evening.

After about ten days of traveling, we eventually landed at March Air Force Base in California on March 13, 2006, having flown through Kuwait, Germany, and the state of Maine. We were home after seven months in Iraq.

EPILOGUE

NGLICO wasn't messing around when we arrived at March Air Force Base that late morning on March 13. We turned in our serialized gear, such as weapons and optics. The headquarters platoon had the process down pat, making things easier for us when we arrived. They checked our equipment and placed it in small Conex boxes destined for Camp Pendleton as everyone laughed and joked, waiting to get on the buses. Some of the headquarters marines secretly brought a few beers and passed them out.

The hour-and-a-half ride felt endless. There is nothing like returning home after a long deployment. We were nervous. When the buses pulled into the parking lot at the 1st ANGLICO headquarters building and opened the doors, none of us rushed out. Truth be told, no one wanted to look like a fool running off the bus and searching for his wife. But hidden by sunglasses, my eyes darted around, seeking Joni.

Pushing through a sea of disoriented, desert-camouflage-wearing marines, I spotted her, and everyone else vanished. As beautiful as I remember, she walked up to me in her light-colored sundress and wrapped her arms around my neck while she stood on her tiptoes. We embraced for what seemed like five minutes. As soon as I found my bags, we headed north towards Newport Beach.

On the other side of the planet, about 7,000 miles away, the soldiers of the 1-506th were mourning the loss of two brothers. I wouldn't realize this until I opened an email written by Staff Sergeant Martinez a few days later.

On March 12, in Ramadi, soldiers conducting a Task Force Dark Eagle mission were exfiltrating their target house after a long day. The streets were dark and quiet. As the men were leaving the house, assembling for the patrol back to Camp Corregidor, they were ambushed. Almost instantly, Joey B., one of the snipers we worked with, was hit in the chest with five rounds from an enemy machine gun. His front SAPI (small arms protective insert) plate and magazines saved his life. Automatic-weapons fire and RPGs hit the men. Staff Sergeant Marco Silva, one of the snipers from the 1-506th, was killed. The QRF responding to the attack was hit by an IED, killing the lead driver, Sergeant Corey Dan. The ambush was chaotic and devastating, considered a mass casualty incident with multiple wounded and two killed.

These operations, which had originally started in December 2005, had dealt a significant blow to the insurgents in Ramadi, but they learned quickly. The enemy fighters realized that attacking the soldiers and marines when they had gone firm in a building wasn't working; after the soldiers were compromised on this mission, the insurgents decided to wait and hit the men at their most vulnerable, during exfil. To guard against this tactic, we had used fixed-wing aircraft to scan the area around our location prior to exfiltration. During this mission, however, the team had departed as the supporting aircraft was refueling. This gap in air support provided an opportunity for the insurgents to get in close to the soldiers to devastating effects.

When I heard about the deaths and the attack on the soldiers, I was home in California, with my wife. I had to read the email a couple times. In the back of my mind, though, I was surprised it had taken this long. These missions were dangerous. It had only been a matter of time. One of the first lessons I learned in Ramadi was that the enemy always gets a vote.

After arriving home, I had five short months before returning with 1st ANGLICO for another tour in Iraq. Joni and I spent as much time together as we could. In July of 2006, I found out that I was going to be a father. A month later, I headed back to Iraq as the OIC for the I MEF personal security detail (PSD), an ANGLICO task. Sergeant Anderson and Corporal Cureton, along with Lance

Corporal Cain, would accompany me; Sergeant Dyer decided to leave the Marine Corps to return to Texas with his wife.

In March of 2007, I came home from Iraq for good. A year later, I left the Marine Corps after a total of ten years of service and dedication. The decision to resign my commission and become a civilian wasn't easy. However, I had decided that I was done leaving my wife and didn't want to say goodbye to my daughter, Scarlett.

I felt that nothing would compare to my time in Ramadi and Hit. The excitement, the fear, the brotherhood, and the frustration and sense of accomplishment simply couldn't be replicated. I hated Ramadi but oddly missed it. I missed the sound of gunfire as it reverberated off buildings and down alleys. I missed the adrenaline of going on patrol and bringing in Cobra gunships and lightning-fast fixed-wing jets. That period of my life haunts me to this day. For a very brief moment in my existence, I was a warrior fighting for and with fellow marines and soldiers.

Over the years, I have been asked if I would do it all over again, knowing what I know now. Without hesitation, the answer to this question is always yes. I would do it all over again. I would be more than happy *Running Towards Gunfire* in the city of Ramadi next to the men on my ANGLICO team.

GUIDE TO TERMS & ABBREVIATIONS

AAV	Amphibious Assault Vehicle
ACOG	Advanced Combat Optical Gunsight
ANGLICO	Air Naval Gunfire Liaison Company
AO	Area of Operations
ASOS	Air Support Operations Squadron
AT4	84mm Antitank Rocket
BCT	Brigade Combat Team
Bingo	Code for when an aircraft is running low on fuel
BFV	Bradley Fighting Vehicle
CAG	Civil Affairs Group
CAS	Close Air Support
CO	Commanding Officer
COLT	Combat Observation Lasing Team
ConOps	Concept of Operation
CONUS	Continental United States
COP	Combat Outpost
CP	Command Post
CQB	Close Quarters Combat
CFR	Crash Fire Rescue
DASC	Direct Air Support Center
Defilade	A unit or position is "in defilade" if it uses natural or artificial obstacles to shield or conceal.
EKIA	Enemy Killed in Action
EOD	Explosive Ordnance Disposal

ESB	Engineer Support Battalion
FAC	Forward Air Controller
FCT	Firepower Control Team
FLIR	Forward-Looking Infrared
FMF	Fleet Marine Force
FOB	Forward Operating Base
FO	Forward Observer
FSSG	Force Service Support Group
FST	Fire Support Team
GPS	Global Positioning Satellite
GRG	Gridded Reference Graphic
HVT	High-Value Target
I MEF	1st Marine Expeditionary Force
IA	Iraqi Army
IDF	Indirect Fire
IED	Improvised Explosive Device
ISR	Intelligence Surveillance Reconnaissance
IZLID	Infrared Zoom Laser Illuminator Designator
JAG	Judge Advocate General
JDAM	Joint Directed Air Munition
JTAC	Joint Terminal Attack Controller
KIA	Killed in Action
LAW	Light Antitank Weapon
LGB	Laser-Guided Bomb
LMAV	Laser-Guided Maverick Missile
LRRP	Long Range Reconnaissance Patrol

LTC	Lieutenant Colonel (US Army)
LtCol	Lieutenant Colonel (USMC)
LZ	Landing Zone
M2	Fifty-Caliber Heavy Machine Gun
M203	40mm Grenade Launcher attached to M16/M4
M240G	Medium Machine Gun; 7.62mm
MAM	Military-Aged Male
MEU	Marine Expeditionary Unit
MGRS	Military Grid Reference System
Mk-19	40mm Grenade Launcher, Heavy Machine Gun
MOS	Miliary Occupational Specialty
MP	Military Police
NCO	Noncommissioned Officer
NPLOC	Nonpunitive Letter of Caution
NVG	Night Vision Goggles
OCS	Officer Candidate School
OP	Observation Post
OPSEC	Operational Security
PFC	Private First Class
PID	Positive Identification
PLC	Platoon Leaders Course
PSD	Protective Security Detail
PT	Physical Training
PX	Post Exchange/Convenience Store
QRF	Quick Reaction Force
RCT	Regimental Combat Team

ROVER	Remotely Operated Video Enhanced Receiver
RO	Radio Operator
RPG	Rocket-Propelled Grenade
SALT	Supporting Arms Liaison Team
SAM	Surface-to-Air Missile
SAW	Squad Automatic Weapon
SNCO	Staff Noncommissioned Officer (USMC)
SOF	Special Operations Forces
SOI	School of Infantry
SOP	Standard Operation Procedure
SVBIED	Suicide Vehicle-Borne Improvised Explosive Device
TBS	The Basic School
TF	Task Force
TOC	Tactical Operations Center
TRAP	Tactical Recovery of Aircraft Personnel
UAV	Unmanned Aerial Vehicle
UCMJ	Uniform Code of Military Justice
VA	Veterans Administration
VBIED	Vehicle-Borne Improvised Explosive Device
XO	Executive Officer